A PASSION FOR
TROUT

This book is dedicated to the two most influential people in my life. Firstly there is my father, who taught me how to fish and started me on a journey which became my passion for fly fishing. Never one to accept second best, he taught me patience, discipline and a desire to win. What greater gift can a father give to his son than to provide him with a platform and passion for learning?

Then there is my wife Rosie. Before we tied the knot, her mother Josie warned her, even at that early stage, that she would always be my second love after fishing. She went ahead and married me anyway. She is my rock.

Finally, this book celebrates the memory of the late James O`Reilly, my very great friend; hiring a boat on Carra will never be quite the same again. And Rod Tye; to a blossoming friendship that was prematurely cut short in 2009.

Young or old, an angler's worst nighmare was to turn around and discover my father observing them fishing, especially when they heard.........

"PRESENTATION, MAN!"

Two words that struck fear into the hearts of us all.

A PASSION FOR TROUT

Mick O'Farrell

A Passion for Trout: Fly fishing and fly-tying experiences shared by Mick O'Farrell with selected photographs by Peter Gathercole.
Foreword by Michael Callaghan.

Text © Mick O'Farrell 2010
Fly photographs © Peter Gathercole 2010

The Author asserts the moral right to be identified as the author of this work.

ISBN: 978-0-9567778-0-5

First published in 2011 by:
Silver Sedge Books
19 Chicksands Avenue
Monkston
Milton Keynes
Buckinghamshire NK10 9DP

www.apassionfortrout.com

All rights reserved. No portion of this book may be reproduced, stored in a retrieval system, or transmitted in any form or by any means, mechanical, electronic, photocopying recording, or otherwise, without the written permission of the author.

Printed by 1010 Printing International Ltd.

Contents

Acknowledgements	vi
Foreword	vii
Flies by design	1
Introduction	2-3

CHAPTER ONE: RESERVOIRS AND LAKES

Stillwater dry-fly	6-17
An unusual catch	18-19
Stillwater nymphing	20-29
A family of Buzzers	30-37
Diawl Bachs	38-43
Draycote Water	44-49
Emergers	50-57
Stillwater wet-fly	58-71
A Season on Pitsford	72-77
Lures and things	78-83
Elinor Trout Fishery	84-87

CHAPTER TWO: RIVERS

The Suir	90-95
Dry-fly on the Suir	96-105
Accidental dry-fly	106,107
Wet-fly on the Suir	108-117
Upstream nymphing	118-125
Some things never change	126-129
Evening fishing	130-137
A beautiful springer	138-139

CHAPTER THREE: LOUGHS AND LAKES

Lough Carra	142-153
A memorable evening	154-161
Behaving like an idiot	162-163
Lough Carrowmore	164-169
Lough Lein	170-189

CHAPTER FOUR: CASTING OFF

Flies and fly-tying	192-203
Competition fishing	204-213
Catch-and-release	214-219
The future	220-225

Acknowledgements

Once I start something I find it difficult to let go; however, without the support and encouragement of my wife Rosie and our four children I could never have completed this book within the timescale that was achieved. A special thanks to my son Danny for his patience in teaching me skills on the computer that I never even thought existed.

A Passion for Trout relates to my experiences on a wide range of fisheries in both the UK and Ireland. The danger in writing this section is that I inadvertently forget to name of one the many friends who provided supporting information and therefore helped make this book possible. If I have committed such an error, then please forgive me.

A special thank you to the following people:
Andrew Flitcroft, editor of Trout and Salmon magazine. His advice on the book's content was invaluable.
Alessandra Imbimbo for assistance with the scanning.
Also I cannot thank Redmond Williams enough for his grit and determination to get things right and also his brother Eamon, for whom nothing is too much trouble.

Lough Carra: Philip Cresham, Chris Huxley, the late James O`Reilly and Rod Tye
Lough Carrowmore: John Cosgrove, Seamus Henry and Mary Barrett
Draycote Water: Keith and Margaret Causer
Elinor Fishery: Edward Foster
The Future: Robert Reilly, Dick Willis, Maurice Willis and Richard Willis
Lough Lein: Malcolm O`Brien, Robbie O'Brien, DJ O`Riordan and Dick Willis
Pitsford Water: Nathan Clayton, Kay Mains, Ian Pow and Jim Collins
River Suir: Kevin Rowe, Willie Burke and Tommy Farrell
The North Western Regional Fisheries Board
The Southern Regional Fisheries Board

PHOTOGRAPHS
This book is all the richer due to the contributions of quality photographs from my many fishing friends. Thank you all so very much.

Fly plates: Peter Gathercole
Lough Carra: Philip Cresham and David O`Farrell
Lough Carrowmore: Mary Barrett, John Cosgrove, Russell Hill (Trout Fisherman Magazine) and Gerry Heston
Competition fishing: Denis Kelleher, Michael Twohig and Milan Hladik
Draycote Water: Andrew Boyd, David O`Farrell, Keith Causer, Steve Cullen (Total Flyfisher Magazine)
Elinor Fishery: Ed Foster
The Future: Robert Reilly, Dick Willis, Maurice Willis, Frank Dempsey and Richard Willis
Lough Lein: Robbie and Malcolm O`Brien, DJ O`Riordan, P.J. O`Brien
Pitsford Water: Nathan Clayton
River Suir: William O`Farrell, Kevin Rowe, Andrew Ryan and Tommy Farrell

Editor/design: Peter Gathercole
Text editor: Mark Williams
Maps: Philippa Swanborough
Caricature: Bill Houston

Foreword

I FIRST MET Mick O'Farrell some years ago when he returned from England to fish in the ITFFA Interprovincial in Killarney. I remember thinking at the time that this must be a very serious angler, going to such trouble to fish for his province.

I got to know him better in my capacity as Team Manager when he qualified to fish for Ireland in the ITFFA Autumn International on the Lake of Menteith in 2007. While he struck me then as one of the most serious and dedicated game anglers I had ever met, what really impressed me was his great sense of joy at having qualified to represent his country at his favourite sport.

He contributed in no small way to team preparations during that International week but more importantly I could see that he was always anxious to learn from other more experienced international anglers. I now realise that this great desire to learn more, to perfect his skills, to try new ideas and to share his experiences with others is something that has been part of Mick O'Farrell, the angler, for a long number of years.

Then some time ago Mick told me he was writing a book and invited me to read and to comment, if I wished, on some of the chapters. The emails began arriving and I started reading. While the initial sections were in draft form, I was immediately impressed. I thoroughly enjoyed what I was seeing and looked forward to the next email with great enthusiasm. I suppose what really impressed me about those early draft sections was the great variety of content. There was a huge amount of information on many English stillwaters and the great loughs of Ireland; there was advice and instruction on how and when to fish them; then there was information on the fly patterns that worked best for him and how to tie them.

I soon realised that Mick observed very closely what was happening on a water and then went home to create a fly pattern which matched what he had seen. As a result we have many original patterns in the book, all brought to life by the wonderful photographs which accompany them. And then there were the little stories and anecdotes which for me bring the whole book to life. It's this variety which makes "A Passion for Trout" so special. So finally after many years of research, planning and hard work Mick's dream is now a reality and those who read this book will be all the richer for his efforts. For the angler there is only one thing better than angling and that is reading about angling. In this regard Mick O'Farrell's "A Passion for Trout" is a welcome addition to the game angler's library and I conclude by congratulating him on bringing his dream to fruition. To you, the reader, happy reading and tight lines.

Michael Callaghan.
Hon. Secretary,
Irish Trout Fly Fishing Association.

Flies by design
Peter Gathercole

FLY CHOICE CAN be a very personal matter. For some anglers, a particular pattern will instil absolute confidence; for others that very same fly is all but useless and, if carried at all, lies neglected in some dark recess of a seldom-opened box. Equally, many fly-fishers like to keep a good range of patterns to hand – there to cope with any circumstance – while others prefer a minimalist approach, carrying just a few tried-and-trusted favourites.

My inclination is to pare down the range of flies that I use to its barest minimum. Mick O'Farrell's take on this is the exact opposite – he revels in having as wide a range of options at his fingertips as he can muster. This is probably why his fly boxes are so impressive, the colours and forms testament to hours of effort at the vice.

The incredible range of Mick's flies reflects a rapacious desire to create new and exciting patterns; ever practical, though, and nearly always effective fish-catchers. For him fly-tying and fly-fishing are inseparable – two sides of the same coin. Each and every fly he ties is designed with a specific purpose in mind, the focus rarely being on the fly itself more on the effect it creates and how it will perform on the water.

This approach isn't always or immediately successful but, for Mick, this is all part of the process and, if anything, merely provides further motivation to make an idea work. Many, if not all, of his patterns are work in progress; even when one has already taken numerous trout, to his mind there is still room for improvement.

While Mick's fly-tying is often coloured by the early influences of Ireland's rivers and loughs, it is by no measure trapped in the past. Coming from what must be considered a very traditional fly-fishing background, he exhibits little sign of hankering for the "good old days." If anything, the reverse is true and he is at his most creative and effective when combining modern materials with fur and feather shaped in prehistory.

For Mick the opportunity to blend colours and combine materials with different textures and effects is a real driving force. Few of the dubbing materials he uses are straight out of the packet, and those that are were obtained from modern masters such as Frankie McPhilips and the late Rod Tye.

Even after having tied flies for almost forty years it seems that his initial passion – yearning to tie a dozen flies for his father – is undiminished. He's open, up-front and generous; happy to share his ideas and flies to anyone genuinely interested; you have only to share a boat or a beer with him to discover this. That said, Mick definitely prefers to plough his own furrow. A keen competition angler, he is at his best when he can make his wet-fly and especially his dry-fly patterns work their magic. If not then he is content to cast what's necessary, but always with a mind to switching back should a few fish show on the surface.

An Irishman by birth, Mick has spent almost 30 years living and fishing for trout in the UK, most of it on the large reservoirs such as Grafham, Pitsford and Draycote. Naturally this has had a major impact on the style of his fly-tying. He has developed a hybrid form; patterns with a modern tang but with a background flavour of Irish loughs and his beloved Suir.

His style of fly is always busy, with teased-out bodies and flowing hackles giving an impression of life. I can vouch for the effectiveness of both his Hoppers and Emergers, though to be honest, I initially thought some of his patterns were rather heavily dressed – certainly for my tastes. I quickly discovered that the trout thought otherwise – even in flat-calm conditions.

If I must confess a bias, it is to this impressionistic style of fly-tying where, rather producing an exact copy of an insect, what is created is a distillation of the most important elements. The result of this seeming paradox is a fly that is practical to use and actually far more imitative than a fly which appears to be a perfect replica of the insect, and far more likely to fool a trout.

In my opinion, any fly-tyer, no matter how experienced, can gain much from practising what Mick O'Farrell preaches, from the choice and application of materials to his methods. Latterly he has become almost evangelical about returning to the traditional styles of wet-flies we once used on UK reservoirs. Angling has always been a broad church but, since first meeting Mick, I find myself increasingly drawn to his faith.

Introduction

I AM A river trout angler at heart whose fate has led him away from home, away from the River Suir. But I love trout fishing, and I fish for them wherever I fetch up.

My angling life began patrolling the banks of the Suir when I was about eight years old. Back then, I was not allowed to fish and served the first few years of my apprenticeship carrying my father's spare rod; he always carried both a salmon and trout rod with him. He maximised his angling time and took his angling cues from what he could see. He would fish for trout mostly when they were rising or for a salmon when it was seen moving in a lie. He rarely wasted his time fishing 'blind.'

On Sunday afternoons and winter evenings I spent a lot of time watching my father tying flies. From time to time he would allow me to select a hackle or two for a fly he was tying but, in over two years' of watching, this was the nearest I ever came to being allowed to tie a fly.

When I look back on those days, I often wonder how – and why – I stuck it out, waiting for crumbs from the Captain's table. Others would have given up and walked away. Somehow, by depriving me of the act of fly-tying, making me wait for so long, my father simply made me more determined to tie my own flies.

My long wait ended one Sunday afternoon. My father left a dozen hooks on the bench and asked me if I wanted to tie some flies. The shackles had finally been removed and I was raring to go. Father went fishing that evening without me; I was on a mission to use every single one of those twelve hooks.

I waited patiently for him to return that evening, bursting with pride at the flies I had tied. He examined my twelve flies, opened his box and stowed them away. The following evening, when we went fishing, he gave the flies to his two fishing buddies who dutifully thanked me and complimented me on the quality of my fly-tying. I was fit to be chained up with temper, especially as I had chosen to tie the Marlodge – this was considered a difficult pattern to tie as a first attempt.

I suppose, with hindsight, my father just wanted to show his friends my early skills at the vice but I didn't see it that way at the time. Just another of my father's tough lessons, I reckoned.

I fished alongside my father for most of my youth. In that time, he imparted to me a huge amount of knowledge about the river, its various moods and the killing flies through the seasons. Many of those patterns, which are still successful today, I am passing on in this book. My father also introduced me to lough fishing, for which I will be forever in his debt, as it my preference in fishing today. The Irish limestone loughs are in my blood but even here, in England, the lessons learned from those huge, wild waters are often carried on to Grafham and Pitsford – the man-made reservoirs now within easy reach of my home. My angling life has taken me down many metaphoric and physical roads. I have made lifelong friends along the way and enjoyed a modicum of success, if success in fishing can be measured in pounds, points or inches.

There will be more chapters to write, I hope, for I am in my 40s and determined to go on achieving and learning more about fly-fishing and fly-tying. Who knows? As I get older I might even learn to relax a little and enjoy my fishing in a less pressured way.

What I didn't want was to allow my father's skills, passed on to me, to languish selfishly in my mind, being of benefit only to my own fishing. These skills are the bedrock of my angling. I have, I think, honed and modified his techniques to suit a modern world, and technology which is far removed from those early days on the Suir.

In deciding to write this book, however, I had to settle my mind as to what I was hoping to achieve before taking on such a mammoth task. Clearly I wanted the book to be considered useful. From the outset it has always been my objective to provide the reader with information that can be used time and again. Should too much dust eventually settle on my efforts then I will have failed.

I suppose, as should be expected with these things, the content and scope of the book has evolved during my time f writing it. My original intention was for the book to become a reference for both beginners and experienced anglers alike, sprinkled with a significant number of trout fly patterns and designs. And I wanted to provide background information on the major rivers, lakes and stillwaters that I have fished.

Then I spoke to my friends about the project and I was encouraged to introduce a human element into the writing. One of them insisted that I include some of my fishing yarns and not become too technical and boring. I hope I have taken that advice on board. Wherever I have offered tips in the book, I have attempted to adopt a commonsense approach and avoid getting bogged down in tedious detail. I hope the book will appeal to a wide range of people as it reflects both my fishing and fly-tying experiences across many diverse fisheries.

This book is not designed to teach people how to fish but some of the observations contained within it may prove beneficial to the reader. I have a tendency to speak my mind and I suspect that there will be areas of this book which may be considered controversial by some; I make no apologies for this.

The core of the book, however, is trout fly patterns. I believe much of my success is down to my fly-tying. After each fishing session I try to analyse what went well and what could have gone better. My mind seldom rests and I have a tendency to be over-analytical. This can have a detrimental effect on my fishing at times. Always looking at problems in depth, I tend to miss the simple things right in front of my nose.

I am also highly competitive, so failure does not sit well with me. I see failures when others have had a pleasant day's fishing. But that is who I am. Nothing gives me greater pleasure, after long deliberation, than to create the solution to a problem in the vice. To then to return to the fishery and prove the flies effective is my elixir. I know, for example, that fishing dry buzzer patterns late into the night on Lough Carra could be successful. It remains a challenge but batches of new flies are ready for next year's confrontation with Carra's big brown trout.

I have been tying flies ever since my father threw down those dozen hooks as a challenge for his young son; I love it with a passion. This book contains over four hundred patterns. Many are well-established flies which need little introduction from me. Quite a number are of my own design, with the remainder being variants to well-known flies. Variants represent evolution rather than revolution but, when it comes to fly-tying, I simply have to tinker round the edges as I continue to strive to create the perfect fly. Should the reader wish to tie any of the patterns illustrated in this book, then the tying 'recipe' should be read in conjunction with the additional information contained in the final chapter of the book, the section titled Flies and fly-tying.

I had been thinking of writing a book for some time and, as my wife Rosie often says, there is a good book in everyone. I was finally inspired when my friend John Lalor completed his second book, this time dedicated to trout and salmon fishing on the River Suir.

It took John four years of hard work to complete his volume. For my part, tying and recording over four hundred patterns was quite an undertaking for one just person. My greatest hope is the end result is rather easier to read than it was to write.

Tight lines.

Michael O'Farrell

Chapter one: Reservoirs and lakes

Contents

Stillwater dry-fly	6-17
An unusual catch	18-19
Stillwater nymphing	20-29
A family of Buzzers	30-37
Diawl Bachs	38-43
Draycote Water	44-49
Emergers	50-57
Stillwater wet-fly	58-71
A Season on Pitsford	72-77
Lures and things	78-83
Elinor Trout Fishery	84-87

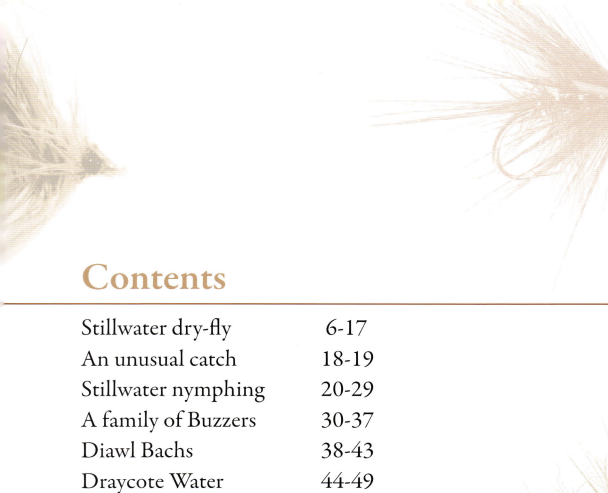

STILLWATER DRY-FLY

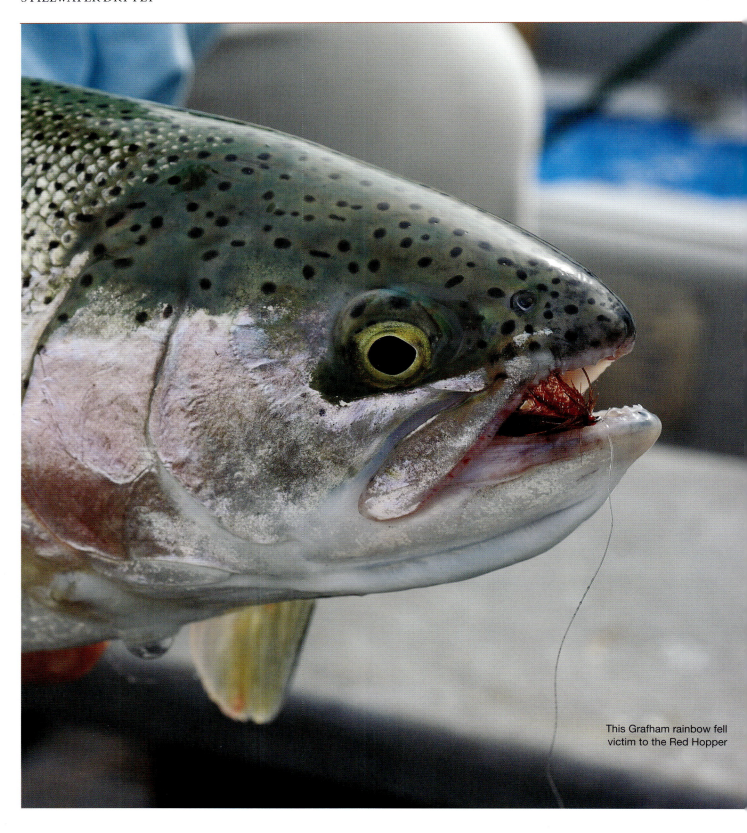

This Grafham rainbow fell victim to the Red Hopper

Stillwater dry-fly

BIG TROUT HAVE seen it all. In the course of their lives, most have experienced a wide variety of flies whizzing past them at differing speeds and depths. Those that succumbed to temptation but survived have learned to be selective in what they eat and particularly wary of an artificial fly.

In my experience – whether you're fishing for wild brown trout or stocked rainbows – the dry-fly is often the way to tempt better-quality fish. Dry-fly fishing on stillwaters can be both fun and frustrating in equal measure. Don't let anyone tell you that rainbow trout are easy to catch because they are 'tame.' I have known rainbows to be incredibly fussy and very difficult to fool.

Just like wild brown trout, rainbows can switch on to a specific food source to the exclusion of all others, and unless you can solve the puzzle as to what they are eating, a frustrating day's fishing lies ahead. I have equally known wild brown trout to practically jump into the landing net when the right conditions prevail.

When trout are preoccupied with feeding on a specific insect on the surface, good observation is the key to success. The ability to identify the natural insect then have an artificial fly close to it in shape, colour and – to some degree – size is what really matters. If you've got the right fly, you already have a good start. Once a cast is made, though, the imitation should behave just as the natural insect does.

Unlike some other methods of fly-fishing, the dry-fly is designed to fool the fish rather than trigger its aggressive instincts. Observing what is happening on the water and then using that knowledge to determine a successful fly selection is for me, the ultimate satisfaction in fly fishing. To me it is the pinnacle of fly fishing techniques and when done from a drifting boat, it can be both exciting and maddening - all at the same time.

Anglers conditioned to other fly-fishing methods often believe that flies require some form of retrieve. For them adjusting to dry-fly fishing can be father difficult. They appear to have an overwhelming desire to be 'doing something' to induce the take.

There are good anglers who swear by giving dry-flies a tweak every now and again to provoke a reaction from the trout. Aside from non-imitative 'dry-flies' like Muddlers and Stimulators, retrieving true dry-flies has never worked for me. I might use a slow figure-of-eight retrieve when I am fishing the dry-fly in darkness, but otherwise I leave them well alone. Presentation, patience and confidence in your flies are the main ingredients for successful dry-fly fishing.

OBSERVATIONS AND TIPS

A common misconception on stillwaters is that trout need to be rising in vast numbers before the dry-fly is considered. Not so. Following a recent eventful period using the dry-fly almost exclusively, I analysed the ratio of blind takes to targeted rising fish. The result of this mini survey was that the number of fish taken on the blind was approximately 70 per cent of the total on each outing. So, fishing the dry-fly then becomes a confidence issue. I have learned to my cost that over-dressed dry-flies and flies that sit too high in the water will result in lots of rising fish but an equal amount of fresh-air strikes. Initially I put this down to striking too fast, as surely there could be no other reason for missing so many explosive takes? Well, there was. I can recall comments from boat partners, such as 'Your flies are floating like corks,' as if this was the supreme virtue of a good dry-fly. This is a common misconception. It seems to me that, when your dry-fly is difficult to see, it is at its deadliest. I'll do anything to get the fly low in the water, including trimming the underside of hackles, especially on Sedge patterns and Hoppers.

STILLWATER DRY-FLY

So when you're preparing a dry-fly before the first cast, don't be over-generous with floatant; a touch of Gink on the back of the fly will suffice. I squeeze a little floatant onto my right wrist and apply it with my left hand. By doing this I avoid the Gink getting on to both hands and inadvertently transferring itself on to my leader. If the fly sits so low you lose sight of it, watch the leader or watch the spot where you last saw it. But don't be tempted to give it a tweak to reveal itself. You must combat any instinct to move the flies. Short casting is the solution, for the following reasons. First of all, short casts will improve presentation and give you flexibility; with a short line out, recasting to a rising fish can be done very quickly and precisely. Secondly, casting a long line will result in more fish being missed or lost.

UNINTENDED CONSEQUENCES

From a drifting boat, putting out a long line is rarely necessary, so why alert the trout immediately in front of the boat by laying fly line over their heads? Even when you do get a rise, it is not as easy to connect with a trout at such great range.

There can be unintended consequences to long lining as I once found out during a major competition fished in Ireland. My boat partner and I were both using dries, but his preference was to cast a long line. Normally I would not have an issue with this. However, my partner, in the stern of the boat would cast directly downwind then, as we drifted obliquely, my partner's dry-flies would swing across and end up in front of me each time. In order for him to retrieve line for the next cast, he had to give the line several sharp pulls, which resulted in the water in front of me being disturbed by him ripping his flies back every few minutes. So, the third reason for maintaining a short line should be out of respect and fairness to your boat partner.

By allowing the boat to drift onto your flies before re-casting there will be minimum disturbance of the water. This method allows the fisherman to cover the angles in front of the boat easily and efficiently.

Striking too soon can also be a problem. Being a river angler, I fall foul of this all too frequently. It takes me hours to adjust to dry-fly fishing on stillwaters after tackling rivers in Ireland. If you are unable to prevent yourself striking on sight, allow a little slack in your line after making the cast. This will build in a buffer between you and the trout and give that half-second delay needed to successfully make contact with the fish. My good friend Willie Burke calls it the 'snaky line'!

Fishing dry-flies that are too big is also another

The superb quality of rainbow that the dry-fly can produce

A PASSION FOR TROUT

On a de-greased leader, dry-flies still work even in a flat calm

common mistake. Just because they are easy to see on the water does not make them any more efficient. As with flies that sit too high in the water, oversized dry-flies will also result in explosive rises but very little contact. If you are getting lots of contact and very few hook ups then downsize to a smaller fly immediately. If fishing a water that is unfamiliar to me I will often start with a size 10 on the point, a size 12 in the middle and a 14 on the top dropper. It doesn't take long to work out where the trout's preference lies then to adapt the remaining flies on the leader to suit. Another important tip is to look out for wind lanes, or slicks as they are sometimes called. You can bet your boots that this is where feeding fish will usually be located.

On bright days with little or no wind to ruffle the water's surface, degreasing the leader is essential. This should be done as often as is required to ensure that the only thing sitting on the surface is your dry-fly. I tend to fish with 0.185mm Grand Max [riverge] fluorocarbon and will have no hesitation going lighter if conditions dictate. I especially like this material for dry-fly fishing; the diameter is very fine and yet I have total confidence in it when playing a big strong fish,

MATCHING THE HATCH

In any typical stillwater season the three main categories of insects that you will encounter are midges, sedges and olives. I am no expert in entomology, and cannot

The Grafham Special: A deadly fly in a midge hatch.

Eyebrook Reservoir. A wonderful water for the dry-fly

recite the Latin names of all our aquatic insects but I still have the knowledge to work out what's hatching and, as importantly, find a dry-fly to suit. You don't need to know the name of a species to work out what to tie on. Given sight of what the trout are feeding on I can usually find something in my box that will match the appearance and behaviour of the hatching insect. I derive the greatest pleasure from this challenge of breaking the code between insect and fish. After even limited success, I leave the water a happy and satisfied angler.

I am often mystified by the lengths anglers will go to determine the colour, size and type of nymph, fish are feeding on. Yet when it comes to the dry-fly, nothing like the same effort is expended. Most stillwater anglers carry just a few standard patterns in their box and if they don't work almost immediately then it's back to the nymphs, even if trout are rising all around them.

Using the right size and colour of dry-fly is often vital and I can recall many times when matching the hatch has made all the difference. On one memorable evening session at Pitsford Water, fishing with my son David, I had moved a few trout to Hopper patterns, just after we'd started, when a breeze was playing the lake's surface.

As the evening went on, the already light wind died away and the trout really came on the feed. I changed to a team of dry Sedges and was soon covering the numerous trout that were rising within range of the boat. Unfortunately, although convinced that I was using the correct imitations I was still unable persuade any of them to have a go. As the evening grew dark, the rise became more intense and we could quite clearly see that the fish were feeding on sedges.

So intense was my concentration that I was not paying enough attention to David when he changed one of his flies. Shortly afterwards, he covered yet another one of trout that was feeding confidently and it immediately sucked down this new dry-fly. In reply to my questioning, David said that a sedge had landed on the peak of his cap and, when examined, he thought, in the gathering gloom, that its body looked distinctly green. So without another thought I changed over to a Green Sedge and caught five trout in quick succession. Originally I had been fishing two Sedge patterns with identical profiles but they had been refused at every attempt. Not until I changed over to the Green Sedge did things begin to happen. Even in the fading light, the correct colour was vital to success

– proof if it were needed that when fishing for selective trout, matching the hatch correctly can mean the difference between success and failure.

ELEGANT UP-WINGED INSECTS

If the sedge is the meat in the dry-fly sandwich, then the olive and midge form the bread. The pond olive and its cousin, the lake olive first put in an appearance around April. The early season olives can be quite large in size; elegant up-winged insects that can vary considerably in colour depending on their environment. Although an overall olive hue, the lake olive in particular is extremely variable and can range from a light greenish olive to the dark, sooty olive of the great Irish limestone loughs.

And as the dry-fly season draws to a close we usually meet the olives again, albeit much smaller in size this time. I have encountered the lake olive on Lough Carra on my early fishing expeditions to Ireland. In the UK, I am lucky in that both Eyebrook Reservoir and Elinor Trout Fishery, two of the waters I most often frequent, have excellent hatches of olives both in the spring and autumn. There are two patterns that I instinctively go for when these particular insects are hatching. When the trout are nymphing, it is difficult to beat the Yellow Partridge on the top dropper especially when tied with a dyed golden olive partridge hackle. For dry-fly fishing, when the trout can be seen picking off the freshly emerged duns I designed the Donegal Hopper. I developed the pattern several years ago and my first trial with it was on Lough Carra. It was an immediate success.

Frankie McPhillips blends some beautiful colours and shades of seal's fur and as soon as I saw his Donegal Olive mix I knew exactly what I was going to use it for – to imitate the lake and pond olives.

On all large waters, locating fish can be a problem. But there are clues if you know what to look for. First, gather as much information as you can before going out on the water. Ask a few questions and make a few phone calls. I am not ashamed to admit to eavesdropping on other boat anglers' conversations from time to time. Voices carry all too clearly across the water…

When out on the water, watch what other boats are doing. The starting up of a lot engines usually means that they are struggling to locate fish but look out for boats returning to make the same drift again and again. If I see gulls or swallows beak-dipping in the water, this normally indicates that insects are hatching, so I am off to fish that area as quick as I can start the motor.

The Donegal Hopper

CONSIDER YOUR APPROACH

Find out which direction the wind has been coming from. There will be a build-up of food in this area and, where there is a concentration of food, there will also be feeding trout. Finally, think about your approach. Cut out unnecessary noise and disturbance and, when presenting your flies, aim the cast above the water not at it. If the flies are well presented, the take will often come very soon after they land on the water.

A freshly emerged pond olive dun

Stillwater dry-flies I

BROWN SNAIL
Hook: Light wire size 12-14
Thread: Brown
Body: Brown seal's fur, hare's fur mixed
Shell back: Brown foam strip
Head: Hare's ear fur
Antennae: Hare's ear fibres

PARACHUTE OLIVE BUZZER
Hook: Buzzer hook size 12-14
Thread: Olive
Body: Olive thread
Rib: Olive Flexi floss
Post: White EPS fibres
Hackle: Grizzle cock, dyed olive

YELLOW SHIPMAN'S
Hook: Light wire size 12-14
Thread: Yellow
Breathers: White EPS fibres
Body: Yellow seal's fur
Rib: Pearl tinsel
Body hackle: Grizzle, reversed

CLARET BITS
Hook: Light wire size 12
Thread: Claret
Body: Claret Mosaic dubbing
Hackle: Natural red cock, underside trimmed

PARACHUTE PHEASANT TAIL
Hook: Light wire size 12-14
Thread: Brown
Tail: Natural red hackle fibres
Body: Pheasant tail fibres
Rib: Fine copper wire
Post: White calf tail
Thorax: Rusty brown Micro Brite
Hackle: Natural red cock

CLARET PARACHUTE
Hook: Buzzer size 12-14
Thread: Claret
Body: Claret seal's fur
Rib: Pearl tinsel
Thorax: Dull orange seal's fur
Post: White calf tail
Hackle: Natural red cock

ORANGE SHIPMAN'S
Hook: Light wire size 12-14
Thread: Orange
Breathers: White EPS fibres
Body: Orange seal's fur
Rib: Pearl tinsel
Body hackle: Grizzle, reversed

OLIVE SNAIL
Hook: Light wire size 12-14
Thread: Olive
Body: Sooty olive seal's fur
Shell back: Green foam with centre coloured brown
Head: Claret seal's fur
Antennae: Hare's ear, dyed olive

PARACHUTE QUILL BUZZER
Hook: Buzzer size 12-14
Thread: Medium olive
Butt: Glo-Brite No4
Body: Black & cream Flexi Floss mixed
Post: White EPS fibres
Thorax: Red holographic tinsel & olive brown seal's fur
Hackle: Grizzle cock, dyed olive

BLACK SHIPMAN'S
Hook: Light wire size 12-14
Butt: Glo-Brite No7
Breathers: White EPS fibres
Body: Black seal's fur
Rib: Pearl tinsel
Body hackle: Grizzle, reversed

GINGER BITS
Hook: Light wire size 12
Thread: Brown
Body: Ginger seal's fur
Hackle: Medium ginger cock, underside trimmed

Stillwater dry-flies II

DARK BROWN SEDGE
Hook: Light wire size 12
Thread: Brown
Body: Hare's ear fur, dark brown, light brown & grey seal's fur mixed
Wing: Deer hair, dyed golden brown, tied over the front, then trimmed
Hackle: Grizzle cock, dyed brown

PARACHUTE DUSTER (MOF)
Hook: Buzzer size 12-14
Thread: Black
Butt: Flat silver tinsel
Body: Grey fur
Thorax: Peacock Micro Brite
Post: Natural CDC
Hackle: Badger cock

ORANGE & GREEN HOPPER
Hook: Light wire size 12
Thread: Medium olive
Body: Olive Mosaic dubbing
Thorax: Orange Mosaic dubbing
Wing: CDC, dyed olive
Legs: Knotted pheasant tail, dyed orange
Hackle: Grizzle cock, dyed fiery brown, underside trimmed

GREY DUSTER
Hook: Light wire size 12-14
Body: Grey Mosaic dubbing
Hackle: Well marked badger cock

CINNAMON SEDGE
Hook: Light wire size 12
Thread: Red
Body: Cinnamon seal's fur
Wing: Pale deer hair tied to form a post
Thorax: Deep orange/red seal's fur
Hackle: Golden ginger cock

GREEN SEDGE
Hook: Light wire size 12
Thread: Olive green
Body: Olive Mosaic dubbing
Wing: Deer hair tied over the front then trimmed
Thorax: Olive Mosaic dubbing
Hackle: Natural red cock, underside trimmed

DADDY LONGLEGS
Hook: Wide gape size 12
Thread: Brown
Body: Foam strip, detached
Wings: Cree hackle tips
Legs: Knotted pheasant tail fibres
Thorax: Grey fur
Hackle: Cree cock

RUSTY BROWN SEDGE
Hook: Light wire size 12
Thread: Brown
Body: Mixed brown seal's fur & hare's ear
Wing: Deer hair fibres tied over the front then trimmed
Thorax: Fiery brown seal's fur
Hackle: Natural red cock

PARACHUTE HARE'S EAR
Hook: Buzzer light wire size 12-14
Thread: Brown
Body: Hare's ear fur
Rib: Pearl tinsel with fine gold wire over
Post: Natural CDC
Thorax: Rusty brown Micro Brite
Hackle: Cree cock feather

HAWTHORN FLY
Hook: Light wire size 12-14
Thread: Black
Body: Black/red seal's fur
Rib: Fine pearl tinsel
Wing: Natural CDC with white DNA strands
Legs: Knotted pheasant tail, dyed black
Hackle: Black cock, underside trimmed

PARACHUTE BLACK BUZZER
Hook: Buzzer size 12-14
Thread: Black
Body: Black tinsel
Rib: Fine silver wire
Post: White EPS fibres
Thorax: Red Micro Brite
Hackle: Black cock

Stillwater dry-flies III

MICK'S BLACK HOPPER
Hook: Light wire size 10-12
Thread: Black
Butt: Red Ultra wire
Body: Black/red seal's fur mixed
Rib: Red Ultra wire
Legs: Knotted pheasant tail fibres, dyed red
Wing: Natural CDC and deer hair with strands of Mirror Flash over
Hackle: Black cock, underside trimmed

CLARET HOPPER
Hook: Light wire size 10-12
Thread: Black
Butt: Red holographic tinsel
Body: Claret Mosaic dubbing
Rib: Fine red holographic tinsel
Legs: Knotted pheasant tail fibres
Wing: Natural CDC, folded over
Hackle: Furnace cock hackle

FIERY BROWN HOPPER
Hook: Light wire size 12
Thread: Brown
Body: Fiery brown seal's fur and brown Glister mixed
Legs: Knotted pheasant tail fibres
Wing: Natural CDC
Hackle: Grizzle, dyed fiery brown

WARSAW HOPPER
Hook: Light wire size 10-12
Thread: Black
Body: Lime green Mosaic dubbing
Thorax: Claret Mosaic dubbing
Legs: Pheasant tail dyed claret
Wing: Deer hair with strands of Mirror Flash over
Hackle: Black cock hackle

DONEGAL HOPPER
Hook: Light wire size 10-12
Thread: Orange
Butt: Flat gold tinsel
Body: Donegal Olive seal's fur blend
Wing: Natural CDC, folded over
Legs: Knotted pheasant tail, dyed golden olive
Hackles: No1 – Light blue cock hackle, No2 – medium red cock hackle

KILKENNY HOPPER
Hook: Light wire size 10-12
Thread: Black
Body: Amber seal's fur
Thorax: Black seal's fur
Legs: Pheasant tail dyed black
Wing: Deer hair dyed black with strands of Mirror Flash over
Hackle: Dark Greenwell's cock hackle

EMERALD HOPPER
Hook: Light wire size 10-12
Thread: Medium olive
Butt: Hot orange Ultra wire
Body: Olive Mosaic dubbing
Rib: Hot orange Ultra wire
Legs: Knotted pheasant tail
Wing: CDC, dyed light olive
Hackle: Medium olive cock

UV BIBIO HOPPER
Hook: Light wire size 10-12
Thread: Black
Butt: Flat silver tinsel
Body: UV Straggle, black/red/black with black seal's fur mixed
Wing: Natural CDC
Legs: Knotted, dyed black pheasant tail
Hackle: Black cock hackle

GREEN PETER HOPPER
Hook: Light wire size 10-12
Thread: Black
Butt: Glo-Brite No 4
Body: Olive green seal's fur
Rib: Oval gold tinsel
Legs: Knotted pheasant tail fibres
Wing: Natural CDC with deer hair strands over
Hackle: Natural red cock hackle

GRAFHAM SPECIAL
Hook: Light wire size 10-12
Thread: Red
Body: Red and orange seal's fur mixed with orange Glister
Legs: Knotted pheasant tail fibres
Wing: Natural CDC with strands of Mirror Flash over
Hackle: Natural red cock hackle

ORANGE & BLACK HOPPER
Hook: Light wire size 10-12
Thread: Black
Body: 1st third, orange seal's fur, remainder, black seal's fur
Wing: Dyed black deer hair with strands of Mirror Flash over
Legs: Knotted pheasant tail fibres
Hackle: Greenwell's cock hackle

MICK'S BLACK HOPPER

UV BIBIO HOPPER

DONEGAL HOPPER

CLARET HOPPER

GREEN PETER HOPPER

FIERY BROWN HOPPER

KILKENNY HOPPER

GRAFHAM SPECIAL

EMERALD HOPPER

WARSAW HOPPER

ORANGE & BLACK HOPPER

An unusual catch

It was, perhaps, only my second year living in England. I was an Irishman who'd washed up in Milton Keynes but, though I may have been an ocean away from my beloved loughs and peaty rivers, I did have Kingfisher Farm nearby.

It was the height of summer and a boiling hot and cloudless day. The fishery was owned and run by a lovely man, John Frisby. It was the usual Friday afternoon routine; I finished work early and headed off to John's trout lake for a few hours fishing along with my brother Willie, and our friend Alf Harrington.

John was a bit of a character and liked to play the odd prank on his regular clients. His favourite pastime was to sit on the wooden porch, sipping a cold beer and dishing out mischievous comments about our inability to catch his fish. Nevertheless, I decided to fish the small lake in front of the fishing hut – within his range – and risk the mickey-taking I knew would follow.

NOT A CLOUD IN THE SKY

He was on top form, delivering a machine-gun rattle of stinging comments. So much so, I eventually moved to the far side of the lake to get a bit of peace. The lake was flat calm and conditions awful, with the sun beating down on us and not a cloud in the sky. The wise thing to do would have been to join John on the porch and drink his beer but the more he taunted me the more determined I was to catch a fish.

A trout would rise very occasionally, barely breaking the surface and causing a small swirl. I found any cover I could and made the odd cast whenever I saw a trout feeding close by.

I noticed a slight dimple straight in front of me but too far out to make a cast, then another dimple, a little closer this time. It looked as if the fish was heading in my direction, so I made a cast in the path of the travelling dimples and waited. Just as my flies were settling in the water, the dimple appeared again, this time right where my leader had landed, so I struck. I was into a fish, accompanied by great cheers from the porch.

To my horror I quickly discovered this was no trout but a snake well over two feet long. Now, being an Irishman, I had never seen a snake in the wild before. St Patrick took care of that particular problem in Ireland hundreds of years ago. To say I am not good around snakes is an understatement. On a scale of one to ten, I am right up there with Indiana Jones; the bloody things make my skin crawl.

OFF LIKE A ROCKET

The snake proceeded to swim towards me and, when it hit dry land, hissed at me. I dropped the rod and took off like a rocket. John, still thinking I was playing a trout, took some persuading that I really did have a snake on the end of my line. He just laughed at me and said it was another one of my Irish stories.

Eventually John and his mate went over to where my rod was laying on the ground, trapped the snake in the landing net, removed the fly from the back of its head and released it. Only then did I reappear from my safe spot behind the shrubs.

After that trauma I started fishing again. The evening began to draw in and by the time it was dark, I had still not caught a trout. I moved to the bottom corner of the lake for the final few casts before John blew the 'all out' whistle. I made another cast, started the retrieve and got a good pull. I didn't need to strike but I got that awful feeling straight away that, whatever was that was on the end of the line, it was certainly no trout.

I eventually landed the fish but in the deep gloom could not identify what species of fish it was. Being the coward that I am, I somehow got the fly out of its mouth without touching it and flicked it back into the lake with my boot.

John was still laughing from my earlier experience when I returned to the hut to complete my catch return. I filled out the card and, after a beer with John, headed off home musing over a very strange day's fishing.

FAME AT LAST

John rang me the following day and asked me to tune into Northampton radio that afternoon. Fame at last. I told my friends that I was going to get a mention on the local radio and everyone tuned in. They all fell about the place laughing when my name was read out. After an announcement of 'The most unusual catch return ever sent in to the radio station,' they broadcast exactly what I had written on my card – one Snake and one Thing.

Stillwater nymphing

HAD I NOT moved to England all those years ago I would never have discovered the real pleasure of stillwater nymphing. It is such a relaxing and rewarding way to fish for trout. There are so many variations in nymph fishing techniques today that the opportunities to experiment are almost endless. With rivers in my blood, my fishing is based on an imitative style, preferring to fool the fish into taking the fly as a natural food form rather than simply triggering its aggressive instincts.

I have been out-fished on many occasions by anglers using sinking lines with Blobs and other lures. Years ago, this caused me some concern – but no longer. If I am confident in the method and flies I am using and enjoy what I am doing then that's where I stay.

Buzzers, especially, have proved incredibly successful on some of the big limestone loughs, including Corrib and Mask. In recent years I've begun to experiment with Buzzers and Diawl Bachs, on various other Irish lakes with some limited success on Lough Lein in Killarney. It seems curious that not all Irish waters respond so well to the nymph though I feel it just needs some more time experimenting with techniques and patterns to truly crack the problem.

Wherever possible my preference is to use a floating line. I usually fish a 7-weight line for nymphs and wet-fly, switching to a 6-weight for the dry-fly. By varying the retrieve and the weight and size of the nymph on the point, I can usually locate the depth that the trout are holding at and, more importantly, keep the flies in that productive zone. If fishing from a drifting boat, line selection will often be critical particularly in varying wind speeds and light conditions.

On slow days, I use a sink-tip or midge-tip line to reach the trout, which will often be lying deeper or in a lethargic mood. Having been brought up on a diet of

One in the net! A good rainbow that took a Cruncher

dry-fly fishing on a river, I prefer to shy away from fully sinking lines wherever possible unless competition fishing, where needs must. Normally I fish a team of four flies and my leaders as long as I can comfortably manage, preferring to keep my flies spaced as far apart as possible provided, of course, that the rod I am using can keep everything under control. My preferred rod for boat fishing is a 10½-foot Sage and a 10ft rod for dry-fly fishing. I seldom fish with anything other than fluorocarbon these days; my preferred material is Grand Max [reverge] 0.210mm for nymph fishing.

FISHING WITH CONFIDENCE

Fishery staff are very helpful and will always give you good advice when asked. I have never been too shy or proud to enquire how the water has been fishing. You will be given an indication of recent hotspots and the depth fish are feeding. Armed with this information, you can start your day's fishing with some confidence. I tend to ignore the detail of advice given on fly selection, as the number of variants of named patterns in terms of colour, shape and size are legion. It is an entirely different matter if I am actually shown the fly that is working.

Boat rather than bank fishing is my preference today. Provided there is sufficient room to allow me a good drift around anchored boats and the wind is suitable, I like to use a drogue to slow the boat as much as possible.

On arrival on any stillwater I would usually start with a floating line. I usually place a Spider-type pattern on the top dropper or a hackled Buzzer. A slim nymph – normally a Diawl Bach or Pheasant Tail – goes on the middle dropper and something with a bit of density, like a Fraser Nymph, Hare's Ear or a heavy Buzzer goes on the point.

This set-up allows me to work different depths with the same team of flies until I begin to learn what the trout are up to. I take a fish or two when friends or family want them, so those first fish are always spooned to gather a little extra information about their diet. I try to avoid the herd instinct, and move away from where the majority of boats are fishing. I prefer instead to search the water with my team of nymphs. If I discover a very productive area, I lower the anchor and cover the fish from a discreet distance rather than continuously drifting over the area and risk putting them down. After all, controlling the speed of your retrieve and keeping your flies at the correct depth is easier from a static platform. It is slightly more difficult to keep everything under control from a moving boat particularly if the trout are holding at a certain depth. If the action stops or there is no major activity for twenty minutes, it is time to move on.

Perhaps it's just me but I have noticed in recent years that the trout on stillwaters prefer a nymph moved at a retrieve so slow that it borders on static. Methods such as suspending a Buzzer from a Bung or the static 'washing-line' method – with a floating fly on the point and the sinking flies hanging between – have become extremely popular and very effective. When Buzzer-fishing, the old rule still applies; however slowly you think you are retrieving, it's still probably not quite slow enough. Maintaining the correct depth on a very slow retrieve then becomes the critical issue.

IT PAYS TO ADAPT

I do feel, though, that competition anglers are at the forefront of innovation and change in fishing techniques. Competition anglers are always looking for a method or a fly pattern that will give them that extra edge. I pay a keen interest whenever top anglers write articles in

No mistaking that this rainbow was feeding well on bloodworm

STILLWATER METHODS

A fine rainbow that fell to a Black Buzzer

fishing magazines, and I often think about the useful tips and methods they describe and try to emulate them in my fishing. It also pays to be observant – to keep a keen eye on what others are doing. The ability to adapt to the trout's behaviour is also very important. I was fishing with my friend and England International Edward Foster in a charity match in 2000. Edward had been taking fish steadily for several hours and then things went quiet.

It appeared as if the fish might be feeding deeper, and I was astounded at the speed Edward changed to a faster-sinking line. I reckoned it took him just over 15 seconds to complete the task. Until that day, I found the task of changing a line too cumbersome and time-consuming to bother with. In the time honoured Irish tradition, I would wait until we beached the boat for lunch before changing the line over. Stillwater fishing is all about adapting to change, I have, in the past, paid the penalty for my lazy approach on many occasions. In angling, just as in life, it often pays to make the effort.

NYMPH PATTERNS

Many of the patterns I have selected in the first plate in this section would be considered point flies, but that is not a rigid rule, the other flies would normally be fished on the middle droppers. Hackled flies are best suited for the top dropper position.

The Cruncher style patterns in particular, when tied on small hooks, make excellent dropper flies. Like all successful flies, over time many variations are spawned from the original pattern. The Quill Cruncher and quill-bodied buzzers work well in April and then again in June when the red buzzer is on the wing. The UV Crunchers tend to fish all year round; the pattern illustrated in this section can be very good indeed late in the season. The Fire Cruncher is a fly I developed recently and so far has worked well for me. I had some fine trout on it at Pitsford Water especially during the summer and also on Lough Lein in Killarney.

The Fraser Nymph is one of my all-time favourite patterns. I put this fly right up there with the best of them. The Fraser Nymph has travelled well for me across many fisheries in the UK, especially the olive variant. Tied on a size 12 hook, it fishes well early in the season when olives are hatching. When up-sized and dressed on a long-shanked hook the Fraser Nymph represents a good imitation of the damsel nymph. The Bloodworm performs best when fished static and is a typical early and late season pattern.

The Cove-style Pheasant Tail Nymph is still deadly, particularly when the trout are lying deep and a slow retrieve is required. The Beaded Buzzer is effective in hot sunny weather and is another deep water pattern. The other Pheasant Tail patterns illustrated here are excellent when the trout are feeding in the upper layers of the water. Rod Tye's Black Nymph is an excellent fly for the top dropper and has taken trout on many fisheries for me.

The Trigger Nymph is a fly I developed with Lough Lein in mind. Simply put, I wanted to create a fly incorporating the most efficient colours for catching trout in Killarney which, in my opinion, are Black, Red, Blue and Orange. I have yet to try the fly out on Lough Lein but fished it several times at the back end of the season on Draycote Water and was very pleased with the results.

The Hot Nymph started out life as a spider pattern for river fishing. Tied on a longshank size 12 this fly has accounted for some quality trout on Grafham Water, when fished on the point.

A Grafham success – the Hot Nymph

Playing a big fish hooked on a Fraser Nymph

Stillwater Nymphs I

CRUNCHER No1
Hook: Kamasan B 175 size 10-12
Thread: Red
Tail: Golden pheasant red neck feather
Body: Pheasant tail fibres
Rib: Fine silver wire
Thorax: Red Micro Brite
Hackle: Dark Greenwell's

MUSKINS
Hook: Kamasan B 170 size 10-14
Thread: Brown
Tail: Greenwell hackle fibres
Body: Pheasant tail fibres
Rib: Fine copper wire
Breathers: White DNA fibres
Thorax: Hare's ear

FRASER NYMPH No2
Hook: Nymph hook size 10-12
Thread: Orange
Tail: Partridge neck feather fibres
Body: Brown turkey feather fibres
Rib: Hot orange Ultra wire
Thorax: Hare's ear SLF
Thorax cover: Turkey feather fibres
Legs: Partridge feather dyed olive

COVE PHEASANT TAIL No2
Hook: Kamasan B 100 size 10-12
Thread: Red
Body: Pheasant tail fibres
Rib: Pearl tinsel with fine copper wire over
Thorax: Green Mosaic dubbing
Thorax cover: Pheasant tail fibres

MONTANA NYMPH
Hook: Nymph hook size 10-12
Thread: Black
Tail: Black goose biots
Body: Black Micro chenille
Thorax: Green Glo-Brite floss
Thorax cover: Dark Nymph Skin
Hackle: Black cock

RED CRUNCHER
Hook: Kamasan B 175 size 10-12
Thread: Black
Tail: Golden pheasant red neck feather
Body: Pheasant tail fibres, dyed red
Rib: Fine silver wire
Thorax: Red UV Straggle
Cheeks: Jungle cock
Hackle: Dark Greenwell's

QUILL CRUNCHER
Hook: Kamasan B 175 size 10-12
Thread: Red
Tail: Golden pheasant red neck feather
Body: Cream and brown Flexi Floss
Thorax: Peacock herl, dyed claret
Thorax cover: Pearl tinsel
Hackle: Greenwell's hackle

HOT NYMPH
Hook: Nymph hook size 10-12
Thread: Orange
Tail: Natural red hackle fibres
Body: Hot orange & hot yellow wire, mixed
Thorax: Rusty brown Micro Brite
Hackle: Partridge brown neck feather

COVE PHEASANT TAIL No3
Hook: Kamasan B 100 size 10-12
Thread: Orange
Body: Pheasant tail fibres
Rib: Pearl tinsel with fine copper wire over
Thorax: Orange Mosaic dubbing
Thorax cover: Pheasant tail fibres

UV CRUNCHER
Hook: Kamasan B 175 size 10-12
Thread: Brown
Tail: Golden pheasant red neck feather
Body: Pheasant tail fibres
Rib: Light silver wire
Thorax: Light grey SLF
Hackle: Medium Greenwell's

FIRE CRUNCHER
Hook: Kamasan B 170 size 10-12
Thread: Fire orange Glo-Brite
Tail: Golden pheasant yellow neck feather
Body: Pheasant tail fibres
Rib: Hot orange Ultra wire
Thorax: Light grey SLF
Cheeks: Jungle cock dyed orange
Hackle: Ginger hen

OLIVE MUSKINS
Hook: Kamasan B 170 size 10-12
Thread: Olive
Tail: Greenwell hackle fibres, dyed olive
Body: Pheasant tail fibres, dyed olive
Rib: Fine copper wire
Breathers: Olive DNA
Thorax: Hare's ear fur, dyed olive

FRASER NYMPH No1
Hook: Nymph hook size 10-12
Thread: Medium olive
Tail: Brown partridge hackle fibres
Body: Light brown turkey feather
Rib: Glo-Brite No12
Thorax: Olive green seal's fur
Thorax cover: Turkey feather fibres
Legs: Brown partridge neck feather

COVE PHEASANT TAIL No1
Hook: Kamasan B 100 size 10-12
Thread: Red
Body: Pheasant tail fibres
Rib: Pearl tinsel with fine copper wire over
Thorax: Blue/grey fur
Thorax cover: Pheasant tail fibres

HARE'S EAR
Hook: Nymph hook size 10-12
Thread: Black
Body: Hare's ear fur, tapered
Rib: Fine gold tinsel
Thorax cover: Pheasant tail, dyed black
Head: Gold bead

CRUNCHER No1

RED CRUNCHER

FIRE CRUNCHER

MUSKINS

QUILL CRUNCHER

OLIVE MUSKINS

FRASER NYMPH No2

HOT NYMPH

FRASER NYMPH No1

COVE PHEASANT TAIL No2

COVE PHEASANT TAIL No3

COVE PHEASANT TAIL No1

MONTANA NYMPH

UV CRUNCHER

HARE'S EAR

Stillwater Nymphs II

RED SPOT BUZZER
Hook: Kamasan B 100 size 10-14
Thread: Black
Butt: Glo-Brite floss No4
Body: Black floss
Rib: Stripped quill from peacock eye feather
Thorax: Black floss
Cheeks: Fine flat gold tinsel

OLIVE BUZZER No1
Hook: Kamasan B 100 size 12-14
Thread: Medium olive
Body: Heron herl
Rib: Olive Flexi Floss
Thorax: Olive floss, varnished
Cheeks: Jungle cock, dyed yellow

QUILL BUZZER
Hook: Heavy gauge size 10-12
Thread: Black
Body: Stripped quill from peacock eye feather
Thorax: Black floss
Cheeks: Fine flat gold tinsel

BLACK NYMPH (ROD TYE)
Hook: Light wire size 12
Thread: Black
Tail: Furnace hackle fibres
Body: Black floss
Rib: Grey Flexi Floss
Breathers: Goose biots, dyed deep orange
Thorax: Peacock green Glister

HOLO QUILL BUZZER
Hook: Heavy gauge size 10-12
Thread: Red
Body: Stripped quill from peacock eye feather
Thorax: Red holographic tinsel varnished over

BLACK HOLO BUZZER
Hook: Kamasan B 100 size 12-14
Thread: Black
Body: Pheasant tail, dyed black
Rib: Fine red holographic tinsel
Breathers: White DNA fibres
Thorax: Black floss
Thorax cover: Red holographic tinsel

BLACK BEAD BUZZER
Hook: Kamasan B 100 size 14
Thread: Black
Body: Black tinsel or floss
Rib: Fine silver wire
Head: Gold or silver bead

OLIVE BUZZER No3
Hook: Kamasan B 100 size 12-14
Thread: Green
Body: Dark olive & medium olive Flexi Floss
Thorax: Black floss
Cheeks: Red holographic tinsel with jungle cock over

CLARET BUZZER
Hook: Heavy gauge size 12-14
Thread: Claret
Body: Claret floss
Rib: Fine pearl tinsel
Thorax: Claret floss, varnished
Cheeks: Orange goose biots
Breathers: White EPS fibres

BOTTLE GREEN BUZZER
Hook: Kamasan B 175 size 12-14
Thread: Black
Body: Bottle green Ultra wire
Thorax: Black floss
Thorax cover: Pearl tinsel

BLACK NYMPH

RED SPOT BUZZER

OLIVE BUZZER No3

HOLO QUILL BUZZER

OLIVE BUZZER No1

CLARET BUZZER

BLACK HOLO BUZZER

QUILL BUZZER

BOTTLE GREEN BUZZER

BLACK BEAD BUZZER

Stillwater Nymphs III

BROWN BUZZER
Hook: Kamasan B 100 size 12-14
Thread: Orange
Body: Gold floss, varnished over
Thorax: Brown floss
Thorax cover: Pearl tinsel
Breathers: White EPS fibres

HARE'S EAR No2
Hook: Kamasan B 175 size 12-14
Thread: Fire orange
Tail: Hare's ear fibres
Body: Hare's ear fur
Flash-back: Flat gold tinsel
Rib: Fine gold wire
Cheeks: Jungle cock

GREEN GREENWELL'S
Hook: Kamasan B 170 size 12-14
Thread: Fire orange
Tail: Greenwell hackle fibres
Body: Veniard's green floss
Rib: Fine flat gold tinsel
Thorax: Blue mole fur
Thorax cover: Pearl tinsel
Hackle: Greenwell's cock hackle

BLACK SPIDER BUZZER
Hook: Kamasan B 100 size 12-14
Thread: Black
Body: Black tinsel or floss
Rib: Fine silver wire
Thorax: Red holographic tinsel
Hackle: Black hen hackle
Cheeks: Jungle cock

BLOODWORM
Hook: Heavy gauge size 12
Thread: Red
Tail: Red Flexi Floss
Body: Red seal's fur
Rib: Fine silver wire

MICK'S OLIVE BUZZER
Hook: Kamasan B 100 size 12-14
Thread: Medium olive
Body: Heron herl
Rib: Orange Flexi Floss
Breathers: White DNA fibres
Thorax: Hare's ear dyed olive

ZEBRA BUZZER
Hook: Kamasan B 175 size 10-12
Thread: Black
Body: White floss
Rib: Black tinsel
Thorax: Black floss
Thorax cover: Pearl tinsel
Cheeks: White goose biots

OLIVE BUZZER No2
Hook: Kamasan B 100 size 12-14
Thread: Medium olive
Body: Heron herl
Rib: Olive Flexi Floss
Thorax: Olive UV Straggle
Cheeks: Red holographic tinsel
Breathers: Grey EPS fibres

SOOTY OLIVE
Hook: Light wire size 12-14
Thread: Black
Tail: Bronze mallard fibres
Body: Pheasant tail, dyed olive
Rib: Red Ultra wire
Thorax: Sooty olive seal's fur
Hackle: Black hen feather
Cheeks: Jungle cock

HARE'S EAR No1
Hook: Light wire size 10-12-14
Thread: Fire orange
Body: Hare's ear & yellow seal's fur mixed
Rib: Fine flat gold tinsel
Thorax: Hare's ear fur
Cheeks: Gold holographic tinsel

A family of Buzzers

THROUGHOUT THE SEASON, the angler's 'buzzer' the Chironomid midge, provides a major contribution to the diet of both rainbow and brown trout. This is how its imitations have gained such a reputation as a top-performing nymphs on stillwaters. Numerous styles of Buzzer patterns have emerged from the fly-tying vice over the years, the majority being tied to imitate the pupal stage of this insect's life.

We have Buzzers that range from super-heavy epoxy-coated tyings to tiny, anorexic patterns, Buzzers tied with straight bodies and others dressed right around the bend. Many styles are hackled Buzzers and Spider-type flies. There are Buzzers fished 'dry' – in the surface film – like the Shipman's. There are parachute-hackled dry Buzzers and tyings, which set out to imitate the emerging fly. The list goes on, and more variations are invented each season. When I first came to England, some 25 or so years back, I must admit I hadn't even heard of the Buzzer let alone fished one. I can remember only one style of dressing for the Black Buzzer back then; a rather simple one with black thread for the body, a rib of silver oval tinsel, peacock herl for the thorax and a tuft of white fibres up front. Today, if there are more variations – aside from colour – to a single fly then I cannot think of one. In the first of these plates, I have put together a selection of twelve dressings for the Black Buzzer in this section alone; I could easily have added a dozen more. Why so many, you might ask? Well, over the course of a season, Black Buzzers will account for more trout than any other colour, and successful flies always generate numerous variations. In the wet-fly world of Ireland, the Green Peter has enjoyed the same fate. The pupal stage of many of the different coloured buzzers may often appear dark in deep water, which is why I suspect that black works well. Light conditions and the silhouette of the nymph may also be a factor in the fish's choice.

I tend to stick to my favourite two or three patterns, as I suspect most other anglers do, too. We each have our favourites – flies that have worked for us on particular waters and which give us great confidence. After black, my most successful Buzzer colours are, bottle green followed by brown, olive and then red. The red and olive patterns are particularly effective when a hackle is added to imitate the emerging insect.

Often we travel to a new water, and are given a special pattern that works well there. Afterwards we go home, tie half a dozen of our newly-found favourite and add them to our growing collection of flies. For me, one such fly was the Traffic Light Buzzer at Grafham Water. Fished on the point, with a Crisp Packet Buzzer on the dropper, it is quite deadly from May to July. In August the Red Buzzer, which I have christened the Grafham Raider, fishes superbly on the top dropper position. However, should I be restricted to fishing only one colour of Buzzer for the entire season, then without question it would be black.

I remember fishing on Lough Lein in Killarney the day before the Munster Championships in 2006. I hooked a good trout which dived under the boat and shot off out

A silver, over-wintered rainbow from Elinor. It took an Elinor Buzzer

Playing a big Farmoor rainbow that took a deep-fished Buzzer

the back. The leader became caught up on the boat's hull and, in the end, I lost both the flies and the trout. I was slightly annoyed with myself for losing the flies; I had been catching trout on a Black Buzzer and I had none of that particular pattern left in my box for the competition next day. The following morning I was still feeling a bit gloomy when my boatman, Robbie, handed me the cast of flies that I thought were long gone. He had dragged the boat up on to the shore after I had left and, luckily for me, rescued from the keel three of the four flies that were still attached to the leader. I put up the same flies later that day, caught six of my nine trout on the Black Buzzer and won the competition.

TACTICS

In the early part of the season, size 10 Buzzers tend to work best. As spring makes way for the summer months, I find a size 12 becomes much more effective. I often fish a size 10 at this time of year but this is usually to anchor the team of flies. As September approaches, a mixture of size 14s and 12s are preferred as the natural insect is now quite small. When fishing Buzzers I only use just two lines; a 6 or 7-weight floating line is my number one choice followed by a similar weight midge-tip. The midge-tip is still an excellent choice when straight-lining a team of nymphs, but is also highly effective when fishing the washing-line method. Total success for me from a day's fishing is when I manage to catch trout on all of the patterns I have selected on the leader. For that reason, I fish with quite a long leader and start off with droppers around 10 inches long. I am forever swopping flies in the quest to find the perfect solution, which is why I need those long droppers. In terms of leader length, my normal set up from line to tip to first dropper is 5 feet then 4 feet to the second dropper. This distance is again repeated for the third dropper and a similar distance to the point fly. Such a set up would give me a total leader length of approximately 17 feet.

The management of a leader this long can prove problematic at times either in a big wind or when the trout are showing a preference for point fly. I feel this is often compensated for by a satisfactory catch return. With the flies well spaced apart, I frequently find myself in a double hook-up situation, which is good fun. I have always disliked flies that are bunched up on a leader; I think this just causes confusion. If buzzers are hatching, I

A good rainbow that took a Black and Copper Buzzer

will tend to fish a hackled fly on the top dropper, a fairly slim Buzzer or two in the middle and, on the point, a fly dressed right around the bend of the hook. This gives me a good variety of flies on the leader and varied sink-rate, which allows me to fish through the depths. Provided the dropper flies are working, I will only change the point fly if I need to correct the depth at which I am fishing. If the trout go deep, after making a cast I will leave the flies settle in the water for longer before starting the retrieve. I also have the option of lengthening the leader between the middle dropper and the point fly to achieve an even greater depth if I need it. All of these are options I will employ before I will consider changing the floating line. I tend not to bother much with Epoxy Buzzers, as I prefer to add a coat or two of varnish to a fly if I need a little extra weight and to gloss the body. It has been said and written many times before but, when Buzzer fishing, always watch the end of your line. It never ceases to amaze me the times other anglers completely miss a take through lack of observation. Even at the other end of the boat, I can spot the movement on the tip of my boat partner's line. I have had to stop saying 'You just missed a take' because of the funny looks that

follow. However frustrating, it is prudent to stay quiet at times. When Buzzer fishing on Farmoor Reservoir some years ago, I experienced a series of incredibly violent takes. The fish were smashing into the flies at an incredible speed. On other occasions, the take can be as gentle as a leaf touching the line and, if you are not in control of your line and flies, the opportunity will be missed. It's vital that everything remains tight on the retrieve, especially from a drifting boat; any slack will result in a failure to connect. When fishing from the bank, selecting a position on the shore where there's a side wind blowing is usually the most productive approach.

If you are familiar with the water and you know of an area with a deep shelf running just off the bank then, this is even better. I love the control that bank fishing affords the angler. One of my very favourite spots for this style of fishing is on the Three Trees shore above the dam on Eyebrook Reservoir. Within a reasonable casting distance of the bank the bottom falls away quite sharply and trout often congregate just here where deep meets shallow. Just cast out, keep everything tight and allow the wind and current to do the rest. The side wind will take the team of flies around in an arc and this is when they are their most

A PASSION FOR TROUT

The Boxmoor Buzzer

which was around 3½ lb. Well, I decided, let's try that one again… but this time without the cigarette. I made my next cast and waited until the line was directly under the boat then started the fastest figure-of-eight retrieve I could manage. Just as the flies broke the surface, I was into another fish. The action lasted for about an hour before quietening off. I landed seven quality brownies in that hectic period. The trout were obviously triggered into taking the Black Buzzer as it raced skywards in an almost vertical ascent. At the time, it was my best day's sub-surface Buzzer fishing on Lough Carra. Normally the Dry Buzzer works much better on this water than the nymph.

The Buzzers patterns in this section are all flies I have fished extensively. I tend to use a hackled Black Buzzer on the top dropper on the stillwaters in England until May. During April and May, huge hatches of black midge can descend on the water. It was on one of these days, a few years back, that I caught a 19lb rainbow trout on Elinor Fishery – it took a size 14 black 'Spider' pattern. It remains the fishery record.

deadly. In spring time, over-wintered fish will often be patrolling the margins and a team of Buzzers allowed to dead-drift in the current can prove deadly for these wily fish so, hang on as the takes often result in runs right into the backing.

BROWNIES BY ACCIDENT

I was fishing Lough Carra in June. It was a lovely day for wet-fly fishing but the trout had been quiet all morning. In desperation I decided to put up some Buzzer nymphs, though my son, David, had tried similar patterns on the lough several times before with only limited success. I then fished for about half an hour with no luck. We were probably drifting a little too fast to fish Buzzers effectively. I was compensating for the speed of the boat by making longer casts… one of the few times I ever consider doing this from a boat. I had attached a sinking braided leader to the end of my floating line; the flies I was fishing were quite small but I wanted them to fish a little deeper.

I made a long cast, then laid the rod down to light a cigarette. I sat for a moment to scan the water and reflect on life, as you do, so by the time I started the retrieve, my flies had sunk very deep. I picked up the slack to find the line had gone directly under the boat. In a hurry to gather the line to make a better cast, I drew the flies up at high speed and, just as the top dropper fly broke the surface, a trout burst out and grabbed it. I landed this beauty,

A study in concentration: Waiting for a trout to take the Buzzer

Buzzers I

BLACK & COPPER BUZZER
Hook: Kamasan B100 size 10-14
Thread: Black
Body: Black floss
Rib: Fine, flat copper tinsel
Thorax: Black floss
Cheeks: Red holographic tinsel

BLACK & GREY No2
Hook: Kamasan B 100 size 12-14
Thread: Black
Body: Pheasant tail, dyed black
Rib: Grey Flexi Floss
Thorax: Black UV Straggle
Thorax cover: Pearl tinsel
Breathers: White EPS fibres

CORRIB BUZZER
Hook: Kamasan B 100 size 10-14
Thread: Black
Body: Black tinsel
Rib: Pearl tinsel, silver wire over
Thorax: Orange seal's fur
Cheeks: Split Jungle cock
Hackle: Black hen, two pearl strands

SEAN'S BUZZER
Hook: Kamasan B100 size 10-14
Thread: Black
Body, Black tinsel
Rib: Silver wire
Thorax: Black floss
Cheeks: Goose biots, dyed yellow
Thorax cover: Pearl tinsel
Breathers: White EPS fibres

BLUE HOLO BUZZER No2
Hook: Kamasan B100 size 12-14
Thread: Black
Body: Black tinsel
Rib: Pearl tinsel-stretched
Thorax: SLF-black
Thorax cover: Blue pearl tinsel
Breathers: White EPS fibres

RED HOLO BUZZER No2
Hook: Kamasan B 100 size 12-14
Thread: Black
Body: Black tinsel
Rib: Silver wire
Thorax: SLF-black
Cheeks: Red holographic tinsel
Breathers: White EPS fibres

BLACK & GREY BUZZER
Hook: Kamasan B 100 size 12-14
Thread: Black
Body: Pheasant tail dyed black
Rib: Grey Flexi Floss
Thorax: Black SLF
Cheeks: Red holographic tinsel
Breathers: White EPS fibres

RED HOLO BUZZER No1
Hook: Kamasan B 100 size 10-14
Thread: Black
Body: Black tinsel or black floss
Rib: Fine, silver wire
Breathers: White DNA fibres
Thorax: Black floss, varnished
Cheeks: Red holographic tinsel

PEARL & GREEN BUZZER
Hook: Kamasan B100 size 10-14
Thread: Black
Body: Black tinsel
Rib: Fine pearl tinsel
Thorax: Black floss
Cheeks: Green holographic tinsel
Breathers: White EPS fibres

TIGER BUZZER
Hook: Kamasan B100 size 12-14
Thread: Black
Body: Pheasant tail, dyed black
Rib: Red Flexi Floss
Thorax: Black UV Straggle
Thorax cover: Pearl tinsel
Breathers: White EPS fibres

BLUE HOLO BUZZER No1
Hook: Kamasan B100 size 12-14
Thread: Black
Body: Black tinsel
Rib: Pearl tinsel-stretched
Thorax: Seal's fur-black/blue-mixed
Wings: White DNA strands
Hackle: Badger cock

BLACK & PEARL BUZZER
Hook: Kamasan B100 size 10-14
Thread: Black
Body: Black tinsel-varnished
Rib: Fine pearl tinsel
Thorax: Black floss
Cheeks: Red holographic tinsel

BLACK & COPPER BUZZER

BLUE HOLO BUZZER No2

PEARL & GREEN BUZZER

RED HOLO BUZZER No2

BLACK & GREY No2

TIGER BUZZER

BLACK & GREY BUZZER

CORRIB BUZZER

BLUE HOLO BUZZER No1

SEAN'S BUZZER

RED HOLO BUZZER No1

BLACK & PEARL BUZZER

Buzzers II

CLARET MIDGE
Hook: Buzzer size 10-14
Thread: Black or claret
Body: Dark claret seal's fur
Rib: Fine flat gold tinsel
Cheeks: Jungle cock, dyed orange
Thorax: Claret Mosaic dubbing
Wing: Grey DNA strands
Hackle: Burnt badger cock hackle

OLIVE MIDGE
Hook: Buzzer size 10-14
Thread: Olive
Body: Olive/brown seal's fur
Rib: Grey Flexi Floss
Wing: Grey DNA strands
Thorax: UV light yellow, Ice Dubbing
Hackle: Medium olive grizzle cock

TRAFFIC LIGHT BUZZER
Hook: Kamasan B175 size 10-12
Thread: Black
Body: Black floss, varnished over
Rib: Stripped peacock quill
Thorax: Black floss
Thorax cover: Pearl tinsel over red tinsel
Cheeks: Orange goose biots

ELINOR BUZZER
Hook: Kamasan B100 size 10-14
Thread: Black
Body: Black floss, varnished over
Rib: Stripped peacock quill, dyed orange
Thorax: Black floss
Cheeks: Orange Crystal Hair

BROWN MIDGE
Hook: Buzzer size 10-14
Thread: Black or brown
Body: Hare's ear fur
Ribs: Fine pearl tinsel and fine gold wire
Body hackle: Cree cock
Thorax: Brown SLF
Wing: Golden pheasant tippets, dyed orange
Hackle: Cree cock hackle
Cheeks: Jungle cock

FLASH ATTACK BUZZER
Hook: Buzzer size 10-14
Thread: Black
Butt: Glo-Brite No 3
Body: Black floss, varnished over
Rib: Stripped peacock quill
Thorax: Black ostrich herl
Cheeks: Pearl Flash Attack tinsel
Breathers: White DNA strands

OLIVE BUZZER
Hook: Buzzer size 10-12
Thread: Black
Body: Medium olive floss, varnished over
Rib: Stripped peacock quill, dyed yellow
Thorax band: Red holographic tinsel
Thorax: Black floss
Cheeks: Strips cut from a Walkers crisp packet

CRISP PACKET BUZZER
Hook: Kamasan B100 size 10-14
Thread: Black
Body: Black floss, varnished over
Rib: Fine silver wire
Thorax band: Red holographic tinsel
Thorax: Black floss
Cheeks: Strips cut from a Walkers crisp packet

PHEASANT TAIL MIDGE
Hook: Buzzer size 10-14
Thread: Red
Body: Pheasant tail fibres
Rib: Red Ultra wire
Cheeks: Jungle cock
Thorax: Brown SLF
Wing: White DNA strands
Hackle: Cree cock hackle

GRAFHAM RAIDER
Hook: Buzzer size 10-12
Thread: Red
Body: Orange and red seal's fur mixed with orange Glister
Rib: White Flexi Floss
Cheeks: Jungle cock
Thorax: Brown SLF
Wing: White DNA strands
Hackle: Cree cock hackle, two turns

BLACK HOLOGRAPHIC BUZZER
Hook: Kamasan B100 size 10-14
Thread: Black
Body: Lureflash Mosaic strands
Rib: Fine silver wire
Thorax: Black floss
Thorax cover: Red holographic tinsel

RED BUZZER
Hook: Kamasan B100 size 10-14
Thread: Black
Body: Stripped peacock quill, No1-natural No2- dyed red
Thorax: Black floss
Thorax cover: Red holographic tinsel

CLARET MIDGE

BROWN MIDGE

PHEASANT TAIL MIDGE

OLIVE MIDGE

FLASH ATTACK BUZZER

GRAFHAM RAIDER

OLIVE BUZZER

TRAFFIC LIGHT BUZZER

BLACK HOLOGRAPHIC BUZZER

CRISP PACKET BUZZER

ELINOR BUZZER

RED BUZZER

RESERVOIRS AND LAKES

Diawl Bachs

PEARL RIBBED DIAWL BACH
Hook: Kamasan B175 size 10-14
Thread: Glo-Brite floss, No12
Tail: Golden pheasant red neck feather
Body: Peacock herl
Rib: Fine pearl tinsel
Throat hackle: Golden pheasant red neck feather
Cheeks: Jungle cock

STANDARD DIAWL BACH
Hook: Kamasan B175 size 10-14
Thread: Black
Tail: Brown hackle fibres
Body: Peacock herl
Rib: Fine copper wire
Throat hackle: Brown hackle fibres

A PASSION FOR TROUT

Which Diawl Bach to try?

ORIGINATING FROM WALES, the Diawl Bach (Little Devil) is an excellent nymph for tempting rainbows and wild brown trout in both rivers and lakes. Sleek lines and a skimpy dressing gives the fly very realistic nymph-like qualities. And, of course, the real beauty of this fly is in its simplicity.

The variations to the original Diawl Bach are legion. The fly is, by its very nature, already quite slim, but some of the variations today have an almost anorexic feel about them. But I actually happen to like that look.

The fact that the Diawl Bach is so successful and versatile is the reason I chose to give so much attention to this fly in this book. Originally known for its effectiveness in catching rainbow trout on reservoirs, this little fly has given me tremendous success on Irish loughs and rivers, when fishing for wild brown trout.

I started experimenting with the Diawl Bach and its variations on the River Suir, many years ago. A combination of small dropper flies dressed on size 16 heavy-gauge hooks and a bead-headed fly on the point can be excellent on its day. Some of the quill-bodied fly patterns can be very effective fished upstream. While the beaded point fly may not work as well in slow, deep water, the trout will readily take the small Diawl Bachs on the droppers.

I have also experimented recently with Diawl Bachs on Lough Lein in Killarney. My preferred method is to fish with a floating or midge-tip line with size 14s attached to the droppers and a size 12 on the point.

On traditional wet-fly fisheries like Lough Lein, if there was little or no wind during the day, conventional wisdom would suggest the chances of catching trout had diminished considerably. Not so. Put up a team of Diawl Bachs and head for the shallow bays, fish a slow retrieve, and enjoy the experience.

On stillwaters, a combination of Buzzers and Diawl Bachs can be absolutely deadly. The Red Holo version of the Diawl Bach will catch trout all season but I find it most effective early in the year and again in the summer months, when red buzzers are hatching. In April and May, black and olive versions can work very well; that said, my most successful Diawl Bach variant in 2009 was a pattern with a quill body plus red holographic tinsel and jungle cock cheeks. I caught some top-quality trout on this fly both on Draycote Water and Elinor Fishery in April and May. Fact is, the original Diawl Bach, with its plain, bronze peacock herl body, will still out-fish many of its variations and should never be discounted in favour of one of its more colourful cousins.

Diawl Bach patterns with stretched pearl tinsel in their bodies have been created with Lough Lein in mind. A body tied with either black or claret herl with blue pearl over can

A Draycote rainbow that took a small Diawl Bach

be outstanding on this lough. On stillwaters today, using the washing-line method with a selection of Diawl Bachs on the droppers can be very effective.

In recent years, especially as the water begins to warm up, I tend to concentrate my fishing around Diawl Bachs in preference to Buzzers. This is certainly a departure from my traditional style of nymph fishing. But, when trout are high up in the water, I find the Diawl Bach much more effective these days. Some years ago, a typical leader formation would have been a Diawl Bach on the top dropper and a team of Buzzers below. Today, from spring onwards, I tend to fish with an Emerger on the top dropper, followed by a couple of Diawl Bachs and a single Buzzer on the point.

Perhaps this is just another one of those confidence issues. But then again, confidence is a huge factor in fly-fishing, as it is in any sport. Though not a style of fishing I enjoy greatly, the Diawl Bach can also be deadly when fished on the bung. I had a particularly cracking day on Elinor Trout Fishery using this method. The trout were holding at a depth of around one foot and wanted the fly presented almost static. I had tried a variety of lines and retrieves with only moderate success. Finally, I rigged up the bung with two quill-bodied Diawl Bachs. The dropper fly was positioned a foot or so below the bung, the point fly at twice that; I immediately started catching fish after fish. Every time the sun broke through, the takes would come on the point fly, but, as soon as I had some cloud cover the takes would switch up to the dropper fly. When depth is the critical factor, using the bung will often out-fish other methods. And of course, as in my recent experience, when conditions alter during the day the takes can come at different depths for prolonged periods and then suddenly change. When fishing the 'washing line' the trick here is to start with the heaviest fly nearest the Booby on the point, if the trout are up in the water. Should the trout go deeper, then switch the heavy fly to the centre dropper and this will create an even greater arc in the leader allowing the cast of flies to fish even deeper without the need to switch lines.

I like to ring the changes and produce a variety of any good pattern. I have put together a selection of Diawl Bachs which I fish. I'll never claim to be the first in anything – in fishing or fly-tying – but some of the flies I've included here are definitely a departure from the norm... and they work!

Two very successful variations on the Diawl Bach theme

Diawl Bachs

BLACK & RED DIAWL BACH
Hook: Kamasan B 170 size 10-14
Thread: Black
Tail: Badger hackle fibres
Body: Peacock herl, dyed black
Rib: White Flexi Floss
Cheeks: Red holographic tinsel
Hackle: Badger hackle fibres

QUILLED DIAWL BACH
Hook: Kamasan B 170 size 10-14
Thread: Red
Tail: Natural red hackle fibres
Body: Stripped peacock eye quill
Thorax: Red holographic tinsel
Hackle: Natural red hackle fibres
Cheeks: Jungle cock

GOLD RIBBED DIAWL BACH
Hook: Kamasan B 170 size 10-14
Thread: Fire orange
Tail: Natural red hackle fibres
Body: Peacock herl
Rib: Fine flat gold tinsel
Hackle: Natural red hackle fibres
Cheeks: Jungle cock

MICK'S OLIVE DIAWL BACH
Hook: Kamasan B 170 size 10-14
Thread: Black
Tail: Greenwell's hackle fibres, dyed olive
Body: Heron herl substitute
Rib: Medium olive Flexi Floss
Hackle: Greenwell's feather, dyed olive
Cheeks: Jungle cock, dyed yellow

BLACK & BLUE
Hook: Kamasan B 170 size 10-14
Thread: Black
Tail: Black hackle fibres
Body: Black silk, tapered
Rib: Blue pearl tinsel
Thorax: Peacock herl, dyed black
Hackle: Black hackle fibres
Cheeks: Jungle cock

SILVER RIBBED DIAWL BACH
Hook: Kamasan B 170 size 10-14
Thread: Fire orange
Tail: Badger hackle fibres
Body: Peacock herl, dyed black
Rib: Fine flat silver tinsel
Hackle: Badger hackle fibres
Cheeks: Jungle cock

OLIVE QUILL DIAWL BACH
Hook: Kamasan B 170 size 10-14
Thread: Black
Tail: Medium olive hackle fibres
Body: Stripped quill from peacock eye, dyed olive
Thorax: Peacock herl, dyed olive
Hackle: Medium olive hackle fibres
Cheeks: Jungle cock, dyed yellow

RED SPOT DIAWL BACH
Hook: Kamasan B 170 size 10-14
Thread: Black
Tail: Black hackle fibres
Butt: Glo-Brite floss, No4
Body: Black Flexi Floss
Thorax: Peacock herl, dyed black
Thorax cover: Red holographic tinsel
Hackle: Black hackle fibres

BLUE DIAWL BACH
Hook: Kamasan B 170 size 10-14
Thread: Black
Butt: Medium blue floss
Tail: Natural red hackle fibres
Body: Peacock herl
Rib: Fine copper wire
Cheeks: Blue holographic tinsel
Hackle: Natural red hackle fibres

CLARET DIAWL BACH
Hook: Kamasan B 170 size 10-14
Thread: Claret
Tail: Furnace hackle fibres
Body: Claret Flexi Floss
Thorax: Peacock herl, dyed claret
Hackle: Furnace hackle fibres
Cheeks: Jungle cock

PEARL RIBBED DIAWL BACH
Hook: Kamasan B 170 size 10-14
Thread: Glo-Brite floss, No12
Tail: Golden pheasant red neck feather
Body: Peacock herl
Rib: Pearl tinsel
Hackle: Golden pheasant red neck feather
Cheeks: Jungle cock

LEIN DIAWL BACH
Hook: Kamasan B 170 size 10-14
Thread: Black
Tail: Black hackle fibres
Body: Peacock herl, dyed claret
Rib: Blue pearl tinsel
Hackle: Black hackle fibres
Cheeks: Jungle cock, dyed yellow

BLACK & BLUE

BLUE DIAWL BACH

BLACK & RED DIAWL BACH

SILVER RIBBED DIAWL BACH

QUILLED DIAWL BACH

CLARET DIAWL BACH

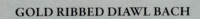

OLIVE QUILL DIAWL BACH

GOLD RIBBED DIAWL BACH

PEARL RIBBED DIAWL BACH

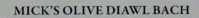

RED SPOT DIAWL BACH

MICK'S OLIVE DIAWL BACH

LEIN DIAWL BACH

RESERVOIRS AND LAKES

Draycote Water

FOR AS LONG as I can remember, anglers from the UK have been making an annual pilgrimage across to Ireland to fish the great western lakes in the quest to land one of those big wild brownies. In recent times that trend has been somewhat reversed; we are now seeing Irish anglers, many of them friends of mine, coming over to fish UK stillwaters. Draycote Water is often on their list of venues. If there is one stillwater I look forward to fishing most, then it has to be Draycote Water – I simply love the place. Over the years it has built its reputation as a top of the water fishery. Insect life and in particular, Buzzer hatches can at times be prolific which leads to lots of surface activity. For the imitative style angler, Draycote is paradise.

For Bank anglers, if Draycote Water had one outstanding feature it is the road which runs around its entire perimeter. And, of course, it has outstanding fishing.

Situated in the heart of the Warwickshire countryside, the reservoir covers a surface area of 600 acres with almost five miles of bank fishing which, thanks to the perimeter road, is made very comfortable. Wind speed and direction can often vary throughout the course of the day but the road around the reservoir allows for easy access to all areas of the fishery. Generous car parking facilities allow anglers the convenience and also the ability to change location quickly.

For those of a more adventurous nature, the fishery operates a fleet of twenty five motor boats which are well maintained and always in excellent condition

The reservoir was constructed in the late '60s, with its primary function being to provide water for the populations of Rugby and Leamington Spa. Water is pumped into the reservoir from the river Leam and the Warwickshire Avon. The deepest area of water is 70 feet

A productive drift off Lin Croft Point

but submerged islands – the 'shoals' – add character to the fishing making for some interesting drifts.

Draycote Water first opened its gates to fishermen in 1970 and has since that time established itself as a premier trout fishery. About 50,000 rainbows are stocked each year, ranging from 1lb 8oz to 10lb. In alternate years, 1,000 to 2,000 small brown trout, about six inches long, are also released into the water and allowed to grow on. These brownies survive in the reservoir for a considerable time and eventually become almost wild. The record rainbow for the fishery weighed in at 23lb and was caught by Dunchurch angler Paul Wally. The biggest brown trout was Bob Wallinger's hefty 14-pounder.

Some ground-breaking survey work was conducted a number of years ago at Draycote. Before being introduced to the reservoir, all of the trout were tagged. Anglers were asked to record the date and location the tagged fish were caught. This provided the management of the fishery with invaluable information on the movement of fish throughout the season and would eventually mould the future stocking policies for the reservoir.

FISHING SEASON
On most stillwaters the trout tend to patrol the margins in the early part of the season. For this reason it is the bank anglers who normally get off to a good start, using a variety of lures on sinking lines. The most popular areas for bank anglers are Rainbow Corner, Flat Stones, Dunn's Bay, Lin Croft Point, Cornfield and Toft Bay.

Patterns with black and green work best in the early-season cold water. A long-tailed Damsel Nymph can also be very effective during the early part of the season along with a White Bodied Montana. Even as early as April, this is a water where I would not hesitate to start with a team of Buzzers fished on a floating line and a long leader. Once the weather warms, around the beginning of May, the trout disperse, spreading out across the whole of the reservoir. Buzzer fishing, with both dry and nymph patterns can be tremendous from this point onwards. I have fished Draycote for many years and have found the hackled Shipman's an excellent dry-fly whenever the adult buzzer is on the water. The trout here certainly do respond well to the dry-fly. A team of Shipman's Dry Buzzers in orange, black and yellow will take trout throughout most of the season. When I visit most fisheries very early in the season, I would probably leave my box of dry-flies at home – not so when I make the journey to Draycote; such are my expectations of this fine water. Even on one a cold April in 2008 the trout were up and taking small black midge off the surface. This was by no means an unusual event for Draycote.

Taking a rest – a female, olive buzzer

DRY-FLY IN THE FOG
I can recall a great day's dry-fly fishing on the water during one of my early season visits several years ago. When I arrived at the shore, the reservoir was shrouded in dense fog, but not one to be easily deterred, I rigged up the rod with some dry-flies and pointed the boat in the general direction of Toft. When the fog finally cleared I discovered that I was, in fact, at the opposite end of the reservoir, quite near the Valve Tower. It just goes to show how disorienting navigating a boat can be in such dense fog. As the mist began to clear the trout came on the feed. I was fishing my usual dry Shipman's

and, on this particular day, yellow was the most effective colour. I finished up with a limit bag of quality rainbows. The dry-fly always appears to attract the better quality fish and these Draycote trout were no exception... they fought like cats.

THE BUNG

In recent years I have noticed many anglers opting to fish the static Buzzer Nymph below a bung – a buoyant non-fly which helps support the nymphs and indicate a take when it occurs. This method, fished with a floating line, works very well on Draycote as the trout here appear to prefer the buzzer nymph offered static rather than the more conventional slow figure-of-eight retrieve. A Booby or similar highly visible pattern is fixed to the top dropper and a number flies or nymphs suspended below. Once the depth that the fish are holding in has been established then the suspended nymphs can be fixed to the leader at the correct intervals. The Bung method can be deadly at times simply because it allows the flies to remain in the productive zone. It is not just nymphs that work well on this method, a standard Wet-fly such as a Silver Invicta fished static below the bung can work surprisingly well at the back end of the season. When fishing buzzers in the more traditional way on a floating line, a dead-slow retrieve is the order of the day. However slowly the angler thinks they are retrieving the fly, it's my guess that it's probably not quite slow enough for this water.

THE FIRST BUZZERS

Bank anglers often utilise a side wind to bring the nymphs around slowly, letting the surface drift do the work. No retrieve is required – just keep the line as straight as possible and concentrate on the end of the fly line, watching for the slightest movement. The first buzzers to appear on this water will usually be black. The Boxmoor Buzzer can be very successful along with a pattern with red holographic cheeks. The Traffic Light Buzzer and the Crisp Packet Buzzer are also top performing patterns on Draycote. Black is then often followed by the olive green and brown buzzers. The

A Black Dabbler accounted for this nice clean rainbow

A good Draycote rainbow that took a Quill Buzzer

early season buzzers can be quite big on Draycote so do not be afraid to fish a size 10 on the point. In summer, a medium olive buzzer can be seen hatching. Brown is also quite a dominant colour at this time of year; a Pheasant Tail Emerger, a rough Hare's Ear and the standard Diawl Bach are all worth a try. One of my favourite patterns is a Buzzer tied with a red butt, a natural peacock quill on the body with a variety of different coloured cheeks. The car park for boat anglers is positioned close to the waters edge, this can be quite advantageous for a little extra information gathering. A good indication of what is happening on the water at any time of year is to examine your car after visiting the fishing lodge. You will find that you have a few welcome visitors after the car has been parked up for ten minutes. This will provide a good indication as to what insects are hatching off, making the task of choosing the right patterns that much easier.

If the trout are in the mood for a chase, try an Orange Blob on the top dropper and a Peach Booby on the point. This will normally provoke a reaction and provide some exciting bow waves as the trout chase the flies back towards the boat. In bright weather conditions, when the trout may be lying deeper in the water, the same flies will work on a sinking line with a variety of Cormorants on the droppers. On difficult days and when all else fails, give a long tailed Fritz Damsel a go – it's a rare occasion when this fly won't catch a fish at Draycote.

The Silver Sedge: A great top-dropper fly for Draycote

DRAYCOTE WATER

Peter Gathercole playing a Cruncher-caught rainbow

In recent years I have enjoyed some tremendous fishing from a drifting boat, short-lining with a team of wet-flies, especially with Dabbler patterns. Black and claret are good colours during the summer months, though for the top dropper I seldom stray from the Silver Sedge or Soldier Palmer. If fishing from a boat some of the more notable drifts are, A Buoy to Musborough Shoal, Draycote Dam to Biggin Bay and Middle Shoal to Toft Bay. A south-west wind provides some excellent drifts along Dunns Bay and also along the Cornfield shoreline and finally on into Toft Shallows. If I do decide to drop anchor then Lin Croft Point and opposite the Inlet are two of my favourite areas to fish on this water. This is also an excellent reservoir for fishing the washing line method, mounting a mixture of Buzzers and Diawl Bachs on the droppers with a Booby on the point.

SPECTACULAR EVENING RISE

There are no fixed rules in fly-fishing, but the most productive technique when fishing the washing line on Draycote is to allow the flies to hang rather than incorporate movement into the retrieve. If conditions are good, the evening rise can also be quite spectacular from May and on right throughout the summer months. Good hatches of brown and olive green sedges can be seen on warm evenings. Dry-flies such as the Rusty Brown Sedge, Green Sedge and Fiery Brown Sedge are all excellent evening patterns. And of course, adult buzzers will be on the wing so, never go out without a selection of hackled Shipman's Buzzers.

In tandem with its reputation as a top-of-the-water fishery, Draycote is also noted for its very big brown trout. A regular visitor from Ireland, my friend Andrew Boyd once landed and released two super brownies within fifteen minutes of each other; both were caught on the Buzzer. The product of this fishery's stocking policy, these grown-on trout weighed 7lb and 7lb 8oz – an amazing catch by any standards. I first fished Draycote Water more than 20 years ago in September and this continues to be my favourite month on this water. Fry feeders normally show in good numbers though there's still plenty of insect life to keep the trout interested in dry-flies and nymphs. Even in years when the daddy longlegs, or crane fly, fail to reach plague proportions, the trout willingly came up for the artificial. I enjoyed some great fishing in September 2007 with the dry Daddy Longlegs and Hoppers. The dam wall was covered with the natural fly and, as the day warmed up, the insects were being blown over our heads off the dam wall on to the reservoir. Some very big trout were up in the water that year, waiting for these large insects to land on the surface. If fishing the wet-fly in September, a Soldier Palmer tied with knotted legs used on the top dropper and a Daddy Longlegs on the point make an excellent team. I would certainly not recommend fishing with anything lighter than 8lb breaking-strain monofilament at this time of year.

THE DETAIL

The fishery is located just four miles south of Rugby in Warwickshire with access gained off the A426. The season opens in late March and closes at the end of October. The lodge is fully manned throughout the season and opens its door to anglers early every morning at 7.30. The staff at Draycote Water are among the most friendly I have ever dealt with on any fishery in the UK. With over thirty years' involvement, much of the success of this water can be attributed to the fishery manager Keith Causer and his wife Margaret.

Steve Cullen with a superb Draycote brown trout

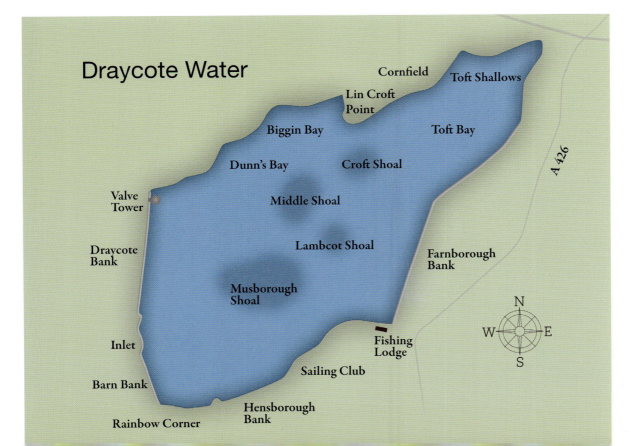

Emergers

IN THE INSECT world, the transformation from pupal stage to adulthood is a risky business By its very nature an emerging insect is extremely vulnerable during this critical stage in its short life. As the winged adult struggles to break free, both birds and fish home in to avail themselves of easy pickings. For this very reason many insects hatch out under the cover of darkness. But on evenings where there is plenty of light left in the night sky this strategy does not always pay off.

The first indication that a hatch is in the offing is when gulls and swifts begin dive bombing the surface. Ducks arrive out on the water from their nesting beds in the reeds and join the banquet and then, when they think it's safe to feed, the trout get in on the act. Knowing where and when a hatch is likely to occur will pay dividends, particularly on a large body of water. For instance it has taken me years to discover some of these hotspots on Lough Carra and I am still learning each time I visit.

A TYPICAL DAY
Another winter has passed, and spring is upon us. This is a time of great anticipation for the imitative style angler. As temperatures begin to rise most fisheries come to life with an abundance of insects on the water. Trout are now beginning to examine the surface of the water for their next meal. It is not unusual in May for the day's fishing to start slowly. The evenings are still cold with the odd frost lingering about; the mornings often kick off with a dose of bright sunshine, so the fishing is likely to be pretty tough.

The early morning tactic is to fish a team of nymphs and explore the depths. The action can be slow, the trout often appear to be quite lethargic and only display a mild interest in the nymphs. Lots of plucks, knocks and bangs, but very few solid hook-ups. This is often a symptom of trout that have enjoyed a recent feast. Examining the surface of the water, it is evident from the number of shucks and other debris lying about, there has recently been a significant hatch. Confidence increases and it is now a matter of waiting and being patient. As the day progresses the cloud cover begins to disperse a little, the sky clears, temperatures rise and the day warms. Happy days, the trout eventually come on the feed. Sight fishing replaces blind casting as your quarry is giving away its presence and can now be targeted. Dry-flies have been mounted on the spare rod in anticipation of this eventuality. Everything is going to plan; it's now only a matter of presenting the flies in the trout's path. After covering numerous rising fish and with every offering stubbornly refused, the problem quickly becomes apparent. The trout are fixated on a particular insect in the food chain to the exclusion of almost everything else. Breaking the code between trout and insect is not as blindingly obvious as first thought. Numerous fly changes are made, in an attempt to find a solution to what the trout are feeding on. Confidence quickly evaporates with each change as the trout continue to be overly selective and every offering is refused.

I have known these difficult and frustrating days. It is quite ironic that trout can so often be at their most difficult to catch when engaged in a feeding frenzy. I have encountered such frustrating days both on reservoirs and when fishing for wild brownies on lakes and rivers. When rainbow trout decide to target a particular insect in the food chain, they can be just as difficult to tempt as any wily brown trout. Having exhausted the armoury of small nymphs and dry-flies with scant effect, the solution is often to resort to pulling a fly at speed through the feeding trout. This final act of desperation is designed to trigger the fish's aggressive instincts. Employing such tactics would indicate that you have in fact, raised the white flag of surrender and grudgingly accepted that on this occasion, you have been beaten!

LOUGH LEIN
Last year I stumbled on one such tough day during a trip to Lough Lein in Killarney. The winds were light, conditions were good and the trout were up and feeding. With just the odd pluck on the small wets, I gave the Diawl Bachs a go but with little success. Then I changed to the dry-fly, anticipating a positive reaction.
Not so; only the occasional trout displayed any interest in my dry-flies and most of those were half-hearted swirls. The solution is normally to go down a size and try a few

This superb rainbow fell to an Olive Emerger

EMERGERS

The Grafham Raider

different patterns. It worked to an extent and I landed a few nice fish. However it was the high percentage of refusals that nearly drove me to distraction. The following day, we encountered almost identical conditions. Overnight I had time to analyse my day's fishing and I decided if conditions permitted, to adopt an entirely different tactic.

I mounted a team of Emergers on a light leader and covered rising fish throughout the day. The results were excellent and I had a cracking time landing and returning loads of fish. The trout clearly wanted the fly presented *in* the surface, and not *on* it. My retrieve was a slow figure-of-eight and the line, a midge-tip. The combination of a light leader and hackled Emergers dressed on light-wire hooks ensured the team of flies remained in the productive zone. It would be fair to say that I have enjoyed more success fishing Emergers on Lough Lein than on any other lough in Ireland. Why that is I'm not totally sure. This is a water where it is generally accepted that the trout prefer the flies moved at speed and yet the Emerger is taken with confidence on a slow figure of-eight retrieve. For a few years the Buzzer worked well in a limited number of shallow bays, it still does to a certain degree. Today, if fishing a team of four flies in a light wind, I will opt for two Emergers on the top droppers and Diawl Bachs on the third dropper and point fly. Black is a dominant colour on Lein so the AK47 is a first choice to fill the top-dropper position on most occasions. During the summer months I would probably swap the AK47 for an olive green pattern and then towards the back end of the season I will opt for a claret fly. The Pheasant Tail Emerger is a solid middle dropper fly that's effective throughout the whole season.

DRY-FLIES WERE IGNORED

If trout are moving on the surface my first preference will be the floating line and a team of dry-flies. But as I have learned from experience, dry-flies are not always the solution to fish feeding on our just under the surface. I recently encountered such a situation during a pleasant summer's afternoon at Elinor Trout fishery. The odd fish was moving on the surface, which is my normal cue to mount a team of dry-flies. I covered a number of rising fish and, much to my surprise, my dry-flies were ignored. Once I was over this initial shock I changed to a midge tip line. With olive buzzers on the wing, I selected the Olive Wasp for the top dropper followed by a Hackled Buzzer in the middle and a Black Buzzer on the point. The Black Buzzer for the most part achieved very little other than to anchor the team of flies. The idea to create the Wasp came from an article that Rod Tye wrote in 2006 for Trout & Salmon magazine. Rod produced a range of flies called "Tye's Reversed Bumbles" (TRBs) I tinkered around the edges of Rod's idea and came up with a number of variations I called the Wasps. That day on Elinor was my first trial with the Olive Wasp and what a success it has turned out to be. I cannot remember how many trout I caught on that particular fly – it was quite a few. I do remember my biggest fish on the Wasp though – it was a beauty of 11lb 2oz. A week or so later I caught another rainbow weighing 10lb, again taken on the Olive Wasp. So, in its first few outings the Wasp had already shown its ability to tempt larger-than-average trout.

When trout are clearly taking insects off the surface of the water then working out what flies to put on the leader is not too difficult. A combination of your own

The 11lb 2oz rainbow that took an Olive Wasp

observations plus acquired knowledge will assist you in the decision making process. It becomes a totally different proposition when trout are rising and yet the surface of the water appears devoid of insect life.

THE INQUISITIVE MIND

We now have an altogether different problem to solve. I consider myself an imitative fly tyer and such problems present an opportunity for the inquisitive mind. Creating solutions in the vice to tempt selective trout can be hugely satisfying, when it works. When fishing nymphs on stillwaters I tend to start with a Hackled Buzzer or Emerger on the top dropper. Initially, this allows me to target the odd surface feeder and also those trout that are lying slightly deeper. An increased number of takes on the top dropper is a good indicator that the trout have moved closer to the surface. If this happens, I will usually change the heavier point fly for a lighter Emerger. It then becomes a matter of selecting the correct colour to match the hatch. Size can also be critical at times, so I tie each pattern on a range of hooks from 10 down to 16s! I look forward to my evenings on stillwaters from April to June and Carra in July. As the winds of the day settle down, the trout often switch on to hatching adult buzzers. It is at this time that the Emerger really comes into its own. There is really no such thing as a definitive solution to surface feeding trout; the perfect fly has yet to be invented. However this range of Emergers will serve to strengthen your armoury against those difficult days when the trout are being very selective and stubborn. The patterns I have selected in this section are excellent on most waters when a hatch is in progress.

Scaling down the size of the fly works well in a light ripple

Emergers I

FIERY BROWN WASP
Hook: Kamasan B 100 size 10-14
Thread: Brown
Body: Fiery brown seal's fur mixed with brown Glister
Body hackle: Grizzle cock, dyed fiery brown
Rib: Fine gold wire
Wing: Golden pheasant tippets
Shoulder hackle: Partridge, dyed orange

MICK'S EMERGER
Hook: Light buzzer size 10-16
Thread: Medium olive
Body: Heron herl
Rib: Olive Flexi Floss
Thorax: Red holographic tinsel and olive Mosaic dubbing
Wing: Deer hair fibres
Hackle: Grizzle cock, dyed medium olive

BLACK DEVIL
Hook: Sedge size 12-14
Thread: Black
Body: Black seal's fur
Body hackle: Black cock
Rib: Fine silver wire
Thorax: Red Straggle
Cheeks: Jungle cock

MICK'S WASP
Hook: Kamasan B 100 size 10-14
Thread: Black
Body: 1st half, orange seal's fur – 2nd half, pale olive seal's fur
Rib: Fine gold wire
Body hackle: Deep red cock feather
Wing: Golden olive pheasant tippets
Shoulder hackle: Partridge, dyed golden olive

QUILL EMERGER
Hook: Light buzzer size 10-16
Thread: Medium olive
Body: Brown and cream Flexi Floss
Thorax: Red holographic tinsel and golden olive seal's fur
Wing: Deer hair fibres
Hackle: Golden olive cock

DUN EMERGER
Hook: Light buzzer size 10-16
Thread: Red
Butt: Glo-Brite floss No 4
Body: Golden olive seal's fur
Rib: Fine gold wire
Wing: Deer hair fibres
Hackles: No1 – light blue dun cock
No2 – golden olive cock

OLIVE WASP
Hook: Kamasan B 100 size 10-14
Thread: Medium olive
Body: Olive Mosaic dubbing
Body hackle: Pale olive cock hackle
Rib: Fine gold wire
Wing: Golden pheasant tippets
Shoulder hackle: Partridge, dyed golden olive

STOKER EMERGER
Hook: Light buzzer size 10-14
Thread: Fire red
Body: Hare's ear fur, dyed olive
Rib: Pearl tinsel with fine gold wire over
Thorax: Red seal's fur
Wing: Deer hair fibres
Hackle: Grizzle cock, dyed medium olive

PHEASANT & ORANGE
Hook: Sedge size 10-14
Thread: Orange
Body: Pheasant tail fibres
Body hackle: Cree cock hackle
Rib: Fine gold wire
Cheeks: Jungle cock
Thorax: Orange Mosaic dubbing

Emergers II

RED HOLO EMERGER
Hook: Light buzzer size 10-16
Thread: Red
Body: Stripped peacock quill
Wing: Natural CDC
Thorax: Red holographic tinsel
Hackle: Cree cock

BLACK DUCK FLY
Hook: Kamasan B 100 size 10-12
Thread: Black
Body: Black/cream Flexi Floss, mixed
Wing: Golden pheasant tippets, white EPS fibres over
Thorax: Red holographic tinsel with black SLF
Hackle: Black hen, one turn

PHEASANT TAIL
Hook: Kamasan B 100 size 10-14
Thread: Orange
Body: Pheasant tail fibres
Rib: Fine silver wire
Thorax: Rusty brown Micro Brite
Hackle: Cree cock
Cheeks: Jungle cock

YELLOW HEAD BUZZER
Hook: Light buzzer size 10-14
Thread: Black
Body: Olive Micro chenille
Rib: Dark olive Flexi Floss
Wing: CDC, dyed olive
Thorax: Yellow foam
Hackle: Grizzle cock, dyed light olive

BIBIO EMERGER
Hook: Kamasan B 170 size 10-14
Thread: Black
Body: Black/red/black UV Straggle
Wing: Elk hair fibres
Legs: Knotted pheasant tail fibres, dyed red

SOOTY OLIVE EMERGER
Hook: Kamasan B 100 size 10-14
Thread: Black
Butt: Glo-Brite floss No7
Body: Pheasant tail fibres, dyed dark olive
Rib: Fine silver wire
Thorax: Sooty olive seal's fur
Thorax Cheeks: Fine flat silver tinsel
Hackle: Black hen
Cheeks: Jungle cock

PALE OLIVE EMERGER
Hook: Wide gape, light wire size 10-16
Thread: Olive
Body: Stripped peacock quill, dyed yellow
Thorax: Red holographic tinsel
Hackle: Cree cock, dyed pale olive
Cheeks: Jungle cock

STRIPEY
Hook: Light buzzer size 10-14
Thread: Black
Body: Pheasant tail fibres, dyed black
Rib: Grey Flexi Floss
Wing: Natural CDC
Thorax: Grey Mosaic dubbing
Hackle: Black cock

OLIVE DUCK FLY
Hook: Kamasan B 100 size 10-14
Thread: Olive
Body: Pale olive/medium olive Flexi Floss, mixed
Wing: Golden pheasant tippets with grey EPS fibres over
Thorax: Red holographic tinsel and rusty brown Micro Brite
Hackle: Medium olive hen

OLIVE EMERGING BUZZER
Hook: Kamasan B 100 size 10-14
Thread: Black
Body: Olive Micro chenille
Thorax: Hare's ear, dyed olive
Thorax cover: Pearl tinsel
Cheeks: Orange goose biots
Hackle: Rusty badger cock

RED HOLO EMERGER

YELLOW HEAD BUZZER

STRIPEY

BLACK DUCK FLY

BIBIO EMERGER

OLIVE DUCK FLY

PHEASANT TAIL

SOOTY OLIVE EMERGER

OLIVE EMERGING BUZZER

PALE OLIVE EMERGER

Stillwater wet-fly

THERE ARE THOSE who will try to convince you that traditional wet-fly fishing no longer works on stocked stillwaters. Don't believe a word of it... not if my experience in the last few years is anything to go by.

When it came to fishing on English stillwaters, my extensive collection of traditional wet-flies had remained dormant in the tackle box for many years. It was only when I travelled to Ireland that these flies would see the light of day. Then, one day, I witnessed a pair of very good anglers on Elinor Fishery making repeated short drifts. From the way that they were retrieving the line I became convinced that they using wet-flies. What's more they were absolutely hammering the trout. I thought, my eyes must be deceiving me, but no, they couldn't be. There was only one thing for it. I removed the nymphs I was using and replaced them with a team of wet-flies. Ready to go, I lifted the anchor and joined in the fun.

WET-FLIES ARE BACK

When I first came to England, some twenty six years ago, the only methods I understood were wet-fly and dry-fly fishing. The majority of my fly-fishing experiences until then had been river based and adapting to stillwaters proved an almighty shock. Lure fishing was pretty big at the time and, like most other would-be English stillwater anglers, I bought a sinking line and gave it a go. But I simply could not get on with lures and sinking lines and I am still very much the same to this day. I retreated to my comfort zone of wet and dry-fly fishing and found that, other than at the start of the season, I could pretty much hold my own on most days with the wet-fly. I used the same flies that worked for me in Ireland; after all, I knew nothing else. These traditional Irish patterns had their moments and I even held the record on my local fishery, Kingfisher Farm, for several years with a 12lb rainbow trout taken on one of those same flies.

In an attempt to learn more about stillwater methods I became an avid reader of nymph-fishing tactics and was fascinated by articles and books written on this subject. The most influential book I read at the time was Arthur Cove's "My Way With Trout" – a book which thoroughly explored the subtleties of fishing nymphs.

When I first took up stillwater fishing, the popular nymphs at that time were very large – size 10 and bigger, and often tied on longshank hooks. Patterns such as the Stick Fly, Montana Nymph and Hare's Ear were catching lots of trout. Then Cat's Whiskers, Dog Nobblers and Tin Heads became all the fashion. When Buzzer fishing took off big time, anglers were using lightly-dressed flies on small hooks, twitched slowly on long, light leaders. Now this was a technique that I could really get my teeth into. Fishing my beloved floating line, I was using flies that imitated a trout's natural food and I was in my element. I am still.

About fifteen years ago, the dry-fly enjoyed a renaissance on the stillwater scene and the Hopper was born. I also love dry-fly fishing and derive the greatest pleasure from tempting a trout to the surface to confidently sip down a well-presented fly. It is such a relaxing and rewarding way to fish.

Over the years, bit by bit, I was weaned off wet-fly fishing to the point where I didn't even bother to include them in my tackle bag. I had become fixated with nymph fishing, particularly with Buzzers. If the trout came to the surface I would revert to the dry-fly, never giving wet-flies a thought. But I am not the only stillwater angler guilty of abandoning traditional wet-fly fishing over the years. Lough-style fishing, in its traditional sense, has been neglected by many excellent anglers in preference to today's modern stillwater methods.

INVESTING TIME

Following that day on Elinor, I started to invest some time fishing the wet-fly on my favourite stillwaters. I began to experiment, tying traditional patterns with modern materials, and also tried out some new patterns that I had been developing. Fortunately at that time I was working in St Neots in Cambridgeshire, little more than 15 minutes down the road from Grafham Water. So, on a summer evening, I would finish work at around 5pm and head to the reservoir.

The wet-fly fishing was so good I didn't even bother setting up nymphs. Those few hours in to dusk made me realise just how much I enjoyed evening fishing, and how much I missed it. Thanks to Grafham, that pleasure has

One to the Limeburst Dabbler

returned. The Silver Sedge and Hot Partridge were two of my best performing flies on Grafham during those evening expeditions, a time when the wet-fly rarely failed me. It is a water I continue to fish at every opportunity having caught some wonderful trout there.

Today, during the summer months, I will normally opt to fish the wet-fly provided there's a reasonable breeze and an overcast sky. Unlike wild brown trout, rainbows do not respond well to a wet-fly in a big wind. The good news is that they will willingly take a wet-fly even in the lightest breeze. I get a great thrill watching the rainbows making a bow-wave, chasing the flies back towards the boat. Just when the top dropper breaks the surface you get that beautiful swirl at the fly and it is only a matter of lifting the rod and you're 'in.'

Regarding tackle, I fish my normal 10½ foot seven-weight boat rod with a ghost-tip line. If the wind gets up, I will at times revert to a DI3 to fish the flies just that little bit deeper. I prefer to use a fluorocarbon leader of around 7lb breaking strain and usually tie on a team of three, or sometimes four, flies on the leader. Each fly will be spaced at least four feet apart. With a further five feet from the fly line to the first dropper, as a result my leader is usually quite long. I feel it is very important to keep the flies well spaced as this will prevent bunching on the leader and avoid confusion for the trout. My preference today is to fish from a boat rather than the bank. I think the ability to move position quickly and without any fuss is what I enjoy most about boat fishing. I also like the freedom of the open water rather than getting that hemmed-in feeling when bank fishing. I tend to fish my first, exploratory drifts without the drogue. This allows me to cover a number of different areas relatively quickly. Once the fish have been located I will set the drogue to slow the boat down and give me more time over each productive spot. I prefer short drifts when wet-fly fishing on stillwaters. As soon as I stop meeting trout, I quickly haul in the drogue and swing round for another drift.

The secret in fishing any team of wet-flies on stillwaters is to hold the rod high at the end of the retrieve and allow the flies to hang for a long period before lifting off the water. I often fish a disturbance fly on the top dropper, something with CDC and deer hair in the wing to create a wake in the water. If not taken during the retrieve, the top dropper will often generate a follow and if allowed to hang, may result in a take further down the leader provided the flies are allowed to sit static for a minute or so. It never ceases to amaze me just how long the flies can sit dormant in the water before a take will come. I have cursed my indiscipline on more than one occasion. Having lifted off to soon, I have been punished by a swirling lunge as a trout makes a final desperate attempt to capture the vanishing flies; another good opportunity lost through lack of focus. Provided that there is adequate cloud cover and the trout are high up in the water, I believe the wet-fly can hold its own against all other stillwater methods.

To support my theory, I will reflect on the 2009 Lexus European Championships. As this was my first major competition in England I decided to put the effort in and practiced on Pitsford Water twice in the build-up to the qualifying heat. I quickly determined the trout were high in the water and in the mood for a chase so I automatically selected a team of wet-flies. On the qualifying day, I finished in second place with 16 trout, all taken on the wet-fly. With only the first two and the captor of the heaviest fish going through to the final, the competition for places was tough. Yet the wet-fly did the trick on the day despite the fact that we fished under very bright conditions for most of the afternoon. I brought trout to the surface all day with Dabblers and the Silver Sedge, hitting five double hook-ups – that's a fish on two flies at the same time – which was amazing fishing even by wet-fly standards. A supposedly out-moded style of fishing outperformed the modern methods. At the very least, I think I may have convinced my boat partner Ian to get behind the vice and start producing Dabblers.

ETIQUETTE

I am always conscious of what other boats are doing around me. It is good practice to scan the water and note the position of successful boats and the methods that they are employing. I am forever mindful when entering an area where other boats are stationed or drifting. I always look out for boats on the drift and attempt to give them a wide berth when motoring back up the reservoir. I have to say that, in my experience, very few of my fellow stillwater anglers bother to take the same precautions. I find the lack of manners so frustrating – to the point of getting rather angry at times.

To this end I had a very disappointing experience on Grafham Water a few years ago. A youth team was out practising on the water before an international match. Each team had an experienced angler in the boat acting as gillie and helping the young lads with advice and general tuition, which I thought was wonderful to see. The boys were being allowed turns driving the boat which I presume was a strategy to get them used to the controls of the engine and how to position the boat correctly for the next drift. I was also drifting at the time, fishing a team of wet-flies. On reaching the end of their drifts, each of these budding young Internationals would turn the boat around and drive straight back up through the other boats – including mine. They never once spared a thought for others by going around in an arc. To my mind, if you discover a productive area it is complete madness to turn the boat around and motor straight back through it. You risk putting the trout down. One boat in particular drove straight up my drift, stopped about 20 feet in front of me, threw out its drogue and started fishing. I was dumfounded and in the end I vacated the area as I was being driven to distraction by the display of bad manners.

 I was very impressed with the effort and commitment being put in by senior anglers to help train and prepare these young Internationals. But it was also a shame and a missed opportunity to educate the young lads on the etiquette of boat fishing. Always attempt to give drifting or anchored boats a wide berth and throttle down the engine as you go past. It's just common courtesy.

The extent of my English stillwater fishing has been rather reduced in recent years, since I have resumed competition fishing in Ireland. My normal pattern now is to fish Elinor during March and April, when the Buzzer fishing is at its peak. Then it's over to Ireland in May for the lake competition in Killarney and some river fishing on the Suir... provided water conditions are being kind to me.

June and July, I am back on my favourite stillwaters. With the exception of September, these are the supreme months for the wet-fly on stillwaters. Early September is normally a mad time for me, taken up with flights back and forth between England and Ireland for competition fishing. Then it's back to the stillwaters in time for the annual hatch of daddy longlegs – the crane fly, which emerges from every grassy bank after a few days of late summer rain. The three main reservoirs I fish are Draycote, Pitsford and Grafham. My experiences fishing wet-flies are based on the summer months and the patterns I have selected in this section reflect these periods in the

Traditional wet-flies – with a modern twist

season. I have also used this section to introduce some of my very latest stillwater Dabbler patterns.

PATTERNS

The key position on any team of wet-flies, is the top dropper. I put a lot of thought into which pattern I attach to that position on the leader. I feel the opposite applies to the dry-fly, where the point-fly is critical.

My favourite combination is to fish a sedge imitation on the top dropper and a Dabbler on the point. Other than floss and tinsel patterns, I prefer the bodies of my wet-fly patterns dressed in seal's fur. In an attempt to breathe life into the fly, the seal's fur should be applied loosely. In this way it will trap tiny particles of air and water in the fibres and improve the attractiveness and performance of the fly.

I have enjoyed some exceptional days wet-fly fishing in recent years, so let me take you through the some of the flies I have illustrated in this section. The Silver Sedge is an excellent top dropper pattern. This is a very versatile fly and is equally effective fished as a dry-fly on river or lake. The trout go crazy for this Sedge when pulled through the surface, often visibly following it and then smashing the fly as it breaks the surface on the lift. I have caught numerous trout on this pattern including two over 6lb, one of which was an overwintered 'bar of silver' that ran my line out to the backing. If the trout are in pursuit mode, you will experience lots of follows on the Silver Sedge, and on some days frustratingly few takes. The fly simply appears to drive the trout mad!

The Green Dabbler is a great fly for the middle-dropper, especially when the damsel nymph is hatching. From June to October, it's difficult to find a better point fly than the UV Claret Dabbler, and I've tried a few! The rainbows and brownies are particularly partial to this fly. On one particular afternoon, I was fishing Pitsford Water and had been moving and catching rainbows on the Silver Sedge. Then the wind got quite strong and the rainbows quickly went down. But, as if by magic, the brown trout came on the feed. I ended up landing six big

In the net. One more to the wet-fly

brown trout, nearly all taken on the UV Claret Dabbler.

The fly has performed even better since I added seal's fur and mixed it with the UV Straggle. The seal's fur tends to tone down the body colour and soften the overall appearance of the fly. I now combine UV Straggle and sea's fur on a number of successful wet-fly and dry-fly stillwater patterns.

The other top dropper fly to compete with the Silver Sedge is the Soldier Palmer. Tied with legs of knotted pheasant tail and a couple of pearl strips over the back this fly fishes well in May but really comes into its own in September. A Soldier Palmer Hopper, if you like.

Another important pattern in the wet-fly angler's armoury is the Daddy Longlegs. Mostly associated with dry-fly fishing and the month of September, a pulling-Daddy, when fished as part of a team of wet-flies, can be quite lethal. It is a great all-round attractor pattern and will take trout from May onwards.

IT'S HARD TO BEAT THE INVICTA

The Black Dabbler will fish on any position on the leader. I usually start with it as a dropper fly and, if the trout are interested, I will then switch it to the point where it usually performs even better.

When sedges are on the water, it is hard to beat the Invicta. I would go so far as to say that in terms of longevity, this fly has outperformed all others for me over the years. The Invicta was responsible for me qualifying for my second Troutmasters Final, tempting a rainbow trout of over 9lb late one evening at Church Hill Farm.

The Cinnamon Sedge and Hare's Ear Sedge are also great flies to try during the summer months. August is the best month for the Cinnamon Sedge. The Silver Invicta, Reversed Red Marlodge and the Pearly Invicta are the patterns to fish when the trout are charging through the shoals of fry later on in the season. The Pearly Invicta will also double up as an effective sedge pattern. The Dunkeld is a great attractor fly, fished either on the top dropper or the point. The Crunchers are simply great patterns, with their nymph-like qualities. These flies can be fished with confidence at varied speeds of retrieve. Once I have worked out the dominant colour of the natural insect being taken, I will include one of these patterns on my leader in an attempt to match the hatch.

Another technique to try is a mixture of a wet Sedge pattern or palmered fly on the top dropper and two Emergers on the middle dropper and the point. For the retrieve, long, slow draws on the line are best. I have also been experimenting with new Dabbler patterns. The

Sunburst and Limeburst Dabblers are some of my latest creations. I struggle with Blobs, but in an effort to compete and find an alternative that's aesthetically pleasing, I have started to create patterns using the successful colour combinations of the various Blobs. The results so far have been outstanding and I have already been thinking about the next generation of stillwater Dabblers.

So, the next time you are on a stillwater on a dull day with a light wind, fill your leader with wet-flies. You just might be in for a pleasant surprise.

A Muddler Daddy was this brown trout's downfall

The Pearly Dabbler

Stillwater wet-flies I

BLACK & PEACOCK SPIDER
Hook: Kamasan B 100 size 10-12
Thread: Black
Butt: Flat silver tinsel
Body: Peacock herl
Hackle: Black hen, one turn
Cheeks: Jungle cock

SILVER INVICTA
Hook: Heavy gauge size 10-12
Thread: Red
Butt: Glo-Brite floss No4
Tail: Golden pheasant crest
Body: Silver holographic tinsel
Body hackle: Natural red cock
Rib: Fine silver tinsel
Wing: Hen pheasant feather
Throat hackle: Blue jay
Cheeks: Jungle cock

SILVER SEDGE
Hook: Sedge size 10-12
Thread: Brown
Body: Flat silver tinsel
Body hackle: Cree cock
Rib: Fine silver wire
Under wing: Deer hair fibres
Wing: Natural CDC
Head hackle: Cree cock
Horns: Stripped grizzle hackle stalks

BIBIO VARIANT
Hook: Kamasan B 175 size 10-12
Thread: Black
Butt: Flat silver tinsel
Tail: Golden pheasant tippets
Body: UV straggle, black/red/black
Body hackle: Black cock
Rib: Fine pearl tinsel
Shoulder hackle: Partridge brown neck feather
Cheeks: Jungle cock

PEARLY WICKHAM'S
Hook: Heavy gauge size 10-12
Thread: Black
Tail: Golden pheasant crest
Body: Pearl tinsel
Body hackle: Natural red cock
Rib: Fine gold wire
Wing: Mallard feather
Shoulder hackle: Orange cock hackle

CINNAMON SEDGE
Hook: Sedge size 10-12
Thread: Gold
Butt: Orange floss
Body: Cinnamon seal's fur
Body hackle: Cinnamon cock
Rib: Fine gold wire
Wing: Pheasant tail fibres
Shoulder hackle: Cinnamon cock hackle

ORANGE CRUNCHER
Hook: Heavy gauge size 10-12
Thread: Orange
Tail: Golden pheasant red rump
Body: Pheasant tail dyed orange
Thorax: Orange seal's fur
Hackle: Greenwell's cock hackle
Cheeks: Jungle cock

MICKY'S FRY
Hook: Heavy gauge size 10-12
Thread: Black
Tail: Bronze mallard fibres
Body: White Ice Yarn
Rib: Fine flat silver tinsel
Throat hackles: Orange/white hackle fibres
Wing: Bronze mallard strips
Cheeks: Jungle cock

RED ARSED GREEN PETER
Hook: Kamasan B 175 size 10-12
Thread: Medium olive
Butt: Red seal's fur
Body: Olive Mosaic dubbing
Body hackle: Natural red cock
Rib: Gold oval tinsel
Wing: Hen pheasant
Shoulder hackle: Natural red cock hackle

Stillwater wet-flies II

VIVA DABBLER
Hook: Kamasan B175 10-12
Thread: Black
Butt: Flat silver tinsel
Tag: Green floss
Tail: Pheasant tail fibres dyed red
Body: Black seal's fur
Body hackle: Black cock
Rib: Fine flat silver tinsel
Shoulder hackle: Bronze mallard strips
Cheeks: Jungle cock

FLASH ATTACK SNATCHER
Hook: Kamasan B100 size 10-12
Thread: Black
Butt: Glo-Brite floss No4
Body: Flash Attack- pearl
Body hackle: Black cock
Rib: Fine silver wire
Shoulder hackle: Burnt badger, two pearl strands over
Cheeks: Jungle cock

SOLWICK
Hook: Kamasan B175 size 10-14
Thread: Red
Tail: Bronze mallard fibres
Body: Rear half – Flat gold tinsel, Front half -Red Micro Brite
Body hackle: Natural red cock
Rib: Fine gold wire

WARSAW DABBLER
Hook: Kamasan B175 size 10-12
Thread: Black
Tail: Pheasant tail fibres dyed red with pearl strips
Body: Front half, bright green Mosaic dubbing – Rear half: claret Mosaic dubbing
Body hackle: Black cock
Rib: Gold oval tinsel
Shoulder hackle: Bronze mallard
Cheeks: Jungle cock

SOLDIER PALMER
Hook: Kamasan B175 10-12
Thread: Red
Butt: Pearl tinsel
Tag: Red floss
Body: Red seal's fur
Body hackle: Natural red cock
Rib: Gold oval tinsel
Shoulder hackle: Natural red cock
Legs: Knotted pheasant tail fibres

SUNBURST DABBLER
Hook: Kamasan B175 10-12
Thread: Black
Tail: Pheasant tail fibres dyed red with pearl strips
Body: Yellow Mosaic dubbing
Thorax: Orange Mosaic dubbing
Body hackle: Orange cock
Rib: Gold oval tinsel
Shoulder hackle: Bronze mallard strips
Cheeks: Jungle cock

INVICTA
Hook: Kamasan B175 size 10-14
Thread: Orange
Butt: Glo-Brite floss No10
Tail: Golden pheasant crest
Body: Yellow seal's fur
Body hackle: Natural red cock
Rib: Gold oval tinsel
Throat hackle: Blue jay
Wing: Hen pheasant feather, dyed golden olive

HARE'S EAR SEDGE
Hook: Sedge, size 10-12
Thread: Black or brown
Body: Hare's ear fur
Ribs: Fine silver wire, fine pearl tinsel
Wings: Deer hair with natural CDC
Thorax: Fiery brown seal's fur
Hackle: Cree cock

UV CLARET DABBLER
Hook: Kamasan B175 10-12
Thread: Claret
Tail: Pheasant tail fibres with pearl strips
Body: Claret UV Straggle mixed with claret seal's fur
Body hackle: Natural red cock
Rib: Fine flat gold tinsel
Shoulder hackle: Bronze mallard strips
Cheeks: Red goose biots

RED SNATCHER
Hook: Kamasan B100 size 10-12
Thread: Black
Body: Red holographic tinsel
Body hackle: Black cock
Rib: Fine silver wire
Shoulder hackle: Burnt badger cock with pearl strips
Cheeks: Jungle cock

YELLOW PARTRIDGE
Hook: Kamasan B100 size 10-12
Thread: Yellow
Body: Pale yellow floss
Rib: Fine silver wire
Thorax: Rusty brown Micro Brite
Hackle: Partridge dyed golden olive

GREEN & ORANGE DABBLER
Hook: Kamasan B175 size 10-12
Thread: Black
Tail: Dyed olive pheasant tail with pearl strips
Body: Olive Mosaic dubbing
Thorax: Orange Mosaic dubbing
Body hackle: Medium olive cock
Rib: Fine flat gold tinsel
Shoulder hackle: Bronze mallard

Stillwater wet-flies III

ORANGE & GREEN GROUSE
Hook: Kamasan B 175 size 10-12
Thread: Green
Tail: Golden pheasant tippets
Butt: Orange seal's fur
Body: Dark olive green seal's fur
Rib: Gold oval tinsel
Hackle: Orange cock
Wing: Speckled grouse tail feather
Cheeks: Jungle cock

UV THUNDER & LIGHTNING
Hook: Kamasan B175 size 10-12
Thread: Black
Tail: Golden pheasant crest
Body: Black UV Straggle
Body hackle: Orange cock
Rib: Gold oval tinsel
Throat hackle: Blue jay
Wing: Bronze mallard
Cheeks: Jungle cock

RED SEDGE
Hook: Sedge size 10-12
Thread: Red
Butt: Red holographic tinsel
Body: Red seal's fur
Body hackle: Natural red cock
Rib: Fine flat gold tinsel
Wing: Deer hair dyed, golden brown
Head hackle: Natural red cock hackle

LIMEBURST DABBLER
Hook: Kamasan B175 size 10-14
Tail: Pheasant tail fibres dyed, golden olive with strands of Mirror Flash underneath
Body: Lime green Mosaic dubbing
Body hackle: Yellow cock
Thorax: Orange Mosaic dubbing
Rib: Oval gold tinsel
Shoulder hackle: Bronze mallard
Cheeks: Jungle cock, dyed yellow

OCTOPUS
Hook: Kamasan B 175 size 10-12
Thread: Fire red
Butt: Green holographic tinsel
Tag: Glo-Brite floss No 11
Body: Golden olive seal's fur
Body hackles: No 1- Golden olive
No 2 – Medium olive
Rib: Gold oval tinsel
Shoulder hackle: Golden pheasant rump feather

GOLDEN OLIVE BUMBLE
Hook: Kamasan B 175 size 10-12
Thread: Red
Tail: Golden pheasant crest
Body: Golden olive seal fur
Body hackle: Golden olive cock
Rib: Fine flat gold tinsel
Shoulder hackle: Blue jay

MALLARD & CLARET
Hook: Kamasan B175 size 10-12
Thread: Black or claret
Tail: Golden pheasant tippets
Body: Claret Mosaic dubbing
Rib: Fine flat gold tinsel
Hackle: Natural red cock
Wing: Bronze Mallard
Cheeks: Jungle cock

CLARET BUMBLE
Hook: Kamasan B 175 size 10-12
Thread: Black or claret
Tail: Golden pheasant tippets
Body: Medium claret seal's fur
Body hackle: Claret cock
Rib: Gold oval tinsel
Wing: Two strands of Mirror Flash
Shoulder hackle: Blue jay
Cheeks: Jungle cock

KATE MACLAREN MUDDLER
Hook: Kamasan B 175 size 10-12
Thread: Black
Tag: Glo-Brite floss No 12
Body: Black seal's fur
Body hackle: Black cock
Rib: Silver oval tinsel
Head hackle: Brown cock hackle
Head & wing: Deer hair

ORANGE & GREEN GROUSE

MALLARD & CLARET

LIMEBURST DABBLER

UV THUNDER & LIGHTNING

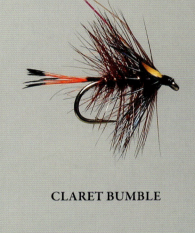

CLARET BUMBLE

OCTOPUS

RED SEDGE

GOLDEN OLIVE BUMBLE

KATE MACLAREN MUDDLER

Pulling Daddies

FLEXI LEGS
Hook: Longshank size 10-12
Thread: Brown
Body: Pheasant tail fibres
Rib: Grey Flexi Floss
Legs: Knotted Flexi legs
Wings: Greenwell's hackle tips
Hackle: Medium ginger cock

PHEASANT TAIL DADDY
Hook: Longshank size 10-12
Thread: Red
Body: Pheasant tail fibres
Rib: Fine gold wire
Wings: Dark cree hackle tips, with two strands of Mirror Flash
Legs: Knotted pheasant tail fibres
Hackle: Cree cock

FOAM BACKED DADDY
Hook: Longshank size 10-12
Thread: Brown
Body: Tan foam, detached
Legs: Knotted pheasant tail fibres
Wings: Cree hackle tips
Thorax: Hare's ear fur
Hackle: Cree cock

CHOCOLATE DADDY
Hook: Longshank size 10-12
Thread: Black
Body: Red chenille, detached
Legs: Knotted pheasant tail fibres
Wings: Dark brown hackle tips
Hackle: Chocolate brown cock

OCTO DADDY
Hook: Longshank size 10-12
Thread: Brown
Tail: Glo-Brite floss No11
Body: Natural raffia
Rib: Gold oval tinsel
Wings: Cree hackle tips
Legs: Knotted pheasant tail fibres
Hackle: Cree cock

SILVER DADDY
Hook: Longshank size 10-12
Thread: Brown
Butt: Glo-Brite floss No4
Body: Flat silver tinsel
Wings: Dark Greenwell's hackle tips
Legs: Knotted pheasant tail fibres
Hackle: Dark Greenwell's

FIERY BROWN DADDY
Hook: Sedge size 10-12
Thread: Red
Body: Deer hair fibres, detached
Rib: Red thread
Legs: Knotted pheasant tail fibres, dyed red
Hackle: Grizzle cock, dyed fiery brown

RED DADDY
Hook: Sedge size 10-12
Thread: Black
Body: Deer hair fibres, detached
Rib: Black thread
Legs: Pheasant tail fibres, dyed claret
Hackle: Grizzle cock, dyed red

A season on Pitsford

RESIDING IN MILTON Keynes, I am spoilt for choice and fortunate indeed to be within easy striking distance of some excellent reservoirs. Pitsford, my favourite wet-fly water, is the nearest of them all. For many river anglers, theirs is a short seven months of pleasure followed by five months waiting for April Fool's Day to come around again.

That's the joy of having somewhere like Pitsford virtually on your doorstep. These big reservoirs and their rainbow trout offer up their sport come rain, hail or shine – even in the snow. The fishing season on Pitsford Reservoir gets under way around the middle of March and extends through to the end of December. If you're tough enough, you can catch rainbow trout there almost every month of the year.

EARLY SEASON

As is usual on most big stillwaters, bank anglers enjoy the best of the fishing in the early part of the season. Fishing with lures for the first two weeks is standard practice and it would be deemed a form of madness not to have a Pitsford Pea fixed on the leader during these first few weeks. The standard, weighted version works well in those early weeks but – if you are trying to achieve extra depth, the Gold Head Pea is an excellent pattern. At this time of year my favourite tactic is to start with a DI3 line with two Cormorants on the droppers and a Pitsford Pea tied with chain-bead eyes at the head. The pattern I use has red holographic tinsel tied in as a flash back over the top of the body. For some reason this extra dash of red in the dressing works well on this water. For the retrieve, I start with a slow figure-of-eight and when I have reclaimed about fifty percent of the line I revert to long, slow pulls and, finally, I then allow the flies to hang. If the takes dry up, I allow the flies to settle deeper in the water before commencing the retrieve. If this

A light ripple: Ideal conditions for nymph or dry-fly

doesn't work a change of pattern and colour is usually required. Black and green Boobies fished on lines from a slow-sinking DI3 to a depth-charging DI7 are worth a go. Even though the trout will be very close into the margins early season, most bank anglers prefer to use shooting head lines which enable them to cast beyond, then bring the flies back in over the trout. The early-season bank fishing hotspots include Stone Barn and Stone Barn Bay, Pitsford Creek and the Pines, The Gorse, Stilton Point and, wind permitting, the Sailing Club Bay. Other areas that are worth a cast include: The Gravels, North Farm Bay and Bog Bay. Out from the jetty, the area known as the Little Half can be fished from the April 1 onwards. At this time of year water levels are usually high. The headroom under the bridge arch through to the Big Half is thus lower than usual, so just keep your head down when motoring through!

EARLY SEASON BUZZERS

Pitsford is renowned for its early-season nymph fishing. The trout on this water quickly switch on to Buzzers... black at first, then green. A Black Buzzer with red or green holographic tinsel in the cheeks can be quite deadly at this time of year. On warmer days and in light winds the occasional trout can be seen picking about on the surface. When this happens, the AK47 or Black Spider Emerger patterns are a good bet for the top dropper, to tempt one of those overwintered, quality fish. In fact, the dry-fly can also account for many trout very early on when other fisheries are still waiting for the trout to move up in the water. I witnessed the most amazing rise of trout one bitterly cold April evening at Pitsford in 2009. Small black buzzers were hatching off in huge numbers and the trout came on the feed, cruising up and down the wind lanes where the pupae had gathered. I was amazed to see so many trout up near the surface and feeding on such a cold evening but I took this as a cue to enjoy two hours of fantastic dry-fly fishing. I practically had the reservoir to myself, as I suspect most anglers thought it wiser to stay at home on such a ghastly evening! The moral here is that even at this early stage in the season, do not be afraid to fish very small buzzer patterns.

As April progresses and the water warms it is usually time to break out the floating line. Bank anglers score well at this time by casting across the breeze and letting the wind slowly bring round a team of small buzzers. On such a set-up, the Traffic Light Buzzer has proved to be an excellent point fly. Pitsford is renowned for the quality of its bank fishing. There are numerous gentle headlands and small bays dotted along its seven-mile shoreline which the bank anglers find so attractive. Should the wind direction change it takes little effort to manoeuvre into a new and suitable position. To enable this, Pitsford has an excellent perimeter road available to season permit holders. It speaks volumes for the all-round quality of the fishing on this reservoir when the bank anglers in 2008 could match their catch returns to the boat anglers throughout the season. On so many waters, bank anglers have a dead time for entire months.

The shallow water in most stillwaters tends to fill with weed in summer and reduce the bank space that can be successfully fished. The inevitable result of excessive weed growth is to push the trout out into deeper water.

WARMER DAYS

Once May has arrived, it's time to think about fishing a Diawl Bach – the Welsh pattern which has proven astonishingly attractive to reservoir rainbow trout. Probably the most successful set-up at this time of year is to position a Cruncher on the top dropper, a Buzzer on the point and a pair of Diawl Bachs on the middle

A deadly summer fly for Pitsford:
The UV Claret Dabbler

Pitsford regular Terry Pancoust with a superb, early-season double

droppers. Should the trout prefer the flies fished static, the 'washing line' method comes into its own. You have to imagine how the leader hangs to understand the name – it's a method which uses a midge tip line, a buoyant Booby lure on the point and, in between, a team of red and green holographic Diawl Bachs on the droppers. Supported by the fly line at one end and the Booby at the other, the leader droops just like a washing line. The standard Diawl Bach and rough Hare's Ear are two of the top-performing nymphs on Pitsford. When the Damsel Nymph puts in an appearance in May, a favourite pattern of mine is the Olive Fraser nymph. Damsel patterns with blue in the dressing can be a bit of a hit and miss affair on some fisheries but not on this water. Should nymphs not be working, it's a good idea to switch the Diawl Bachs for a pair of holographic Cormorants then increase the speed of the retrieve.

On bright days, a combination of a Gold-head Fritz Damsel on the point and some Crunchers on the droppers, using long slow pulls on the retrieve will work. As water temperatures begin to increase in midsummer, the trout tend to go deeper. At this time, fishing a variety of flies and nymphs static, suspended below a 'bung' – a very buoyant pattern or even a strike indicator – will take trout. Personally, I do not find this method very appealing but for those who do enjoy this style of fishing it appears to work well on this water throughout most of the season. And of course Blobs will always catch trout when fished on any line ranging from a midge-tip to a DI7. The Sunburst and Tequila Blobs tend to be among the favourite colour variations on Pitsford.

WET-FLIES

Because of its long and narrow shape, this reservoir suits my style of fishing. Depending on wind direction, areas like The Narrows can often be quite sheltered and provide excellent shorts drifts for dry-fly fishing. A north east or south west wind will afford much longer drifts along both shorelines of The Narrows. This is productive water all season long and ideal for nymphing or short-lining with a team of wet-flies. As the water warms up in summer, the trout tend to migrate towards the main bowl of Pitsford Reservoir. It was in this area in June and July 2007 and 2008 that I enjoyed some of the best wet-fly fishing on any stillwater in years. Using a ghost tip line, I caught numerous top-quality trout with a Silver Sedge on the top dropper and the UV Claret Dabbler on the point. These flies accounted for some superb trout, including two over-wintered rainbows of around 6lb, both of which took my line out to the backing. I would go as far as saying that Pitsford has been my best wet-fly fishing venue of the last three years. Other successful wet-fly patterns are the Sunburst Dabbler, Silver Invicta, Green Dabbler and Soldier Palmer. Short-lining with a team of wet-flies can be pretty exciting; the rainbows create a Jaws-like bow wave as they chase the flies back towards the boat. When the trout are high in the water, a great many takes come just after the flies have landed. It has happened to me on more than one occasion when a trout burst through the surface to grab the wet-flies before they even reached the surface. There can be nothing better than that to get the adrenaline going. The key to getting the most from this surface wet-fly fishing is not to lift the flies out of the water too early as they come to the boat. Allow them to hang, static, for a few seconds before lifting them clear and making the next cast. I particularly enjoy fishing the wet-fly when Anglian Water – in hot weather – turn on the aerators, or 'boils,' which send streams of bubbles and food from the lake bed to the surface. The trick here is to cast the flies into the current created on the surface by the seething water, the trout will often attack as soon the flies touch down. With the drogue set, a south east wind will allow the boat angler to drift slowly along the line of aerators. The force of the water from the aerators will often push the boat back which means you can hold over this productive area for longer than normal. Trout are often seen rising in the calmer water around the edge of the the boils and these feeding fish are well worth a few casts with the dry-fly.

DRY-FLIES

I normally set the rod up with a team of three dry-flies using 0.185mm fluorocarbon as my preferred leader. This low-diameter monofilament breaks through the surface tension quite easily just the way I like it. I fish a very short line in front of the boat so that there are no issues with the fluorocarbon dragging the flies under the surface. For dry-fly fishing on Pitsford in summer, the Claret Hopper, CDC Emergers and Hare's Ear Shuttlecock-style patterns are among the most successful. Other notable dry-fly patterns are the Claret Bits, Orange Hopper and Orange & Black Hopper. If the wind gets up, try a team of foam-headed Suspender Buzzers. Black patterns such as the UV Bibio and, again, the Hare's Ear work best. One memorable September's day I teamed up with Peter Gathercole for a boat fishing session. The weather was kind to us and perfect for the dry-fly – overcast with a light south westerly breeze. We concentrated our efforts in the middle of the reservoir, making short drifts across the Narrows. Although it took me far too long to cotton on to the presence of the small black midge, I eventually put up the UV Bibio which from that point on accounted for every trout we caught. There were two very interesting things about that day on Pitsford. We hardly saw a fish moving all day and yet we boated over twenty trout on the dry-fly. I also had four double hook-ups – that's two fish on at the same time. Even on good days when trout are feeding well on the surface this had never happened to me before when fishing dry-flies. On summer evenings, as the light begins to fade and the surface becomes calm, the trout will normally switch on to sedges – moth-like fluttering flies in a huge variety of sizes. Small green and brown Dry Sedge patterns tied on fine-wire size 12 hooks will then take trout on most evenings. Another successful evening pattern is the Orange Sedge. I mix orange seal's fur with hare's fur to achieve the realistic looking body I'm after.

LURES

Fishing 'on the rudder' is very popular both at Pitsford and Draycote Waters. It's a simple way of directing a boat on the drift. By attaching a rudder to the stern of the boat, close to the engine, you can get the boat to drift with the bow pointed straight down-wind. A variety of sinking lines are used in an attempt to establish the depth the trout are holding at, usually casting at right angles to the direction of drift and allowing the line to swing back round behind the boat, when you polish off with a fast retrieve.

The standard patterns are Tube Flies, generally very large (in trout lure terms) and used to imitate fish fry. Big trout, especially brown trout, are the intended quarry of many rudder-anglers. After their introduction to the water, these brown trout grow to a couple of pounds then tend to 'disappear' in reservoirs. It is usually the rudder angler who locates them, because at that stage, the big browns feast almost entirely on small fish. Rudder fishing can be employed at any time during the season provided there is an adequate wind but really comes into its own in autumn. It's at this time that the trout – all trout – will move back into the margins and start piling on the weight by fry-feeding. The foam-backed Silver Fry is still a good dry-fly pattern when fished in and around weed banks. By autumn, lure fishing with sinking lines will again become one of the most productive methods. White and Grey Minkies are the best patterns for this time of year. Also take a range of Sparklers, Gold-head Cat's Whisker and Pearl-bodied Cormorants. For the imitative style angler, the Corixa is also a good end of season nymph and accounts for many top-quality

The black and green Psuedo Cormorant

PITSFORD RESERVOIR

The Narrows is a productive area throughout much of the season

trout right into November and December. Buzzers will continue to hatch when suitable conditions prevail but will be very small. Black and dark green are again the dominant colours later in the year.

ANGLING CLUB

Founded in 1952, the Mid Northants Trout Fishers Association is one of the oldest and most renowned fly-fishing clubs in the UK. Since its inception, the MNTFA has engaged with and maintained very close links with the local water company and considers Pitsford Reservoir its home trout fishery. The club has around 80 members from all backgrounds including Vice President and winner of two world championships, Bob Church. This is a club with a stunning record of producing internationally capped anglers, five of whom have had the honour of captaining their country, these being Bob Church, Jim Collins, Mick Stevens, Bob Draper and Jeanette Church. In addition to the serious side of competition fishing, the club also maintains a strong social culture. Many of the members meet up for a pint and a chat every Monday evening at The Pioneer pub in Northampton. A few seasons ago I was invited by Ian Pow, the club's Competition Secretary, to come along and meet some of the members at the pub. We talked about fishing trips and successful methods – information which was freely disclosed. New expeditions were planned and some social fly-tying was part of the evening. And, of course, there is the banter and the usual leg pulling; there are very few secrets in any angling club!

Over the winter, the committee provides a programme of guest speakers who are invited for an evening's discussion with the members on a chosen topic. A number of very well-known anglers have attended these sessions over the years.

To encourage the youngsters in the area, the club offers free membership to all juniors up to the age of 16. Also, any angler attending an Anglian Water beginner's course is rewarded with a first year free membership of the club. The club is also affiliated to the Confedertion of English Fly Fishers which means all are welcome to enter the open eliminators and hopefully go on to represent their country. In 2009 I set myself the task of joining a club and taking up some competition fishing in the UK. I'm pleased to say that MNTFA accepted my application and I've since had some real fun taking part in their competitions as well as a fair degree of success. So yes, this is a plug for MNTFA but I'd make the case for every angler to join the club closest to their favourite water – the benefits go way beyond the fee.

ABOUT PITSFORD

Pitsford Reservoir covers an area of 750 acres, and is owned and managed by Anglian Water Authority. It is situated 10 miles north of Northampton and entry to the fishing lodge is off Brixworth Road and, for those using satellite navigation, the postcode is NN6 9SJ.

The reservoir was constructed to supply water to the Northampton and Milton Keynes districts and was opened by the Queen Mother in 1956. Pitsford first opened its gates to anglers in 1962 and has maintained a reputation as a high-quality trout fishery ever since. Aside from the excellent bank fishing, there's superb boat fishing: nothing finer, as Ratty said, than messing about in boats! Pitsford operates a fleet of 25 well-maintained boats. I was first introduced to Pitsford Reservoir about 15 years ago by my friend Martin Fairbrother and have returned there to fish every year since. I enjoy fishing Pitsford because the trout move up in the water very early in the season and mostly stay there. As a result of this I have experienced some wonderful sport with my favourite floating line.

Approximately 30,000 rainbows are stocked each year along with 1,500 brown trout. All of the brown trout introduced to the water are of a takeable size but because so many of these fish are released by anglers, many grow to an impressive size and some on into double-figures. The record rainbow weighed in at 15lb 11oz, and was caught by Tim Sparks in 2004. The biggest fly-caught brown trout was landed by Rob Layton in 2002; it hit the scales at 14lb 3oz.

To help every angler get the very best from Pitsford Reservoir, the management team offer a range of professional coaching programmes, from beginners' courses to top-up refreshers for anglers who want to lose a few bad habits and gain some new skills.

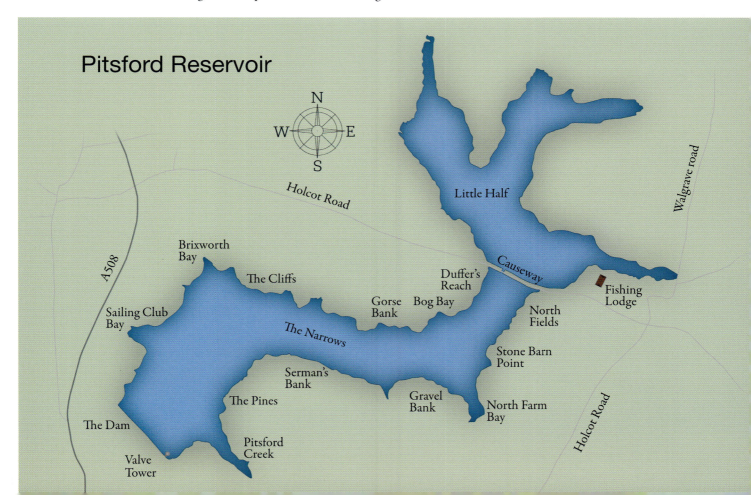

Lures and things...

I AM CERTAINLY not the best authority on trout fishing with lures – those flies, the majority of which resembling nothing in nature, which set out to stimulate the trout's aggressive instincts to attack.

I recognise their effectiveness, but being essentially a river man at heart I simply do not enjoy fishing with sinking lines for prolonged periods. However, on days when the rainbow trout go deep, pulling lures is often the most productive method of catching trout. Even though I know this, I tend to seek out a calmer corner of the reservoir and fish with a floating line or midge-tip because it is my preferred style of fishing. But there are days when you do not have the luxury of making that choice. Yet again, it was competition fishing that opened my eyes to the potential of using lure patterns that I find acceptable, namely because of the restriction on the size of hooks that can be used. These smaller lures have a greater appeal for me and can be successfully fished on a variety lines and retrieves. More often than not, weather conditions will dictate the tactics an angler will employ on the day. If conditions are kind, we often have a choice of methods but on bright, windy days the trout may well go deep and to be successful you will have to follow them down. In such conditions one of the best ways to achieve this from a drifting boat is to use a sinking line and pull lures. And there is no doubt that the Blob is the top-performing lure in modern stillwater fishing. And of course I cannot mention successful lures without highlighting the Minkie. Now here we have a lure which is designed to imitate a natural food source. Grafham angler Dave Barker invented the Minkie along with the Deer Hair Perch Fry some thirty years ago, and what a success story those two patterns have been. It's not just on stillwaters where the Minkie has built its reputation. On some Irish Loughs, traditional, early-season methods have been replaced by big lures fished on fast-sinking lines. Some very big wild brown trout are taken in spring on the Humungus and Minkie. Lures have also found their way on to my home river in Ireland. In high water conditions local anglers have taken to fishing Streamers on sinking lines with some measure of success. In fact my brother Willie recently caught and released two salmon on the Streamer.

Since joining Mid Northants Trout Fishers Association I have taken up competition fishing at local club level for the first time. My boat partner on a number of these outings has been Ian Pow. Ian is the Competition Secretary for MNTFA and is, for his sins, what I call a Blob man. Ian tries to convince me that Blobs actually represent something in the trout's natural food chain – daphnia feeders is a common claim. Needless to say, I have a very different point of view. However I have to admit I actually carry a few of the damned things in my box. I have yet to create a Blob on the vice so, Ian and I do swaps. I part company with a few Silver Sedges and Hoppers and in return I receive Blobs; somehow I think I've got the worst end of the deal! Thanks to Ian's powers of persuasion I now carry a selection of sinking lines in my tackle bag. The DI5 still hasn't seen the light of day but, I am starting to enjoy fishing the DI3 from time to time. On a day out on Grafham, 'Powie' held his head in his hands with despair when I out-fished him using a Black Blob. The poor soul thought that day would never dawn; it serves him right for teaching me the Dark Arts. But as they say - "needs must."

Lures account for a great many fish at the start of the season

A Minkie-caught rainbow hooked close to a large weed bed

CHANGE

I seldom, if ever, fish a team of lures, preferring instead to mix and match with some nymphs or Crunchers. My latest experiment in competition fishing is to fish a team of wet-flies and a small un-weighted lure on the point. By adopting this method, I am both fishing for resident trout and also recently-stocked fish at the same time.

The added attraction to using competition-sized lures is that they can be very effective when fished on a slow retrieve. I have caught plenty of trout on these small lures using a slow, figure-of-eight retrieve. It's a very productive technique for catching fish, comparing well with the more recognised 'sink and draw' lure fishing method. Lure fishing was traditionally linked with sinking lines and limited times within the fishing calendar. The start of the season was associated with fast-sinking lines and big lures, returning again at the back end when the trout would be packing on weight by feeding on fry. But today, modern lure-fishing techniques on stillwaters do not recognise any such time restrictions or boundaries.

In recent years, traditional methods have been turned on their head. For example, the much-publicised washing-line method involved suspending two nymphs between one or two Boobies, initially using a floating line or midge-tip. Today this method can be fished on the vast array of sinking lines. In many cases the nymphs are often substituted by Cormorants. Equally, many nymphs are now fished on deep-sinking lines. The tendency is to mix-and-match various categories of lines with different styles of flies. I feel this break with tradition has been driven by the competition angler who is always looking to achieve an edge through maximum flexibility.

Competition anglers tend to think outside of the box and do not get bogged down with tradition. For example, when I qualified for the Lexus final in 2010 it was by fishing a DI3 line with Hoppers. It was a bright, windless day and the trout had gone deep. I fixed a Booby on the top dropper, and spotting red buzzers on the water, I tied on Red Hoppers behind it. It worked; the trout followed the Booby in, and then turned to take the Hoppers below it. A week or so later I watched a very good angler fishing a small Booby on the point with a pair of dry-flies as a team; he was taking fish with great regularlity on all three patterns. This is something I would never have dreamt of doing. You live and learn.

A successful tactic on Grafham has been to fish two Dabbler patterns below a Blob on a sweep line. In September on the same water, I caught some cracking trout on two Silver Invictas fished below a Blob. There are simply no hard and fast rules. Lure fishing some years ago was confined to fast-sinking lines. No longer; these small, modern lures are accounting for trout all season, especially the Blobs, Boobies and Cormorants, which can be fished on a range of lines and rates of retrieve.

LURES AND THINGS

An early-season Ravensthorpe trout hooked on a slowly-fished Fritz Lure

COMMON TACTICS

A typical stillwater season gets underway around mid-March. Water temperatures will be well down, with the majority of fish hugging the shoreline. Early-season lures will be dominated by colours such as black and green, black and white and green and white. The tactic here is to start with one colour of lure and then change when the trout become wary or tire of that particular colour. This change in behaviour is often indicated when solid takes revert to just plucks and follows. Around midday, or early afternoon, the water will often warm up a little. A common tactic when this happens is to attach a Booby to the team of lures to bring the flies up in the water. Even at this early stage in the season, it is not all about sink-and-draw. The trout will often prefer small lures presented on a slow figure-of-eight retrieve. I feel the secret here is not to adopt a single method of retrieve; it is better to alter the speed of the fly coming back during each cast, speed up, and then slow down. If I was offering advice to a beginner it would be to assume that a fish is following your fly after every cast. Vary the retrieve, and always hang the flies at the end of each cast. I cannot emphasise enough the importance of 'the hang' in stillwater fishing. It is amazing at times just how long the flies can be held static at the end of a retrieve before a take will occur. Having allowed the flies to hang for a determined period, commence a slow figure-of-eight retrieve and bring the flies up in a vertical ascent and then hold once more before recasting. This second hang is often the deadly one. As the fishing year progresses, the big, early-season lures are quickly replaced by smaller and more brightly coloured patterns, such as the Tequila, Orange and Sunburst Blobs. These colours are also very effective when fished as Booby patterns with the washing line method. The Booby is often placed strategically on the leader to keep the team of flies in the productive zone, depth being one of the critical issues in stillwater fishing. I know I keep banging on about depth when fishing lakes and reservoirs, but it is just so important. Arriving on any fishery, most stillwater anglers quickly try to determine the depth fish have recently been taking the fly. "What line are you using" must be the most frequently asked question on reservoirs. Sometimes such information is not readily available so, to establish the depth at which the fish are feeding, some anglers choose to start with a sinking line and work their way up through the layers. I, on the other hand tend to start with a floating line or midge-tip and, if unsuccessful, work my way down. Once the takes dry up or conditions change, the process should start all over again.

Boobies are often taken static; the Cormorant Booby, for example, can be an effective pattern when trout are feeding on snails. The Sparkler Booby is another good example; this works well when the trout switch on to fry. Recently-stocked fish quickly become conditioned to the standard-coloured lures, simply because they are hooked or tipped so many times. New colours are then introduced, such as coral, pink and peach; these can be very effective at times when the fish become more wary. However, it would be foolish to discount a Black and Green Lure at any time in the season.

There is some debate as to whether the Fritz Damsel is a nymph or a lure. Whichever camp you belong in, there can be little argument about the effectiveness of this pattern. The long-tailed Damsel is one my best-performing patterns and will take fish all year round. I have even fished the Damsel as a point fly with a team of wets. It is also a great pattern for employing multi-speed retrieves. When fishing this type of fly, I often start with a slow figure-of-eight retrieve. Having drawn in the line about half way I change to long, fast pulls. If a trout is following, this change of speed and depth is often the trigger-point for a violent take. From early season onwards right to the very end, the Cormorant and its many variations can be excellent. As you can see from the patterns I've selected in this section I like this small lure simply

The Fritz Damsel

because it is so versatile. Fished fast or slow, mixed with nymphs or wet-flies, the Cormorant is, undoubtedly, a very effective mini-lure.

CHANCE OF A TROPHY

As the season draws to a close, the focus will be on fry-imitating patterns. This will be one of the best opportunities in the fishing calendar of landing a big trout as they are often seen hunting the margins and weed beds for fry. Fishing along the edge of the weedbeds during autumn is exciting stuff. Big brown trout which have spent the season sulking in the deeps put in an appearance, increasing the chance of a trophy fish before the season ends. There are many lures that imitate natural fry but, I feel it is hard to beat the Minkie for end-of-season lure fishing.

The patterns I have selected here have all caught trout for me on a number of stillwaters in the UK. The majority of these flies would be regarded as small lures that fall within major competition rules. The Emerald Cormorant and Snow White have been particularly effective patterns on Pitsford and Grafham during the early part of the season. I have taken the liberty of adding a hackle and jungle cock cheeks to give these flies more of a wet-fly look. These variations to the original tying impart additional movement into the flies. They also give the patterns extra appeal when fishing for wild brown trout.

Lures

VIVA CORMORANT
Hook: Kamasan B175 size 12-10
Thread: Black
Tag: Silver tinsel
Butt: Green floss
Body: Peacock herl
Rib: Fine flat silver tinsel
Wing: Black marabou
Hackle: Black hen feather
Cheeks: Jungle cock

ZEBRA CORMORANT
Hook: Kamasan B175 size 12-10
Thread: Black
Tail: Black marabou
Body: Red holographic tinsel
Rib: Flat pearl tinsel
Wing: Black marabou with strands of red Crystal Hair
Hackle: Black hen feather
Cheeks: Jungle cock

EMERALD CORMORANT
Hook: Kamasan B 175 size 12-10
Thread: Black
Body: 1st half, green floss - 2nd half, peacock herl
Wing: Black marabou
Cheeks: Lime green goose biots
Head band: Flat silver tinsel

RED STRAGGLE CORMORANT
Hook: Kamasan B175 size 12-10
Thread: Black
Tag: Flat silver tinsel
Butt: Mosaic Lureflash
Body: Red UV Straggle
Wing; Black marabou
Hackle: Black hen hackle
Cheeks: Jungle cock
Head band: Flat silver tinsel

BLACK & GREEN
Hook: Kamasan B 175 size 12-10
Thread: Black
Tag: Flat silver tinsel
Butt: Mosaic Lureflash
Body: Green Straggle
Wing: Black marabou
Hackle: Black hen hackle
Cheeks: Jungle cock
Head band: Flat silver tinsel

FLASH ATTACK CORMORANT
Hook: Kamasan B175 size 12-10
Thread: Black
Body: Flash Attack pearl tinsel
Wing: Black marabou with FAP strips
Cheeks: Jungle cock

PEARL CORMORANT
Hook: Kamasan B175 size 12-10
Thread: Black
Body: Pearl tinsel
Wing: Black Marabou
Throat hackle: Red hen hackle
Cheeks: Jungle cock

HACKLED WHISKERS
Hook: Kamasan B175 size 12-10
Thread: Red
Tail: White marabou
Body: Bright green chenille
Body hackle: Grizzle cock hackle
Rib: Silver oval tinsel
Wing: White marabou

CORMORANT VARIANT
Hook: Kamasan B175 size 12-10
Thread: Black
Tag: Silver tinsel
Butt: Lureflash Mosaic
Body: Peacock herl
Hackle: Black hen hackle
Wing: Black marabou with strands of red Crystal Hair
Cheeks: Jungle cock
Head band: Flat silver tinsel

RED HOLO CORMORANT
Hook: Kamasan B175 size 12-10
Thread: Black
Tail: Red holographic strands
Body: Red holographic tinsel
Wing: Black marabou
Throat hackle: Black hen feather
Cheeks: Jungle cock

SNOW WHITE
Hook: Kamasan B175 size 12-10
Thread: Black
Body: 1st half, white floss - 2nd half, peacock herl
Wing: Black marabou
Cheeks: Lime green goose biots
Head band: Flat silver tinsel

UV BLACK CORMORANT
Hook: Kamasan B175 size 12-10
Thread: Black
Butt: Red holographic tinsel
Body: UV black Straggle
Wing: Black marabou
Cheeks: Jungle cock, dyed yellow

BLACK & GREEN

VIVA CORMORANT

CORMORANT VARIANT

FLASH ATTACK CORMORANT

ZEBRA CORMORANT

RED HOLO CORMORANT

PEARL CORMORANT

EMERALD CORMORANT

SNOW WHITE

HACKLED WHISKERS

RED STRAGGLE CORMORANT

UV BLACK CORMORANT

Elinor Trout Fishery

LIKE MANY OTHER trout fisheries, Elinor is a medium-sized gravel pit. But while most are unprepossessing places, Elinor has carved itself a very special niche in the trout angling psyche. Astute management by forward-thinking manager – and England team member – Ed Foster has created a healthy environment that provides Midlanders with angling of impressive quality. I just love the place.

Located near Thrapston, Northamptonshire, the lake was dug in 1969/70. Elinor lies in the Nene valley, which supplies the springs that feed its 50 acres. In all, it has 1½ miles of bank fishing. The five underground springs entering at various points account for the gin-clear water in the lake. This well-oxygenated lake experiences some fantastic insect hatches providing rich feeding conditions for the trout throughout the season. The atmosphere at this fishery is unlike any other I have encountered in the UK. While there is no angling club associated with Elinor, the number of regulars give it a really friendly 'club' feel. There's always plenty of good natured banter going on at the Elinor, whether on the bank or over a cup of tea in the fishing cabin.

The world of competition fly-fishing is often shrouded in secrecy – particularly when it comes to successful flies and methods – but not so on this fishery, despite manager Edward Foster being one of our finest competition fly fishermen. There is a spirit of openness here and you will often hear the regular anglers sharing information throughout the day. Productive flies and tactics are freely disclosed to all who ask or who care to read the chalkboard. It's a credit to Edward, who has controlled the lease on this fishery since 1990. Edward was introduced to fishing at the age of seven by his dad, Harold. After a short spell trying his hand at coarse fishing Ed caught his first trout when he was just eight years old... aptly, on Elinor Trout Fishery. It was at Elinor that my son, David, learned to fish the fly. Ed has a policy of allowing budding young anglers to fish without charge alongside a senior, thereby reducing the cost to parents and encouraging young people to take up the sport of fly-fishing. There is a common thread running through the stillwaters I have chosen to write about in this book, they are all recognised top of the water fisheries. But, Elinor beats them all hands down for surface action. In reasonable weather conditions, fish can be seen rising right at the beginning of the season. I recently fished the lake in late October on a chilly day off the bank. As I walked to my chosen spot, I noticed the grass was covered with layers of gossamer. Numerous trout were rising in front of me so I gave the dry-fly a go but, my offerings' were steadfastly ignored. I continued to downsize my dry flies until I was fishing a pair of size 18 midges, yes I did say it was late October! Examining the surface of the water I discovered it was covered in tiny black spiders and the trout had homed in on this food source to the exclusion of almost everything else. From ten in the morning till late afternoon trout were rising in front of me. I had never encountered rainbows feeding on spiders before and I threw everything at them but the kitchen sink. It proved to be a tough but ultimately rewarding day – that is why enjoy fishing the Elinor so much.

THE SEASON AND TYPICAL FLIES

Elinor's season opens at the end of February and closes at the end of December. Like the majority of fisheries today, the lake is stocked with triploid rainbow trout. In the past, out-of-condition black cock fish were what you encountered in spring. Now sexless, triploid trout have made those ugly, flabby fish a thing of the past and, because these fish have no urge to breed, the season has been extended. No genetic engineering is required; the fertilised eggs of the rainbow hens get a short heat

Elinor is well renowned for its free-rising fish

A beautiful spring day at Elinor

treatment which persuades the dividing chromosomes to 'triploid' – split in XXY, sexless formation. It's fishery management at its finest. Approximately 15,000 trout are introduced into the lake annually, of which 500 are (fully sexed) brown trout. The fish range from a minimum size of around 1lb 4oz to double figures.

FISHING ELINOR

With the season opening so early, the water is generally very cold and the trout remain close to the margins in the warmer water. Elinor is fed by water filtered through the gravel seam; it is crystal clear, at all times apart from the occasional high summer week when algae colours it. For this reason, the use of fluorocarbon leaders is pretty much essential on this fishery. The best method in early Spring is a slow retrieve with an intermediate line… the most productive flies are lures, with a combination of black and green or white and green in the dressing. Towards the end of March, the Apps Bloodworm fished under a 'bung' – a strike indicator – on a floating line can be deadly on this water. Takes may be delicate, and the bung helps detect them. Other early-season patterns include the gold-beaded Hare's Ear, both in its natural colour and dyed olive. These nymphs accounted for huge numbers of trout in 2009, when the fish were feeding on the then prolific hog louse. A Cruncher with a pearl thorax will also perform well in March and is a good imitation of the corixa – the lesser water boatman. As the water begins to warm up in early April, buzzers begin to hatch. The black buzzer is the first to appear followed by the olive green variety. The effective method is, again, using a very slow retrieve with a slow intermediate fly line, ghost tip or even a floating line. The most effective size of Buzzer at this time of year is tied on a 10 or 12 hook. I had some fantastic fishing with the Buzzer nymph in April 2008 using two quill-bodied Buzzers on a floating line. One had red 'holographic' cheeks and the other gold. On most dull days in April, the olives will hatch and the fish will quickly switch on to this food source to the exclusion of most others. I have found a Lemon Partridge Spider tied with a partridge hackle dyed golden olive a brilliant fly during this early-season period. The trout will also take a good imitation dry-fly freely when the hatch is on. During April evenings, the trout will again venture in close to the margins to feed and, provided the weather is not too cold or windy, the rise can be excellent. This is when the dry-fly comes into its own. Size is a critical factor when dry-fly-fishing

Blue damselflies are a common sight during the summer at Elinor

on Elinor at this time of year. Big flies attract plenty of splashy rises and swirls but very few connections. I was dry-fly fishing the lake in early May, 2009. Conditions were excellent, with the trout up and feeding all day. I was fishing my version of the Black Shipman's Buzzer tied quite small, on a size 12 hook. For every 10 trout I rose to the dry-fly, I connected with only one. Eventually, after hours of frustrating fresh-air strikes I traded down to a skimpy, size 14 and ended the day landing 35 trout. So size does matter! Staying with the evening dry-fly fishing, the trout will continue to feed on Black Buzzer and then, later in the evening, will switch over to the adult Midge. A hackled Olive Shipman's is a good imitation to use when the fish are feeding on the adult buzzer along with the dry UV Bibio. Later in the month, a size 14 'shuttlecock,' or parachute dry-fly, will work well during the evening rise. Daytime fishing in May on Elinor is all about the Damsel Nymph. A fly dressed with a light-coloured olive Fritz body and a copper bead-head has always been the best performing pattern for me. Even in bright conditions, trout will be seen surface-feeding on the emergent damsel. The evening rise often suffers as a result of the trout gorging themselves throughout the day on damsels. The Olive Fraser Nymph is also an excellent fly on this water at this time of year. The Buzzer patterns will continue to perform well when dressed on smaller, size 14 hooks. Green and black will still be work-

ing along with red and pearl Diawl Bachs. If you want to trigger the aggressive instinct of the rainbow trout, the Sunburst Blob is the most successful lure on this water throughout the season. It is also a good pattern when the trout are feeding on daphnia. In June and July, the trout will be feeding on the adult damsel but, if conditions allow, a team of wet flies can be an excellent option. The Silver Sedge fished on the top dropper position has accounted for many quality trout for me in the last couple of seasons. The Green Dabbler is also a good imitation for the olive Damsel. In fact, from April right through to the season end, a team of wet flies will take trout. Other good patterns include the Soldier Palmer, Silver Invicta, Bibio and Golden Olive Bumble. In July, the trout will continue feeding on the adult damsel during the daytime. The evening rise can be sporadic at this time of year as the trout will be stuffed full of damsels. There will often be a good hatch of sedge on the water and, apart from the obvious dry flies, the Amber Nymph is a favourite on this lake during the summer months. During hot weather, the trout will often concentrate in the centre of the lake where the water is at its deepest, returning once again to the margins to feed late in the evening. During these bright warm days a small size 14 Black Buzzer with a bead head fished deep on a long leader, and retrieved very slowly, can work well. I combine the Beaded Buzzer with the Elinor Buzzer, a fly I developed a few years back specifically for this fishery. By the time September arrives, the damsel fishing will be almost over. Buzzer hatches will be diminishing with the nymphs now very small. This is the month for the daddy longlegs, also known as the crane fly to distinguish it from the spider that shares the same name. Elinor is surrounded by grassland on all sides, and the crane fly lays its eggs in turf to hatch as larvae which feed on grass roots, before turning into the gangling, adult insect. It is because of this that fishing Daddy Longlegs patterns on the lake can be

The Elinor Buzzer

The author with a fine 7lb rainbow taken on a dry-fly

superb. The trout here appear to prefer a slightly sunken Daddy rather than the standard dry pattern. In fact, a team of flies, with a sunken Daddy on the top dropper and a Minkie on the point, make a great September combination on this water. As the season draws to a close, the water temperature drops away and the lake becomes very clear. The optimum time to fish at this time of year will be from around 11am to 2pm. On calmer days the Bloodworm and small Buzzers suspended from a bung will catch fish. Small lures such as the Cormorant and the Montana Nymph work better in windy conditions.

UNLIMITED CATCH-AND-RELEASE

Twice voted Best Medium Sized Trout Fishery in the UK, Elinor is a great destination for anglers who want to use imitative fly patterns.

The record rainbow trout for the fishery weighed in at 19lb... and I caught it. I have, by dint of luck, held this record for several years. The huge fish took a size 14 hackled Black Buzzer. The biggest brown trout weighed 10 lb 5oz; this record has stood since 2007. The fishery opens from 7am and can be fished until one hour after sunset. Ed operates a fleet of 16 boats and allows the use of electric outboard motors. Float tubes are also welcome on the Elinor. Elinor was one of the first fisheries in the UK to allow unlimited catch-and-release. This proved to be a significant catalyst for change in attitudes towards catch-and-release policy. Catch-and-release has, interestingly, proven to be the perfect antidote for the 'limititis' disease – the compulsion to kill a limit bag of trout – which effected most day ticket fisheries at one time.

The pressure to catch your limit, or otherwise be deemed to have failed, has now disappeared. Thank Heavens. A full range of permits are available to suit all preferences. Most anglers prefer to retain just a couple of trout and release the rest, and the day ticket options reflect this. This change in culture has led to many fish growing on in the lake, leading to some exceptional catches of big fish throughout the season. Tuition can be arranged for anglers of all backgrounds. Coaching sessions can be tailored for beginners or experienced anglers and top-up and improver-courses are also available.

Chapter two: Rivers

Contents

The Suir	90-95
Dry-fly on the Suir	96-105
Accidental dry-fly	106,107
Wet-fly on the Suir	108-117
Upstream nymphing	118-125
Some things never change	126-129
Evening fishing	130-137
A beautiful springer	138-139

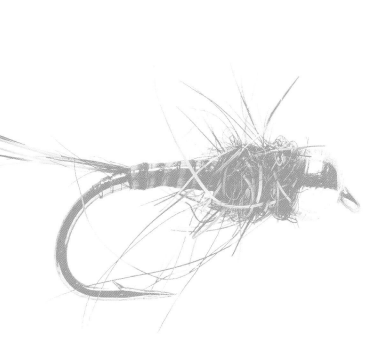

The River Suir

ALWAYS THOUGHT TO be one of the very best salmon rivers in Ireland, today the Suir is also widely recognised as a premier brown trout fishery. In its heyday, the river thrived on a reputation for big salmon. It has held the Irish record since 1874 with a fish weighing in at a staggering 58lb.

From its source in the Devil's Bit mountains, the river runs for 114 miles before entering the sea at Dunmore East, just below Waterford city. The particular stretch of water where I first learned to fish is controlled by Cahir and District Anglers' Association. This section of the river has recently been designated a 'centre of excellence' for brown trout fishing.

Founded in 1935, the club either owns or manages the fishing rights of 14½ miles of excellent fishing waters on the Suir and a further two miles on the River Aherlow, which is a major tributary of the River Suir. The Aherlow flows into the Suir several miles above the town of Cahir. The confluence of the two rivers, know as The Point, is a great spot for a salmon. The salmon tend to rest up here in floodwaters before continuing their journey upstream.

Both rivers contain a healthy stock of wild brown trout, and to encourage a self-sustaining population, the size limit on Cahir waters has been 10 inches for some years now. A recent survey carried out by the Central Fisheries Board on the River Suir Catchment area has indicated a healthy population of large brown trout. Significant numbers of fish from 12 to 20 inches were evident with trout over two feet long and weighing 5lb also recorded. This can only be good news for local and

A beautiful stretch of the Suir, just below Liamy's Lane

visiting anglers alike.

The fishing season opens for both salmon and trout on the March 17 and closes on September 30. Since 2007, salmon fishing on the Suir has been 'catch and release' only. This is in response to the serious decline in stocks over the years.

LIGHT AT THE END OF THE TUNNEL
Salmon runs in the river were devastated some thirty years ago by the Ulcerative Dermal Necrosis (UDN) disease. Over a period of several years I watched thousands of salmon succumb to UDN. It was a heartbreaking sight and one which I shall never forget. Excessive netting, pollution both agricultural and human and climate change have all taken their toll on stocks. However there is light at the end of the tunnel now that the initiative has been taken to remove the nets at sea. Salmon stocks will, hopefully, begin to recover in time, provided the river anglers co-operate, of course. Despite the difficulties it has endured over the years, the Suir was still ranked as the fourth-best salmon fishery in Ireland in 2005, and this was before netting ceased.

The club is actively engaged every year with bank clearance work and other ancillary activities such as stile maintenance and repairing the small bridges which span the many streams entering the main river. With upwards of 20 miles of river banks to manage, this is a never ending task. With a membership of approximately one hundred and fifty anglers most of this work each season is carried out by the usual dedicated few. The older generation anglers always carried a small bow saw with them and would often take a break from the fishing to do a little bit of bank clearance work. This continuous maintenance ensured good clean banks all year round.

The Suir is renowned for the superb quality of its dry-fly fishing, especially during summer. The trout are free-rising and of a good average size. Combine these two points with the fact that the river offers good access for vehicles and you can see why the Suir has hosted so many major championships.

The club has a strong tradition in competition fishing; its current membership contains no fewer than nine international anglers. My uncle, Liam, won the Munster

Sweet memories- salmon leaping the Bakery Weir

River Championships on no fewer than five occasions and the club have honoured his achievements by naming his favourite stretch of river after him, Liamy's Lane.

Until 2005, my father had been the only member of the club to win the Munster Lake Championship. My brother Tommy has qualified to fish on the National team twice. So as you can see, I hail from a family steeped in the Suir's angling history.

VISITING ANGLERS
Fishing was so good on the river that at one time it supported both my uncles with employment during the fishing season. The two hotels in the town and those in the outlying districts would fill up with visiting anglers from all over the world arriving for the summer months' fishing. Both my uncles, Liam and Tommy, were engaged as guides by the hotels.

I enjoyed meeting these foreign anglers and was always fascinated by the different techniques and equipment they would bring to the river. My uncles were often left a gift or two by these visiting anglers as a token of their appreciation. Uncle Liam would be given the latest samples of leader material and modern flies. Uncle Tommy was not always so appreciative of these gifts. He preferred the liquid type...

But Tommy somehow always ended up with additional fishing gear by relieving his new-found friends of any-

THE RIVER SUIR

Choosing the right fly. Uncle Tommy on the right with French angler Pierre Poux

thing heavy prior to their return journey. You would need eyes in the back of your head when that fellow was about!

The Americans were always very polite, and extremely good dry-fly anglers. The English have a long association with the Suir and always enjoyed their visits to the river. The Dutch, Spanish and especially the Germans were top-class anglers but could not understand the locals taking trout for the table. The whole thing was a total mystery to them.

A GAME OF CAT AND MOUSE

And then there are our friends from France. No nation can ever be tarred with a single brush, but these guys were the bane of our lives. They would turn up year after year, fishing any method, regardless of the fishery rules and almost always without buying a permit. I put scores of these so-called anglers off the water only to find them on the river the next day doing exactly the same thing. It was a constant game of cat and mouse, but quite unnecessary if some international respect was shown.

In the interests of fairness, it was two French anglers, Nicole and Pierre Poux who were instrumental after my Uncle Liam's death in having his favourite stretch of water named after him, Liamy's Lane. These two anglers visited the Suir for well over 20 years and left a sad gap since they passed away. Unfortunately, when the troubles in Northern Ireland escalated, the number of visiting anglers to the river diminished significantly, which was a shame for all concerned. It would be good to see the river being promoted, and visiting anglers returning in number once more.

In more recent years the club officials have had their share of difficulties managing the recent influx of Eastern Europeans. Scales or feathers, if it can be caught, it can be eaten!

The other visitor to the river which is a very unwelcome is the cormorant. These sea birds have travelled inland in ever greater numbers over the years. Some club members have counted over 90 cormorants in just one area of the river. If each one of these birds is taking two to three small trout per day, which is feasible, in just one month there will be as many as 9,000 fish killed. This threat to the river has been steadily building up over the years and is adding unsustainable pressure to trout and salmon fry stocks in the river. Some greater form of control of these birds must be introduced soon.

It just does not add up for me: what is the point of introducing additional conservation measures to protect salmon stocks if the real beneficiaries are the cormorants? The salmon fry are particularly vulnerable to these incredibly voracious birds.

The cormorants have travelled inland in search of food because their natural habitat is being destroyed. This problem needs to be cured at source. I hardly think that the solution lies in allowing one threatened species to decimate another. It appears, as so often seems to happen, that the lunatics are running the asylum.

MY ROOTS

My journey into fishing began with my father when I was just eight years old. We didn't have the luxury of a car back then, so the standard mode of transport was the bicycle. I didn't even get my own bike, at first, I shared the journey on my father's, riding on the crossbar. There were days when this can't have been much fun for him. He would have to negotiate the hills home with rods, a basket full of trout on his back, me on the crossbar and occasionally a salmon hanging on the handlebars. But they were good days and full of great memories.

Apart from the standard services which any gillie is required to perform, my other regular duty was to look out for any salmon rising in the river and report back. If there was any doubt at all in my father's mind regarding the accuracy of the sighting then the questioning would be more than a little severe.

At a very young age I had already learned to place a stick in the ground to mark the exact spot opposite where I saw a salmon showing. The river has a way of playing tricks on a young mind and only now do I admit to not reporting all of the salmon I witnessed.

The coward's way out was the easier option. The interrogation would eventually make me doubt something I had actually seen only minutes earlier. All my father would have to say is: "I have never seen a salmon laying there before," and doubts would come rushing into my mind. Thankfully, on the odd occasion I would prove him wrong.

STICKLER FOR DETAIL

After hours of persuasion he would finally make a cast where I'd seen the salmon and go on to catch it. I would then be given some justifiable reason why the fish had been in that position in the river and not the correct spot where it should have been. My father was a stickler for detail, so the easiest solution at times was just to play dumb. My two brothers will know exactly what I mean as they, too, went through a similar apprenticeship.

After a few years of rod carrying and making the tea, I was rewarded with a single-handed rod and allowed to start wet-fly fishing. I was still not allowed to wade into the river and it would be some time later before I was presented with a secondhand pair of thigh waders.

In those early days I would amuse myself fishing in shallow water from the bank catching small trout and salmon fry. At times it was like hauling mackerel as the salmon fry in the river were so plentiful. It was certainly great fun for a young kid learning how to fly fish.

Whenever he needed to cross the river, my father would haul me up on his back along with the rest of the gear and off we would head across stream. I would be designated a position to fish, and that is where I would remain until the Boss returned.

Fishing with wet-flies in the height of the summer was not the easiest of methods. Only the odd kamikaze trout would fall for a wet-fly at this time of year. But I learned to persist and sometimes would get my revenge on those trout late into the night. I fell in love with late evening fishing for this reason... a passion which still exists to this day. There is no better tranquillity to my mind than being in a stream in the dark of night with a full moon up. This style of fishing sharpens the senses and brings one closer in touch with your surroundings.

After a few years of wet-fly fishing I was finally allowed to venture out fishing on my own. I had to adhere to strict time limits, otherwise I would be grounded.

I recall one such incident as if it was only yesterday. It was a Sunday, my father had a band engagement, and it was certainly one of the first times I was allowed out fishing on my own.

I was under strict orders to be home by three o'clock. The usual Sunday afternoon film would start at 3pm, and this particular afternoon it was a war film, and I never missed a war film! I cycled down to The Park and fished with my wet-flies to no avail.

Eventually I ended up in Ballyheron and had one of

A well-marked Suir brown trout that fell to a Nymph

those fishing flukes that come around every so often. I cast out my wet-flies and in making the cast I managed to wrap the line around the stem of the reel. While I was concentrating on unravelling the line, the rod was nearly jerked out of my grasp.

I somehow ended up hooking a trout close to 2lb and, after a battle for what seemed like ages, I landed the fish. That was it, time went out the window and I fished my head off for the next few hours. The only time I stopped casting was to show any passing angler my trophy trout.

After a few hours I looked around to find my father standing on the bank. Boy, was I in trouble. My mother had become worried, especially when the war film had started and I was nowhere to be seen. My father was instructed to search the river and locate me. He was not impressed when he eventually found me.

I was rescued from a serious rollicking when a fellow angler told my father about the big trout I had caught and was full of praise for me. He also eased the situation by loading the two bicycles into the boot of his car and giving us both a lift home. It was weeks before I was cut loose on my own again. That same childhood excitement returns again before every fishing trip to this very day.

My window into the world of fishing opened fully when I first started tying flies. Sitting behind a vice provides the angler with valuable thinking time and brings out the creative side. I waited patiently for years to start tying flies and, when the opportunity came, I grabbed it with both hands.

My father netting a good trout in The Park

I started off by tying basic Spider patterns for the river and eventually moved on to dry-flies. The real challenge came when I first started dressing lake flies. Getting the shape and colours in the correct order was certainly difficult at first. For a brief period in my late teens I started tying salmon flies using traditional materials. However, a couple of sessions with a professional tutor were required in order to be successful. A traditionally-dressed salmon fly is a thing of true beauty and, as I was unable to master the art, I left it alone. I could not tolerate anything less than perfection. Perhaps one day!

I derive great pleasure from being creative, as I hope can be seen from the patterns I have selected for this book. Some people find tying flies a chore; to me it is a great stress buster.

I also discovered I had a flair for teaching people how to tie their own flies. Even as a teenager I was teaching several local anglers to tie flies, some of whom are accomplished tiers today. Those training sessions were conducted in the kitchen of my parents' house and were frequently interrupted by my father coming in to make a cup of tea, which was really an excuse to start telling fishing stories. End of fly-tying session!

LIKE AN EXCITED CHILD

I was then introduced to lake fishing on Lough Lein in Killarney. The trout season in Killarney extends for eleven days after the Suir is closed to fishing on September 30th. We would attend the lake for the last two weekends of the fishing calendar, and the build-up to these trips was just amazing

My father would be tying flies and preparing casts for weeks beforehand. Everyone would be given a selection of the best patterns when we arrived on the lake shore in Killarney. My father absolutely loved lake fishing; he

The Master at the vice

would be like an excited child prior to making his annual trip to Loughs Lein or Melvin.

A gang of us from the Cahir club would head for the lake at the end of each season and I have the most wonderful memories of those weekends in Killarney, many of which cannot be recorded here.

Some years, a novice would join the team and the fun would start after the first days' fishing. The initiation ceremony of the first nights' drinking would commence. Every trick in the book was pulled to get the poor individual plastered. Some of these unfortunate devils were preselected by the rogues to share a room with my father and there would be merry hell to pay at the breakfast table. At some crazy wee hour, my father's bedroom door would have been quietly opened and the victim pushed, staggering, into the bedroom. You can only imagine the laughter in the hallway outside as the gang waited for the anticipated explosion that would happen in the room soon afterwards. Most of those novices never made it to the second day's fishing. Those that did, like me, wished they had stayed in bed.

My brother Tommy has now taken over my father's mantle as chief storyteller. Whenever we all gather in the pub, the inevitable tales about those trips to Killarney are revisited. Even though I have heard these stories hundreds of times before we all die laughing when Tommy takes us back down Memory Lane.

My brother Willie displaying a 9.4lb Suir monster

As I reflect on the years of my apprenticeship, I now understand how each stage of my training was carefully managed. I could have given up in frustration at any time, and perhaps that was the ultimate test of my endurance set for me by my father. Nothing ever came easy for his generation and I suppose he imposed those standards on us. For some, to be denied the right to progress is the green light for giving up. For me, it only made me more determined to beat the system. Those early years were incredibly character forming. Today, I'm always impatient to get on, never one to do things by halves, often ending up with both feet in the trough. I do not see doors, I see openings, and I charge in – sometimes for the better, sometimes not.

Andrew Ryan fishing down a nice stream for salmon

Dry-fly on the Suir

THE RIVER SUIR rightly holds the reputation as one of the premier dry-fly rivers in Ireland. Like all rivers, the Suir has its floods but it is at its most productive in low-water conditions, following a prolonged period of warm, settled weather. This is when the Suir's fishing is at its finest, and not just because it is productive. It is in these conditions that the dry-fly comes into its own.

Rising in County Tipperary, the Suir meanders east and along with the Rivers Barrow and Nore, reaches the sea at Waterford. The section of the river known as Swiss Cottage flows south of the town of Cahir. Local fisherman call it simply 'The Park' and it is among the most famous of all stretches on the Suir, being fished by anglers from all over the world.

This section of the river is controlled by Cahir and District Anglers Association, and runs through some of the most fertile terrain in Ireland. The river once enjoyed prolific aquatic insect hatches but, like many other waters – and to our shame – these hatches have diminished significantly due to agricultural and human pollution. But, even now, the trout on the river are free-rising and – given the right conditions and settled water levels – the Suir still has impressive numbers of olives and sedges.

EARLY YEARS

When I began fishing the river as a boy, the stocks of wild brown trout were simply amazing. With so much competition between them for food, it was not uncommon to see trout rising throughout day. When the trout truly came on feed, it was a sight to behold.

The local anglers used the term 'boiling' – quite an

Returning a well-marked Suir trout

accurate description as the water erupted, with rising fish everywhere. Indeed, in one place on the river known as Carrigatata, the trout would shoal up during summer evenings below the weir and make their way upstream, sipping flies from the surface. The backs of their heads could clearly be seen as they rose above the surface, gorging themselves on the main hatch.

Once the fish reached the turbulent waters under the weir, they would submerge and, minutes later, reappear downstream to start the process all over again. I have witnessed this behaviour only on the Suir, though I did observe something similar on Lough Carra early in the morning when shoals of trout of up to fifty strong were feeding on an incredible hatch of caenis.

Historically, anglers on the Suir would carry no more than a dozen dry-fly patterns, and these would suffice for the whole season. Any more fly patterns would have been deemed unnecessary. This was not an attempt by the local anglers to keep things simple but a reflection of the incredible stock of trout the river held, all competing with one another to reach the next meal.

Provided the weather was settled, you could set your watch by the arrival of the insect hatches throughout the season. The key to success, then as now, is identifying the hatch and adapting the fly and method accordingly.

The number of dry-fly patterns used on the Suir today is far too extensive to record here. Of the flies illustrated in this section, some are specific to the Suir, while many of the others are internationally-recognised. Being an angler who loves to develop, tie and fish new flies, I have used every one of the patterns I've listed. Like everyone, I have my favourites; they are currently the Greenwell's Glory, Ginger Quill, Sherry Spinner, Blue Winged Olive, Red Quill, Badger Quill, Badger Grey and the Yellow Spider. These eight flies are versatile enough to cover most of your needs for daytime and early-evening fishing. I use special patterns for late-evening dry-fly fishing, and these are dealt with elsewhere in the book.

The Cahir waters do not enjoy a significant hatch of mayfly, which is why I have not included any mayfly patterns. You will have to travel further upstream to the Camis and Golden waters to encounter a good mayfly hatch. The usual selection of small Wulffs and up-winged dry-flies, along with some emergers and nymphs, will normally work here.

The Swiss Cottage

TACKLE

For fishing the Suir, the lighter the tackle you use, the better. The double-handed split-cane rod, which used to be the weapon of choice for the locals, has now been replaced by single-handed carbon-fibre rods, in line ratings from 4 to 7. The critical factor is to match rod and line. Accurate and delicate casting with the dry-fly is all about presentation, and mis-matches of line and rod will work against you. A good-quality floating line is also essential. The Suir trout snatch at flies and reject them in fractions of a second. If the tip of your fly line is prone to sinking, the brief delay the slack introduces into the line will mean a missed fish. And forget the old adage about delaying the strike. Strike on sight on the Suir. Any pause will surely result in failure. Dick Willis, one of the finest anglers to have ever come out of Ireland, considers the trout on the Suir to be some of the most difficult he has ever fished for, and not without good reason.

I prefer to fish with a 6-weight rod, reducing to a

The September Dun

THE RIVER SUIR

Short-lining with the dry-fly

5-weight in low water conditions. Reel selection is not important here; you certainly don't need masses of backing, as short casting is the usual form. Leader or tippet choice is very important. My preference at one time was Orvis Mirage 4 ¾lb fluorocarbon on 25-metre spools. This was a beautiful leader material, especially so for dry-fly fishing, and I enjoyed tremendous success with it on rivers and lakes. It is a shame Orvis stopped making it.

In competition fishing, I always felt this leader gave me an edge and I have not been able to find its equal since it was taken off the market. I had no difficulty with this leader submerging and dragging the flies under, as is common with other dense, fluorocarbon line. Orvis have now introduced new monofilaments with even thinner diameters for their breaking-strain. I cannot speak for others, but the results were disastrous for me. I ended up with lots of breakages and, even worse, left flies in trouts' mouths. If it ain't broke, don't fix it, they say and, in my experience, this was one of those occasions when things would have been best left alone.

In low-water conditions it is best to reduce your leader strength to 4lb but only if you are comfortable with such light leaders. In summer, the Suir experiences massive weed growth. A hooked trout, given half a chance, will run into a weed bed and may well be lost if you don't have the tackle to horse it to the bank.

WADING
Some anglers appear convinced that all of the trout in the river lie under the far bank. Adorned with chest-high waders, these water babies only appear to be happy when they are submerged up to their necks in the river.

I am neither attempting to be elitist nor old-fashioned here, but I was taught to fish the dry-fly in a pair of thigh waders, and it was a good discipline. Yes, it meant that the far bank of some broader sections of the river was inaccessible to us; the only cure then *was* to increase the length of the cast, but that usually ended in tears.

But today I see anglers standing in the very pools they should be fishing; I was taught to wade only when necessary. If wading is required, manoeuvre around the edge of a pool rather than plough through it, even after you've fished it. There's no point in disturbing the trout unnecessarily, especially if you want to return later for another cast.

Any attempt to move quickly in the water wearing thigh waders usually results in a wetting. Some of the worst of the chest-wading nuts must be on steroids or have an outboard motor strapped to their backsides, the speed they move through the river. Whatever happened to heron-like stealth? Trout will endure some disturbance but aggressive wading will force them to move off and seek out a quieter spot. After all, who would choose to live next to a noisy motorway?

APPROACH
While there is always an element of luck attached to any form of fishing, to be truly successful with the dry-fly on the Suir you need to be familiar with its insect life. Good observation is important; you will need to be able to adapt quickly to change. The Suir can often be a difficult river. On many an occasion I've thought I had picked the right main course, then the trout would suddenly choose to dine from another menu. I often failed to recognise that the trout had switched on to a new food source and continued casting with the same flies to no avail. The fun and the challenge of dry-fly-fishing is ability to recognise that a change has occurred and to keep pace with it. When the rise form changes from a splash to a sip, the fish stop rising or begin to splash at the fly without taking it, you must have a rethink. Stop fishing for a while to watch, and perhaps see the fly the trout are taking. Or sit and think, then change your flies until you crack the code.

A stealthy approach and, above all, good fly presentation are essential. This may be stating the obvious but, in a river, we know the trout are facing upstream, so your approach to feeding trout is always from behind or slightly from the side – something that is rarely possible on stillwaters. These are wild creatures and to avoid sending them scurrying, you must move slowly and use any bankside cover you can. If they know you're around, they are much less likely to feed. When trout are preoccupied, you won't cause a problem by using the wrong fly. If your presentation is good, the trout will simply allow your unappetising fly to pass by and simply carry on feeding. But a bad or impatient cast – no matter which fly is on the leader – and the trout will immediately sense danger and go down. It may well be some time before they reappear and have the confidence to start feeding again.

For me, the key to presenting the dry-fly is to cast above the water and not at it. Using the old Kingfisher silk lines, my father was a joy to watch when dry-fly-fishing. His line would land gently on the water followed by his two dry-flies, parachuting slowly down to the surface. I use the same technique when fishing from a boat; a short line, aimed high and allowed the flies to drift through the air on to the water.

If the trout are near the surface, this casting style will often induce a take straight away. The natural insect does not descend onto the water with the speed of a missile and neither should our imitations. If you have been stealthy and you're happy with your presentation, avoid the temptation to move on when you don't raise a fish straight away. Be patient; there are usually enough trout close by if you can work out what they're eating.

FLY SELECTION

Fly selection is generally about matching the hatch. The local anglers tend to fish dry-fly in pairs spread roughly three feet apart. Replicating both the male and female of the insects that are hatching on the same leader is always a good idea.

I have found some of the most successful partnerships that work for me are a Parachute-style fly on the dropper and a normal Spider or up-winged fly on the point. It's certainly a good starting point if you want to use two dry-flies together. The ultimate selection depends on what is happening on the water, of course, but here's a run-down of flies I would normally team up on the same cast. Early season, a combination of the Greenwell's Glory and Black Spinner work well. The Greenwell's will imitate any olives on the water and the Spinner will work for the midge ball, which often appears in April. The other early-season combination is the Black Quill and Iron Blue Dun. I had a terrific day's dry-fly fishing in April a few years ago when the trout came on the feed in the afternoon. A big hatch of black midge came off and they were rolling across the surface of the water, in a hatching frenzy, in tiny balls. I tied on two small Black Spinners and landed 25 trout in just a few hours.

The Blue Dun Spinner will work well as a dropper fly in tandem with the Iron Blue Dun. And, finally, for early-season fishing a pair of Olive duns, tied with light and medium olive bodies, will always catch trout.

Later in the season, the Ginger Quill comes into its own when pale olives arrive on the water; teamed with the Pale Olive Dun, you have a very effective pair of dry-flies. In June, the Red Quill arrives, and both patterns shown here are very effective when fished together. June also sees the first blue winged olives hatch. Any combination of the BWOs indicated here fish well with the Claret Spider – a terrific little fly invented by my brother, Tommy.

In July, the two Sherry Spinners in the fly plates make an excellent combination when the hatch goes spent. The black midge will also reappear very early on July evenings, when the Badger Grey and the Black Midge are the team required. My father loved the combination of the Yellow and Orange Spiders for June and July and, aside from Ginger Quill, these two flies accounted for majority of his trout at this time of the year. The Red and Brown Ant make an obvious team, and can work well in July if the ant is on the water.

Through trial and error it took me several years to develop my version of the August Dun. Teamed up with the Pale Evening Spinner, these are your August dry-flies, along with small, Dry Sedges for the late-evening fishing.

September can be either feast or famine depending on the rainfall and subsequent water conditions. Two of the best combinations here can be the Red Spinner and Red Quill No 2, or the Badger Quill and September Dun. For several years in succession, I was fortunate enough to fish the Suir in September and, over these years, I developed the September Dun – a terrific dry-fly during daytime fishing. The almost-forgotten Gold Partridge can also fish well in September. I enjoyed some success in club competitions with this fly many years ago. Since then, I have carried out some development work to the pattern in order to turn it into a successful dry-fly.

A lesson in stealth and patience, on the Wier in Cahir

Suir dry-flies I

CADDIS No1
Month: July – August
Hook: Light wire size 12-14
Thread: Light olive
Tail: Deer hair
Body: Yellow/olive SLF
Wing: Deer hair

GINGER QUILL No1
Month: May – August
Hook: Light wire size 14 -16
Thread: Light brown
Butt: Flat gold tinsel
Tail: Pale ginger cock hackle fibres
Body: Stripped quill from peacock eye
Wings: Light blue hackle tips
Hackle: Pale ginger cock hackle

OLIVE DUN
Month: April –May
Hook: Light wire size 14
Thread: Light olive
Tail: Medium dun hackle fibres
Body: Medium olive SLF
Wing: Natural CDC
Hackle: Medium olive cock, underside clipped

BLACK MIDGE
Month: April & July evenings
Hook: Light wire size 14-16
Thread: Black
Body: Black tinsel or black thread
Wings: White EPS fibres
Hackle: Black cock

GREENWELL'S GLORY
Month: April –September
Hook: Light wire size 14
Thread: Yellow
Tail: Greenwell's hackle fibres
Body: Well-waxed yellow thread
Rib: Fine gold wire
Wing: Natural CDC
Hackle: Greenwell's cock hackle

SEPTEMBER DUN
Month: September
Hook: Light wire size 14
Thread: Orange
Butt: Flat gold tinsel
Tail: Golden olive
Body: Stripped quill from peacock eye
Wings: Dark blue hackle tips
Hackle: Golden olive cock hackle

SHERRY SPINNER No2
Month: Late June –September
Hook: Light wire size 14-16
Thread: Orange
Tail: Light blue dun hackle fibres, split in V- shape
Body: Burnt orange thread
Post: Grey DNA fibres
Thorax: Rusty brown Micro Brite
Hackle: Medium blue dun cock

CADDIS No 2
Month: July –August
Hook: Light wire size 12-14
Thread: Grey
Tail: Deer hair
Body: Light grey fur
Wing: Deer hair

AUGUST DUN
Month: August – early September
Hook: Light wire size 14-16
Thread: Light olive
Butt: Flat silver tinsel
Tail: Cree hackle fibres
Body: Stripped quill from peacock eye dyed yellow
Wings: Light blue hackle tips
Hackles: No1 Cree cock
No2 Light blue cock

IRON BLUE DUN
Month: April – May
Hook: Light wire size 142
Thread: Black
But: Red floss
Tail: Iron blue dun hackle fibres
Body: Blue mole fur
Wing: Mallard dark wing feather
Hackle: Iron blue dun cock

BLUE DUN SPINNER
Month: April – June
Hook: Light wire size 14
Thread: Red
Butt: Flat gold tinsel
Tail: Blue dun hackle fibres
Body: Stripped quill from peacock eye
Wings: Light grey EPS fibres, tied spent
Hackle: Blue dun cock hackle

CADDIS No1

GREENWELL'S GLORY

CADDIS No 2

GINGER QUILL No 1

SEPTEMBER DUN

AUGUST DUN

OLIVE DUN

SHERRY SPINNER No 2

IRON BLUE DUN

BLACK MIDGE

BLUE DUN SPINNER

Suir dry-flies II

BLACK QUILL
Month: Late April – early May
Hook: Light wire size 14-16
Thread: Black
Butt: Flat silver tinsel
Tail: Black hackle fibres
Body: Stripped quill from peacock eye
Hackle: Black cock hackle

SUIR DUN
Month: June – September
Hook: Light wire size 14
Thread: Red
Butt: Flat gold tinsel
Tail: Dark blue dun hackle fibres
Body: Stripped quill from peacock eye
Wing: Natural CDC
Hackle: Dark blue dun cock

YELLOW SPIDER
Month: June – September
Hook: Light wire size 14-16
Thread: Black or yellow
Tail: Grizzle hackle fibres
Body: Swan quill dyed yellow
Rib: Black thread, doubled & waxed
Hackle: Grizzle cock

CLARET DUSTER
Month: June – September
Hook: Light wire size 14-16
Thread: Light olive
Tail: Light blue dun hackle fibres
Body: Dark claret seal's fur, clipped short
Post: Grey DNA fibres
Hackle: Grizzled cock hackle

PALE OLIVE DUN
Month: June – August
Hook: Light wire size 14-16
Thread: Light olive
Tail: Pale olive hackle fibres
Body: Heron herl fibres
Rib: Yellow horse hair
Wings: CDC dyed olive
Hackle: Pale olive cock hackle

GOLD PARTRIDGE
Month: September
Hook: Light wire size 14
Thread: Brown
Tail: Natural red hackle fibres
Body: Flat gold tinsel with clear horse hair over
Hackles: No1 Partridge brown neck feather – No2 Natural red cock

CLARET SPIDER (TF)
Month: June – September
Hook: Light wire size 14-16
Thread: Bright claret
Tail: Grizzle cock hackle fibres
Body: Dark claret seal's fur, clipped short
Hackle: Grizzle cock hackle

BADGER GREY
Month: June – July
Hook: Light wire size 16
Thread: Black
Tail: Grizzle hackle fibres
Body: Black tinsel or black floss
Hackle: Grizzle or badger cock

RED QUILL No2
Month: June and September
Hook: Light wire size 14-16
Thread: Red
Butt: Flat gold tinsel
Tail: Natural red hackle fibres
Body: Peacock eye quill, dyed red
Hackles: No1 Natural red cock
No2 Grizzle cock

GINGER QUILL No2
Month: July – August
Hook: Light wire size 14-16
Thread: Light brown
Butt: Flat gold tinsel
Tail: Light blue dun hackle fibres
Body: Stripped quill from peacock eye
Hackles: No1 Light blue dun cock
No2 Medium ginger cock

ORANGE SPIDER
Month: July – August
Hook: Light wire size 14-16
Thread: Orange
Tail: Grizzle hackle fibres
Body: Orange floss
Rib: Black thread, doubled and waxed
Hackle: Grizzle cock

PHEASANT TAIL
Month: July – August
Hook: Light wire size 14-16
Thread: Brown
Body: Pheasant tail fibres
Rib: Fine gold wire
Post: Grey EPS fibres
Thorax: Rusty brown Micro Brite
Hackle: Medium ginger cock

BLACK QUILL

PALE OLIVE DUN

RED QUILL No2

SUIR DUN

GOLD PARTRIDGE

GINGER QUILL No2

YELLOW SPIDER

CLARET SPIDER

ORANGE SPIDER

CLARET DUSTER

BADGER GREY

PHEASANT TAIL

Suir dry-flies III

RED SPINNER
Month: September
Hook: Light wire size 14-16
Thread: Red
Tail: Natural red hackle fibres
Body: Red floss
Rib: Fine gold wire
Hackles: No1 Blue dun cock
No2 Natural red cock

PALE EVENING SPINNER
Month: July –August
Hook: Light wire size 14-16
Thread: Light olive
Tail: Light grey hackle fibres
Body: Pale watery SLF
Rib: Fine gold wire
Wings: Grey DNA fibres, tied spent
Hackle: Light grey dun

RED ANT
Month: July
Hook: Light wire size 14
Thread: Red
Body: Red thread, well varnished
Wings: Grey EPS fibres
Hackle: Natural red cock

BADGER QUILL
Month: July – September
Hook: Light wire size 14-16
Thread: Black
Butt: Flat silver tinsel
Tail: Badger cock hackle fibres
Body: Stripped peacock eye quill
Wing: Natural CDC
Hackle: Badger cock

CLARET DUN
Month: May – June
Hook: Light wire size 14-16
Thread: Red
Butt: Flat gold tinsel
Tail: Dark grey hackle fibres
Body: Red/claret floss
Wing: Natural CDC
Hackle: Dark blue dun cock

RED QUILL No1
Month: June
Hook: Light wire size 14-16
Thread: Red or brown
Butt: Flat gold tinsel
Tail: Deep red hackle fibres
Body: Stripped quill from peacock eye
Wing: Natural CDC
Hackle: Dark red/brown cock

JENNY SPINNER
Month: June – August
Hook: Light wire size 14-16
Thread: White
Tail: White hackle fibres
Butt: Red
Body: White floss with clear horse hair over
Wings: Grizzle hackle points
Hackle: White cock hackle

BLUE WINGED OLIVE No2
Month: June – August
Hook: Light wire size 14-16
Thread: Light olive
Tail: Medium dun hackle fibres split in V-formation
Body: Yellow/olive SLF
Rib: Yellow thread
Wings: Dark blue/grey synthetic
Hackle: Medium blue dun

HARE'S EAR & BADGER
Month: July – September
Hook: Light wire sedge size 14
Thread: Black
Tail: Hare's ear fibres
Body: Hare's ear fur
Rib: Fine flat gold tinsel
Post: Natural CDC
Hackle: Badger cock hackle

SHERRY SPINNER No1
Month: June – September
Hook: Light wire size 14-16
Thread: Orange
Tail: Light blue dun hackle fibres, split in V-formation
Body: Burnt orange floss
Rib: Fine gold wire
Wings: White DNA fibres
Hackle: Medium red cock hackle

BROWN ANT
Month: July
Hook: Light wire size 14-16
Thread: Dark brown
Body: Dark brown floss, varnished
Wing: Grey EPS fibres
Hackle: Dark brown

BLUE WINGED OLIVE No1
Month: June – September
Hook: Light wire size 14-16
Thread: Orange
Tail: Medium blue dun hackle points
Body: Dark orange thread
Wings: Dark blue hackle points
Hackle: Medium blue dun cock, underside clipped

Accidental dry-fly

IT WAS SEPTEMBER on the River Suir, way back in my dim and distant past, and the local fishing club was holding the final competition of the season the very next Sunday.

Aside from fishing, my father's great passion in life was music, he being Band Master of the town's brass band for many years. Normally father would not miss a chance to compete but unfortunately for him, the band had an engagement to play the same Sunday as the fishing competition. I knew what the consequences were for me – band engagements always took precedence over fishing, as far as my father was concerned, and that meant there would be no way that I'd be fishing.

SO I GROVELLED

I was very young at the time, probably no more than ten or eleven years old, and was not even allowed to be near the river bank unaccompanied, let alone left to fish on my own. But this would have been my first proper fly-fishing competition and I was absolutely desperate to take part. However, not surprisingly, despite my very best efforts to persuade my father to let me fish, he refused point blank. I could think of only one way to get round him, so swallowing my pride I grovelled to my Uncle Liam, who thankfully intervened and volunteered to look after me for the day. After another bout of begging and pleading father finally relented and let me fish.

On the morning of the competition, I sneaked into my father's fishing shed and 'borrowed' two dry-flies from his box. I was still not allowed to fish the dry-fly at this time but I knew my Uncle Liam would not spill the beans even if he caught me fishing them so I decided to chance my arm.

Uncle Liam decided that we would fish upriver, above the town of Cahir in a place called White's, and he set me up to fish in a spot under Darcy's Weir. I will never forget the look on his face when I asked for his permission to fish the dry-fly; Uncle Liam always was a bit more flexible than my father and so I got the go ahead to fish whatever flies I liked, with no trouble at all.

There wasn't any such thing as a floating line back then, at least, not for us. We were fishing the old Kingfisher silk lines which, if they were to float, had to be thoroughly greased before starting fishing. My father was the type of man who liked to make everything himself, including his own version of the line grease Mucilin.

I got out the tin of fake Mucilin and home-made cloth and greased the line. I then tied my leader on, obviously getting everything the wrong way round. The inevitable result was grease all over my line, and me.

The iron discipline instilled into me still forced me to put up a cast of three wet-flies even though I knew that the dry-fly was the best method of catching a trout. Even with my uncle's permission I still didn't have the nerve to start with the two dry-flies I had borrowed earlier that morning. It was almost as if I was expecting to turn around and find my father standing behind me.

But off I went, bursting with excitement at the prospect

The original Gold Partridge; an "accidental dry-fly"

of fishing my first competition. I waded into the water just below the weir, made an upstream cast and, much to my surprise, the wet-flies drifted back down on the surface, floating like corks. I had made such a mess of greasing the line that the bloody stuff was all over the flies. I was even more shocked when a trout came up and took the Greenwell's Glory. I struck and hooked a beautiful little brown trout which I landed a couple of minutes later. I had just caught my first fish on the dry-fly even if it was by total accident!

FEELING VERY BRAVE

Needless to say I greased my wet-flies again and, in the next hour or so, had another four 'accidents' on the Greenwell's and on a Gold Partridge. By now I was feeling very brave and decided to change to the two dry-flies I had borrowed that morning... a Red Ant and a Red Spinner. I moved upstream to a place called Neil's Field, a favourite spot of mine. Feeling decidedly cocky, I wondered at the great mystery surrounding dry-fly fishing. I waded into a spot called the Slip and fished upstream, under the bank in the lovely fast-flowing riffle there. I ended the day having caught five more trout on the dry-fly and won the juvenile competition. Had I been eligible to fish in the seniors that day, I would have finished in second place behind my Uncle Liam, who caught just two trout more. I returned home later that evening as proud as punch secretly replacing the two dry-flies into my father's box. It was important that he didn't find out what I'd done as to father taking flies from his box was little short of a crime. To this day I'm still convinced that he never did discover what I'd done.

I knew that whatever happened I would still be reduced to fishing wet-flies again for the rest of the season but I was so made up after my unexpected success that for now at least I really didn't care. I had just won my first ever competition and now had a little secret up my sleeve.... and all over my hands, shirt and trousers. That tin of home-made Mucilin.

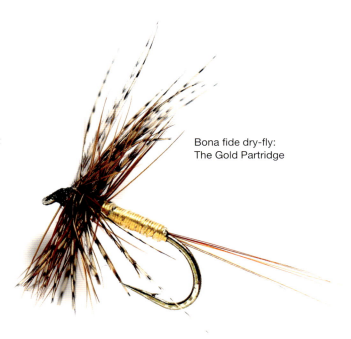

Bona fide dry-fly: The Gold Partridge

A BONA FIDE DRY-FLY

Some years later while fishing the senior river competition, again in September, I was having a particularly bad day of it. None of my usual 'banker' patterns would work and I was feeling more than a little desperate. It was then I remembered my episode with the accidental dry-fly. I took out a standard Gold Partridge from my fly box and trimmed the underside of the hackle. I then added some flotant and fished it as a dry-fly. It seemed that the magic from all those years past hadn't been lost for I went on to finish second in that particular event.

Since then, I have carried out some development work on the Gold Partridge covering the body with clear horsehair to impart some translucency, and adding a second hackle of natural red cock to support the brown partridge feather. It has now become a bona fide dry-fly.

I am not absolutely sure why the fly works so well in September; perhaps it resembles one of the small sedges that are so prevalent on the water at this time of the year.

I am reasonably confident though that this little gem of a fly would perform well on other rivers and streams in Ireland and the UK and may well be worth a try on tough days in September, almost anywhere. What I do know for certain is that the effectiveness of the Gold Partridge is really no accident after all.

Wet-fly on the Suir

AT FIRST GLANCE wet-fly fishing on a river would appear to be one of the simplest of all forms of fly-fishing. The cast is made at an angle across the stream and as the current picks up the line, it swings the flies around in an arc. This procedure is repeated and unless they are intercepted by a trout, the flies and line will eventually arrive back under your own bank. But like all forms of fly-fishing, to be successful with the wet-fly requires excellent river craft, presentation skills and the ability to recognise the most important insect species.

Compared to the summer months, when your quarry is often visibly seen feeding on the surface, trout in the early part of the season have different behaviour patterns when river levels are running high and water temperatures are low. In fact wet-fly fishing requires more effort and hard work to initiate a take as the trout will often hug the bottom and be quite lethargic in cold water conditions. I have known many wet-fly anglers in my time, but then again I have also been lucky enough to meet a few very good ones. These few 'lucky' anglers are in a league of their own because they understand how to do the basics well and are consistent in their approach and methods.

JUST A NYMPH IMITATION

Wet-fly fishing is not all about cast and hope; the skill is in knowing where the trout will be in high water conditions and presenting the flies to them. My father was a brilliant exponent of the upstream wet-fly. Today the technique is much the same but the wet-fly has been replaced by the Beaded Nymph. It is not without good reason that my father tied all his wet-fly patterns very slim and with the minimum amount of hackle. "What is a wet-fly, other than just a nymph imitation?" he often used to say. This older generation of anglers knew the basics well and were upstream nymph fishing long before it became such a well publicised method.

Another great wet-fly angler is my good friend Dick Willis from Mallow. I was in conversation with Dick some months ago and we were discussing fishing in general over a pint. He related a tale to me about a particular day's wet-fly fishing on his native River Blackwater. He had invited a friend to join him on the river for some trout fishing. Dick, always the gentleman, set up his friend's rod for him and mounted a team of flies which were suitable for the river at that particular time. Dick also tied identical flies to his own leader.

After a few hours fishing they met for lunch. Dick had caught a handsome bag of trout whilst his friend had no luck at all. On realising how well Dick had done, his friend was a little put out and insinuated that Dick had tied improper flies on his leader. On hearing this and with a slight touch of temper Dick replaced his own rod for the one his friend was using and proceeded to catch another basket of trout in the afternoon. His friend still ended the day fishless. This is what I mean when I describe the qualities of a good wet-fly angler.

THE SUIR

The Suir, particularly the stretch that flows through the town of Cahir, is a classic wet and dry-fly water. With the exception of a couple of miles of river above the town which is deep and slow the remainder of the river is a mixture of fast-flowing, shallow streams, interspersed by a number of small rocky weirs and flowing glides.

The bed of the river is limestone and the stone bottom makes for a non slippery surface which is ideal for safe and comfortable wading. Traditionally the wet-fly season would commence on the river Aherlow, which is a major tributary of the Suir. The Aherlow is then generally abandoned by the local anglers once water conditions on the main river become favourable.

CHANGE

Wet-fly fishing in the early season was always excellent on the Suir and Aherlow. Major hatches of March Browns and Large Dark Olives were ever present on the water in the early spring. These were followed by Medium Olives, Iron Blue Duns and Black Quills in April. After a hard winter, the trout would gorge themselves on these prolific hatches of insects in the milder

Fishing the upstream wet-fly at Liamy's Lane

spring weather. These happy days are now confined to the past. Insect hatches in the early part of the season have diminished significantly for reasons stated elsewhere in this book. Weather patterns have also changed and this is having a dramatic effect on the ecological balance of the river.

The inevitable outcome of all this change is that the trout have adapted their feeding behaviour and have reverted to bottom feeding in order to survive and grow. In recent winters the traditional frosts and snowfalls have been replaced by excessive and prolonged bouts of rainfall and the river has suffered as a result. The surrounding land becomes soaked and is unable to cope and slow down the natural drainage of rainfall into the river. This results in prolonged periods of high water levels much to the frustration of the local anglers.

For three years in succession my fishing trips to the river suffered from this excessive rainfall. I arrived in Ireland in May just prior to the annual Munster, Lake Championships hoping to get some fishing on the river only to be greeted by a flood on each occasion. I now know how visiting salmon anglers must feel; all that anticipation, preparation and dreaming of what might be ahead is destroyed when arriving on the water to discover the river is in full flood. This is how fragile our rivers have become in recent years. It has to be a real dilemma for those salmon anglers as to whether to go ahead and book a week's fishing for the following year. Trout anglers like me can always head off to the nearest lough to get our fix. They can't.

RESEARCH

About fifteen years ago I started spooning the trout from the river and was surprised to find a high percentage of nymphs amongst the contents of the trout's stomach. The spooning of trout on the Suir was uncommon back then and surprisingly, still is to this day.

Living in England has always had an influence on my thinking and fishing methods. Combined with an inquisitive mind, I am always interested in what is going on in the water. Such measures as the spooning of fish had always been deemed unnecessary in the past. Weather

WET-FLY ON THE SUIR

Two classic Suir wet-flies: The Badger Quill and Ginger Quill

patterns were settled and the anticipated hatch of insects duly turned up on time as expected. As long as the angler knew what to expect and could recognise the change in insect cycles, then they would normally be successful. The other noticeable difference I have seen in recent times is that water temperatures appear to remain much colder in the river. This must be in part due to the lack of prolonged periods of warm weather, which we used to call our summers. Even on the odd warm day as the sun begins to dip over the horizon, air temperatures drop away very quickly and quite often a cold breeze springs up. All of these changes in weather patterns are effecting how we go about our fishing today. If the trout are altering their feeding habits then we must adapt along with them in order to be successful. Such changing conditions are challenging and provide an opportunity for the innovative angler and fly-tyer. Many anglers on the Suir today will tell you that early season wet-fly fishing is finished.

This conclusion has been arrived at simply because the trout are no longer feeding on the surface as they used to and many of the traditional hatches of insects have disappeared. I remain unconvinced; I feel the local anglers have become preoccupied with fishing Beaded Nymphs to the total exclusion of the more traditional methods. And of course, the last four or five years of persistent high water levels have to be a factor in these considerations. There can be no doubt in my mind, that damage must have been caused to insect life in the river as a result of the continuous floods over recent years.

THE METHOD

Traditionally, wet-fly fishing would involve starting at the head of a stream, with a cast of three or four flies mounted on a slow sinking line, or even a floating line in warmer weather. The actual technique is not too dissimilar to salmon fly-fishing. The stream should be fished step by step lengthening the cast as you go. This type of blind fishing for trout can be a bit laborious but can still be rewarding with a little luck and perseverance. The real skill is in slowing the flies down at the critical time allowing each pool to be fished properly. I usually fish with four flies mounted on fluorocarbon leader of around 5lb breaking strain. On a windy day it is best to reduce the team to three or even two flies. Winged wet-flies are not as popular on the Suir as they are on other rivers; local anglers tend to prefer Spider patterns instead. And finally there is the Beaded Nymph which will achieve an even greater depth when required. A combination of anorexic wet-flies on the droppers and a beaded fly on the point can be very successful at times.

The beaded fly, if cast to the correct spot, will allow the other flies to work efficiently through the pool by raising the rod tip at the critical time. In terms of fishing these flies, I have replaced the floating line with a sink-tip. This is a reaction to the trout generally lying deeper in the water in recent years. Instead of the traditional across-and-down method I cast the flies slightly above me. I then mend the line immediately after making the cast and then once more as the current picks up the line. The second mend will slow the rate the line swings across the current and allow the flies to fall and rise in the water, simulating the action of the natural insect. On a set up like this, short upstream casting under the near back can also be very rewarding.

Finally, there is no need to strike the trout when fishing wet-fly on the Suir. You will know when a take occurs; a steady lift of the rod is all that is required. If you do not feel the trout following a rise, do not strike. Change the angle of the cast and the chances are you may well get a second opportunity.

SOME TIPS AND COMMON MISTAKES

Pools must be fished slowly and worked from different angles. Impatience leads to halting the cast before the full width of the river has been covered. Overly-long casts are made to the far bank as 'apparently' this is the only place where trout can be found in the river. Long casting will reduce the conversion rate between takes and solid hook ups. Remember, too, that trout are often found under the near bank as well! Equally, excessive and unnecessary wading never helps catch fish.

The stream should not be fished too fast. When it has been thoroughly worked, across and down, the angler should turn around and present the flies back upstream and fish the known pools once again. The line should be mended at least once, after the initial cast has been made, to allow the flies to sink deeper. Always present the flies from different angles and don't overdress wet-flies; skimpy patterns work best. As a general rule-of-thumb, winged wet-flies should be fished on the top dropper only. Leaders should be made up of different sizes and weights of flies to allow greater flexibility when fishing different current speeds and depths. Matching-the-hatch is still very important even when early-season fishing.

THE PRESENT DAY

So how do we adapt to these difficult and changing conditions on the river? First we must consider the flies we fish. For some years now I have tied nearly all of my wet-flies on heavy-gauge hooks so that they sink faster and deeper. In addition, since spooning the trout all those years ago, I also dress most of these flies round the bend of the hook. The Kamasan B100 is an ideal hook to achieve the extra weight required. The profile of the hook also lends itself to dressing the fly round the bend. I have also introduced a thorax to most Spider patterns which never existed in the traditional dressings. These changes are made to reflect and imitate the nymph stage rather than the adult insect.

Additionally I have taken a range of standard wet-fly patterns and developed them by giving them even greater nymph-like qualities. I have enlarged the thorax and used a material such as Nymph Skin for the thorax cover. The hackle is now tied in at the throat only and is quite sparse. These Unweighted Nymphs are fully described in the section on upstream nymphing.

A ROUGH GUIDE TO FLY PATTERNS

I have indicated in the detailed tying descriptions my preferred position for each fly on the leader. As a general rule of thumb when wet-fly fishing on the Suir, the Grouse patterns will perform best in the colder weather and the Partridges when temperatures begin to rise. Pale yellow is a dominant fly colour on the river and is quite probably a reflection of the terrific hatches of olives that once graced this water.

The Gold Partridge is one of the most consistent and all round patterns and should never be discounted from the leader. This point fly has probably accounted for more trout on the river than any other pattern over the years. I landed my first ever spring salmon on the river Aherlow on the Gold Partridge. In tandem with the

The Stonefly: Highly effective in April, on the Suir

Grouse flies, the other early season patterns would be the Quill March Brown, Dark Greenwell's, Black Spinner and Iron Blue Dun. The Orange & Green Grouse was a particular favourite of my father's; he would often fish this pattern late at night during summer.

April is generally a month associated with black flies. The Black Spider fishes well whenever the midge ball is on the water followed by the Black Quill which can also be good in early May. If the water is slightly coloured the Orange Grouse and the Red Grouse will perform well. The Orange Grouse fishes again during the first two weeks of July as a late evening sedge imitation.

WARM SUNNY DAYS

The Greenwell's patterns, both dark and standard forms work when olives are on the water. The Woodcock & Greenwell's and also the Stone Fly are particularly effective patterns on warm sunny days, both as top dropper flies. The Stone Fly is a great favourite of mine whenever I see trout rising to medium olives, I always think of this pattern even when fishing stillwaters in the UK. I suspect if tied as a beaded nymph, it could do very well, one to keep in mind for the future.

The Yellow Partridge is a brilliant fly in windy conditions, and fishes its best when a strong wind is blowing waves back up the river. I have had great success in the past with a pair of Yellow Partridges on the leader on windy days even in the height of summer, particularly on the river Aherlow. The Badger Quill, Ginger Quill and Pale Olive Quill are generally April and early May flies when the trout are up in the water and feeding on light olives. The Red Spinner is a great June and September fly.

The Hot Partridge, a fly I invented a few years ago, and the Orange Partridge are very consistent patterns and will fish again later on in the year in September if the river is running high. The Hot Partridge is one of a number of patterns from my own vice which I have included in this selection. I have tied a variation of this fly as a beaded nymph for deep river fishing and another variation tied on a long shank hook for stillwaters. All have been very successful.

Other patterns include Mick's Dun, the Pearly Patridge and the Hare's Ear & Orange. The Pearly Partridge has been around for many years now and is a great point fly particularly when fished using an upstream cast and allowed to float down in the current. The thinking behind the Hare's Ear & Orange stemmed from my stillwater experiences. The Hare's Ear and its many variants are much underutilized patterns on the river Suir in my opinion. Mick's Dun follows a similar theme with the use of hare's ear fur in the body. The use of brightly coloured wires in both patterns highlights the body segmentation seen in many natural insects.

Flies like the Purple Partridge and the Snipe & Purple have a limited window in the early season. The trout on the Suir will often switch on to this colour sometimes to the exclusion of all others.

A MASSIVE DIFFERENCE

I was fortunate enough some years ago to take almost three weeks leave from work and I managed to spend most of those delightful days on the river Suir. For the first few days I spooned every fish I caught and placed the contents in a jar of water for examination. The trout were stuffed with olive and pale brown nymphs. I was big into dressing my wet-flies around the bend of the hook at the time and as I had my fly-tying kit with me, I tied up some imitations of what the trout were feeding on. The patterns I tied up made a massive difference to my catch rate over the next few weeks. On one particular day I was fishing above the bridge at the Swiss Cottage and by lunch time had landed sixteen quality trout. Around 3pm the trout came on the feed and I enjoyed some brilliant wet-fly fishing. There were a number of anglers fishing the opposite bank of the river who, clearly, were struggling to find the answer. I, on the other hand, had a fantastic day. I put this down to doing my homework and not that my fishing skills were superior to the other anglers who were on the river that day. If you know what the trout are feeding on, then you are already half way there. Matching the hatch is vital, even when early season wet-fly fishing. Having done my homework, those three weeks on the Suir were amazing and will live in my memory for a long time. As it happens, my brother Tommy informed me that the river had fished its socks off for the whole of that season and he had some wonderful evening-fishing later in the season catching some very big trout in the process.

In years past there was always great anticipation during the build up to a new season. I would often patrol the banks of the river watching the trout feeding and counting down the days until I could get at them. I was like a kid in a candy store with no money, driving myself to distraction waiting for the opening day.

In recent years this great anticipation has sadly been replaced by impending gloom because of the incessant rainfall. However every now and then a year comes along which provides exceptional fishing on the river all season long. What triggers this frenzy is a mystery to me but as each new season gets underway hope springs eternal that this will be one of those very years.

Quill-bodied flies are deadly on the Suir. (left-right) The Pale Olive Quill and the March Brown Quilll

Suir wet-flies I

ORANGE GROUSE
Position: 2nd dropper
Hook: Kamasan B100 size 14
Thread: Orange
Tail: Natural red hackle fibres
Body: Orange floss
Rib: Fine, flat gold tinsel
Thorax: Rusty brown Micro Brite
Hackle: Grouse neck feather

PURPLE PARTRIDGE
Position: 2nd dropper
Hook: Kamasan B 100 size 14
Thread: Purple
Tail: Natural red hackle fibres
Body: Purple floss with pearl tinsel flashback
Rib: Fine, silver wire
Thorax: Hare's ear & grey fur mixed
Hackle: Partridge, brown neck feather

WOODCOCK & COPPER
Position: Point fly
Hook: Kamasan B100 size 12-14
Thread: Black or brown
Tail: Greenwell's hackle fibres
Body: Flat copper tinsel
Rib: Fine, copper wire
Wing: Woodcock
Hackle: Greenwell's cock hackle

GINGER QUILL
Position: Top dropper
Hook: Kamasan B100 size 14
Thread: Brown
Butt: Flat gold tinsel
Tail: Golden ginger hackle fibres
Body: Stripped quill from peacock eye
Thorax: Rusty brown Micro Brite
Wing: Wood pigeon
Hackle: Medium ginger cock hackle

ORANGE & GREEN GROUSE
Position: 2nd dropper
Hook: Kamasan B100 size 12-14
Thread: Green
Tail: Natural red hackle fibres
Body: Rear third-orange floss remainder green floss
Rib: Fine, flat gold tinsel
Thorax cover: Small jungle cock
Hackle: Grouse neck feather

RED GROUSE
Position: 2nd dropper
Hook: Kamasan B100 size 14
Thread: Red
Tail: Natural red hackle fibres
Body: Red floss
Rib: Fine, flat gold tinsel
Thorax: Rusty brown Micro Brite
Hackle: Grouse neck feather

CRUNCHER
Position: Point or 2nd dropper
Hook: Kamasan B100 size 12-14
Thread: Orange
Tail: Greenwell's hackle fibres
Body: Pheasant tail fibres
Rib: Fine, silver wire
Thorax: Rusty brown Micro Brite
Hackle: Greenwell's or badger cock hackle

DARK GREENWELL'S
Position: 2nd Dropper
Hook: Kamasan B100 size 14-16
Thread: Green
Tail: Greenwell's hackle fibres
Body: Bottle green floss
Rib: Fine gold wire
Thorax: Rusty brown Micro Brite
Thorax cover: Pearl tinsel
Hackle: Well marked Greenwell's hackle

ORANGE PARTRIDGE
Position: Top or 2nd dropper
Hook: Kamasan B100 size 14
Thread: Orange
Tail: Natural red hackle fibres
Body: Orange floss
Rib: Pearl tinsel/silver wire over
Thorax: Rusty brown Micro Brite
Hackle: Partridge, brown neck feather

GOLD PARTRIDGE
Position: Point fly
Hook: Kamasan B100 size 12-14
Thread: Black or brown
Tail: Natural red hackle fibres
Body: Flat gold tinsel
Rib: Fine gold wire
Thorax: Rusty brown Micro Brite
Hackle: Partridge, brown neck feather

WOODCOCK & GREENWELL'S
Position: Top dropper
Hook: Kamasan B100 size 14
Thread: Yellow
Tail: Greenwell's hackle fibres
Body: Well-waxed yellow thread
Rib: Fine gold wire
Wing: Woodcock wing feather
Hackle: Greenwell's cock hackle

BLACK QUILL
Position: Top dropper
Hook: Kamasan B100 size 14-16
Thread: Black
Butt: Flat silver tinsel
Tail: Black hackle fibres
Body: Stripped quill from peacock eye
Wing: Starling feather
Hackle: Black hen hackle

Suir wet-flies II

BLACK SPIDER
Position: Top dropper
Hook: Kamasan B100 size 14
Thread: Purple
Body: Black tinsel
Thorax: Hare's ear, grey seal's fur mixed
Thorax cheeks: Pearl strands
Hackle: Black hen hackle

HARE'S EAR & ORANGE
Position: 2nd dropper
Hook: Kamasan B100 size 14-16
Thread: Orange
Tail: Natural red hackle fibres
Body: Hare's ear fur
Rib: Ultra wire, hot orange
Hackle: Partridge feather dyed golden olive

GREENWELL'S GLORY
Position: Top or 2nd dropper
Hook: Light wire size 12-16
Thread: Yellow
Tail: Greenwell's hackle fibres
Body: Well-waxed yellow thread
Rib: Fine, gold wire
Wing: Starling feather
Hackle: Greenwell's hackle

BLUE DUN
Position: Top dropper
Hook: Light wire size 14
Thread: Black
Butt: Gold tinsel
Body: Blue mole fur
Wing: Wood pigeon
Hackle: Blue dun hen hackle

MICK'S DUN
Position: 2nd dropper
Hook: Kamasan B100 size 14-16
Thread: Yellow
Tail: Blue dun hackle fibres
Body: Hare's ear fur
Rib: Ultra wire, hot yellow
Hackle: Iron blue dun hen

HOT PARTRIDGE
Position: Point or 2nd dropper
Hook: Kamasan; B100 size 12-14
Thread: Orange
Tail: Natural red hackle fibres
Body: Ultra wire, hot orange/hot yellow
Thorax: Rusty brown Micro Brite
Hackle: Partridge, brown neck feather

YELLOW PARTRIDGE (TF)
Position: Top or 2nd dropper
Hook: Light wire size 14
Thread: Yellow
Tail: Ostrich fibres dyed white
Body: Yellow floss
Rib: Silver oval tinsel
Hackle: Partridge, brown neck feather

RED SPINNER
Position: Top or 2nd dropper
Hook: Light wire size 14 *Thread:* Red
Tail: Natural red hackle fibres
Body: Red floss
Rib: Fine, flat gold tinsel
Wing: Starling feather
Hackle: Natural red cock

BLACK SPINNER
Position: Point or top dropper
Hook: Kamaan B100 size 14
Thread: Black
Tail: Black hackle fibres
Body: Black floss
Rib: Fine, flat silver tinsel
Wing: White EPS fibres
Thorax: SLF-black
Hackle: Black hen hackle

PEARLY PARTRIDGE
Position: Point fly
Hook: Kamasan B100 size 12-14
Thread: Red
Tail: Natural red hackle fibres
Body: Pearl tinsel
Rib: Fine, Gold wire
Thorax cover: Small jungle cock
Hackle: Partridge brown neck feather

WICKHAM'S FANCY
Position: Point or top dropper
Hook: Light wire size 14
Thread: Black
Body: Flat gold tinsel
Body hackle: Natural red cock
Rib: Fine, gold wire
Wing: Mallard wing feather

IRON BLUE DUN
Position: Top dropper
Hook: Light wire size 14
Thread: Black
Tail: Iron blue hackle fibres
Butt: Red floss
Body: Blue mole fur
Wing: Blackbird feather
Hackle: Iron blue dun cock

Upstream nymphing

I WOULD NEVER be silly enough to claim to be first in anything relating to either fishing or fly-tying. However, there is always some innovative thinking going on leading to an event... and then there is a tale to tell.

For many years, trout fishing on the River Suir has been fairly traditional; repeating themes throughout the season with very little diversion. The season would start with wet-fly fishing on either a floating or slow-sinking line – a method which would return in late September, depending on water conditions. In the intervening summer months, the dry-fly would reign supreme. Nothing much had changed in generations of anglers on the river.

My brother Willie was one of the first to attempt something different a few years ago. Having lived and worked in England for many years, he eventually returned home to Tipperary. I believe the time spent in England influenced his thinking regarding fishing methods and techniques. Fishing on stillwaters in the UK had really taken off, and the pace of change was quite astonishing.

The pioneers of stillwater fishing challenged everything to the extent that it was often hard to keep up with new techniques and methods being publicised in the angling press.

For the first few years following his return, Willie enjoyed tremendous success fishing nymphs downstream. This was a departure from the traditional wet or dry-fly and he certainly grabbed everyone's attention with the bags of trout he was catching.

A beautiful Suir brown that took a size 16 Olive Nymph

His approach was particularly successful in low-water conditions. While the dry-fly anglers were obediently waiting for the anticipated time in the day for the trout to feed, Willie was out on the water catching trout. His nymphs worked throughout the day.

Visiting anglers, particularly from abroad, would appear on the river using unheard-of flies and innovative methods of fishing. Some of these excellent anglers had great days on the water but such events were usually frowned upon by the locals, and considered lucky. And it would be fair to say that, in the long term, the traditional river methods would generally out-fish all others.

Then the fishing got tough. Hatches of aquatic insects began to decline noticeably, weather patterns changed and the trout were no longer feeding on the surface as frequently as they once did. Something new and different was required.

A NEW APPROACH

It was April and I was in Ireland on one of my annual fishing trips. I was on the bank at Ballyheron watching my brother Willie fishing the downstream nymph. We got talking afterwards and I enquired whether anyone had thought about fishing beaded nymphs upstream with a floating line, in a similar fashion to dry-fly. His negative reply came as no surprise to me.

Living in England had opened my eyes and my mind to alternative methods of fishing. I am also an avid reader of books and magazines on the subject. There was a lot of publicity at the time surrounding the Poles' and Czechs' use of heavy nymphs in rivers, which had set me thinking about the River Suir.

So, after the conversation with my brother, I decided to put my thoughts into practice. A few days later I journeyed downstream to a place called Ross' Slip with upstream nymph fishing in mind. This is a beautiful stretch of fast-flowing, shallow water with lots of rocky pools and rapid changes in depths.

I tied three size 16 nymphs on the leader. A hackled Olive Nymph occupied the top dropper, a Hare's Ear Nymph the middle and a Pheasant Tail Nymph went on the point. I waded into the water at the bottom of the stream and cast the flies up under some overhanging tree branches. The flies were drifting down nicely towards me in the current when I saw the line give a slight jerk forwards. I struck, but was too late and missed the trout. Or had I merely snagged the bottom?

The Quill Bodied Hare's Ear

I made a second cast, this time slightly further out and, again, as the nymphs were drifting back towards me the line stopped dead in the water. I struck again. This time I was rewarded with a good brown trout. I was now getting a bit excited: two casts and two trout had taken the fly. Had I latched onto something clever, I wondered?

I was having some difficulty watching the end of the line, as the weight of the nymphs was dragging the tip of the floating line under the surface. Bear in mind, these were only tiny, size 16 flies.

My problem with seeing takes was compounded by the glare on the surface, making sight fishing difficult. I rooted around in my wading vest and found some brightly-coloured wool that I had been using in England for fishing static Bloodworm on stillwaters. I 'Ginked' the wool with the universal flotant and tied it into the junction between the line and leader. I was now able to detect the slightest movement of the line.

I fished upstream under the bank until I reached the top of the stream. I was spraying casts above me and slightly outwards, covering each rocky pool from different angles. I resisted the temptation to cast any further than halfway across the river. I quickly learned that by raising the tip of the rod I could at times induce a take.

Having reached the top of the stream I returned to the spot where I had originally started, crossed the river, and started the whole process again. I was meeting trout with almost every cast and had landed sixteen by the time I had reached the top of the stream again. It was only at this juncture that I noticed my brother, Willie, sitting by a clump of reeds. I had no idea how long he been there watching as I had become preoccupied with my fishing.

UPSTREAM NYMPHING

A good brown trout that fell to the charms of a Red Bead Pheasant Tail

I waded back across the river to have a chat and, as I reached him, Willie commented: "I see you've never lost it with the dry-fly." I explained that I may have been casting upstream but I was fishing tiny nymphs. After the usual natter and a couple of cigarettes, I moved upstream to the next glide. I continued fishing the tiny nymphs, with Willie following me, step by step, observing everything and asking loads of questions. He stayed with me for about an hour and then said his goodbyes.

I'd had a brilliant first day fishing the upstream nymph, landing 23 quality trout. I had learned quite quickly how to fish this new technique and was already looking forward to the next day on the river.

The following morning I decided to try a different location and headed for Liamy's Lane – where the river has a superb small weir, followed by a deep glide then a fast, streamy section. I thought it the perfect spot to continue my experimentation with the nymphs.

The problem was that my brother Willie and a friend from France were already fishing the water. And to my complete shock, both of them were fishing the upstream nymph – but using large, bead-headed Pheasant Tail Nymphs with a chunk of knitting wool attached as a strike indicator. Both of them were pulling trout out from all over the place.

I have to give my brother some credit here. He learns fast. The only other angler on the river at that time who might possibly have been in possession of some beaded nymphs would have been Pierre from France; Willie must have sought him out almost immediately after our conversation the previous afternoon.

The rest is history, as they say. Word got round fairly quickly. Within two years, it seemed like every angler on the river was fishing the upstream nymph. This method of fishing has now become extremely successful on the River Suir. Even a salmon or two have been hooked on the beaded nymph. However, I feel there is more scope for improvement and further innovation is required. Hopefully some of the flies illustrated in this section of the book will aid that development.

Whenever big trout of 2lb to 4lb are caught, their stomachs are stuffed with crayfish. It is also noticeable that very few of these big trout in the river are caught on the standard beaded nymphs. So there's food for thought for the innovative fly-tyer!

TECHNIQUES

There is very little to say about the actual method of upstream nymphing; it's self-explanatory. Good presentation and short-lining are the key factors.

The critical issue is to be adaptable; varying currents and depths present different challenges, and demand alternative flies and slower line recovery. Good rivercraft is another essential factor in nymph fishing. Water conditions will continue to vary throughout the season and trout will move about in the river adapting to these conditions. It is also helpful to know which pools the trout prefer to occupy as they come on the feed.

I've lost count of the number anglers I have watched charge out into the water creating bow waves then start casting beaded nymphs so large they look like depth charges going in, only to snag the bottom with every cast. They seem oblivious to water depth and general rivercraft and appear to be content to strike at the stones all day long. At times it leaves me scratching my head in sheer bewilderment.

In deep water, it is a good idea to attach a size 16 nymph to the hook of a larger or heavier fly. A sort of sunken New Zealand style, if you like. The larger nymph is used to get the smaller fly down quickly through the depths, and for all intents and purposes is the sacrificial nymph. This allows the smaller size 16 to tempt the fish.

I still feel that a combination of a hackled nymph on the top dropper, an 'anorexic' Diawl Bach on the middle dropper and a beaded nymph on the point will out-fish the normal method of suspending a single fly below an indicator. At least this way the angler is hedging his or her bets by fishing at varying depths.

Fishing with this team of flies I would normally start at the bottom of a stream making short casts and working the different depths feeling the river as I make my way upstream. By changing the size of the beaded nymph on the point, I can adapt to changes in the speed of the current or to different depths. Should the trout move up in the water, a change to a size 16 on the point or the removal of the beaded nymph altogether will adapt quickly to fish more effectively.

The local anglers on the Suir in Cahir appear to have become fixated with fishing the beaded nymph suspended below some form of indicator. Some years ago, when this method came onto the scene, some great bags of trout were recorded and still are today by a few, fine anglers. But such prolific catches have become less frequent. The method I have described earlier will catch more trout but requires a little extra skill and patience.

Finally, there is the matter of fly selection. The best anglers on the Suir are expert in recognising the major aquatic insect species and set great store in knowing exactly which imitative dry-flies to mount on the leader throughout the season.

However, it's a pity the same effort is not being put into what is happening beneath the surface. It is as important to understand the life cycle of nymphs as it is the winged insect. There is far too much dependence on fishing the Pheasant Tail and Hare's Ear Nymphs when there are so many other patterns to try. My brother has told me that the trout in the river have become very wary of these 'standard' nymph patterns. This is to be expected if everyone is fishing the same flies and the trout are getting pricked by them regularly. An opportunity exists for further innovation to catch these wily trout.

Brown trout find their food, primarily, on or near the riverbed. They will come up to the surface to feed only if it is worth the effort. It is easier to 'match-the-hatch' when you can see the insects the trout are taking from the surface but even without visual clues It's not too difficult to work out what the trout are feeding on when they are grubbing around on the bottom.

Take a few minutes to lift some stones from the riverbed and see what's crawling around underneath; usually there will be caseless caddis larvae and olive nymphs. Or spoon fish throughout the season, examine the stomach contents in a jar of water, and make a note of the seasonal ebb and flow of nymph species. The more difficult but rewarding task is to then imitate these insects and present them to the trout in a natural manner.

An imitation Crayfish: A pattern to possibly tempt big, Suir brown trout

Beaded nymphs

BLACK SPINNER NYMPH
Hook: Kamasan B100 size 14-16
Thread: Black
Tail: Black hackle fibres
Body: Pheasant tail dyed black
Rib: Fine, flat silver tinsel
Thorax: Black SLF
Head: Black tungsten bead

GHOST NYMPH
Hook: Light wire size 12-14
Thread: White
Tail: White goose biots
Body: Fine silver wire
Thorax: Grey fur
Thorax cover: Pearl tinsel
Legs: White partridge fibres
Head: Silver bead

BLACK & SILVER
Hook: Kamasan B100 size 14-16
Thread: Black
Tail: Black goose biots
Body: Black floss
Rib: Medium silver wire
Thorax: Mole fur dyed black
Thorax cover: Pearl tinsel
Head: Silver bead

PHEASANT TAIL No 4
Hook: Heavy gauge size 12-14
Thread: Brown
Tail: Crystal hair
Body: Pheasant tail fibres
Rib: Fine copper wire
Thorax: Rusty brown Micro Brite
Thorax cover: Pearl tinsel
Head: Copper bead

GREY GOOSE
Hook: Heavy gauge size 14-16
Thread: Grey
Tail: Heron quill fibres or substitute
Body: Heron herl or substitute
Rib: Fine copper wire
Thorax: Blue mole fur
Head: Copper bead

PHEASANT TAIL No 1
Hook: Kamasan B100 size 14-16
Thread: Olive green
Tail: Pheasant tail fibres
Body: Pheasant tail fibres
Rib: Fine copper wire
Thorax: Mole fur dyed olive
Thorax cover: Pearl tinsel
Legs: Short pheasant tail fibres
Head: Red bead

JONAH BUG
Hook: Kamasan B 100 size 14-16
Thread: Brown
Tail: Natural red hackle fibres
Body: Ultra wire, hot orange/hot yellow
Thorax: Hare's ear fur
Head: Gold bead

HARE'S EAR
Hook: Kamasan B175 size 14-16
Thread: Brown
Tail: Natural red hackle fibres
Body: Hare's ear fur
Rib: Fine flat gold tinsel
Thorax: Hare's ear fur
Thorax cover: Pearl tinsel
Head: Gold bead

OLIVE BUG
Hook: Kamasan B100 size 14
Thread: Olive
Tail: Heron herl or substitute
Body: Heron herl or substitute
Rib: Olive Flexi Floss
Thorax: Hare's ear dyed olive
Head: Gold bead

COPPER BUG
Hook: Heavy gauge size 14
Thread: Brown
Tail: Brown goose biots
Body: Copper wire
Thorax: Peacock herl
Thorax cover: Pearl tinsel
Legs: Grouse feather fibres
Head: Gold bead

PHEASANT TAIL No 5
Hook: Heavy gauge size 12-14
Thread: Black
Tail: Pheasant tail fibres dyed black
Body: Pheasant tail dyed olive
Rib: Fine copper wire
Thorax: Rusty brown Micro Brite
Thorax cover: Pearl tinsel
Legs: Short pheasant tail fibres
Head: Black tungsten bead

PHEASANT TAIL No 2
Hook: Heavy gauge size 14-16
Thread: Brown
Tail: Pheasant tail fibres
Body: Pheasant tail fibres
Rib: Fine copper wire
Thorax: Mole fur dyed olive
Thorax cover: Pearl tinsel
Legs: Short pheasant tail fibres

GREY GOOSE

OLIVE BUG

BLACK SPINNER NYMPH

PHEASANT TAIL No 1

COPPER BUG

GHOST NYMPH

JONAH BUG

PHEASANT TAIL No 5

BLACK & SILVER

HARE'S EAR

PHEASANT TAIL No 2

PHEASANT TAIL No 4

Unweighted nymphs

BLACK & YELLOW
Position: 2nd dropper
Hook: Kamasan B 100 size 12-14
Thread: Black
Butt: Silver tinsel
Tail: Black hackle fibres
Body: Stripped peacock eye quill, dyed yellow
Thorax: Mole fur, dyed black
Thorax cover: Dark Nymph Skin
Hackle: Black hen feather

GOLD PARTRIDGE
Position: Point fly
Hook: Kamasan B 100 size 12-14
Thread: Black
Tail: Natural red hackle fibres
Body: Gold holographic tinsel with black tinsel over
Rib: Fine gold wire
Thorax: Hare's ear fur & red seal's fur
Thorax cover: Dark Nymph Skin
Hackle: Brown partridge feather

BLACK SPINNER
Position: Point fly
Hook: Kamasan B 100 size 14
Thread: Black
Tail: Black hackle fibres
Body: Pheasant tail, dyed black
Rib: Fine flat silver tinsel
Thorax: Black SLF
Thorax cover: Dark Nymph Skin
Hackle: Black cock

BLACK PARTRIDGE
Position: Top dropper
Hook: Kamasan B 100 size 14
Thread: Black
Tail: Natural red hackle fibres
Body: Black floss with pearl strip over
Rib: Gold oval tinsel
Thorax: Hare's ear fur
Thorax cover: Dark Nymph Skin
Hackle: Brown partridge feather

PHEASANT TAIL No 1
Position: Point fly
Hook: Kamasan B175 size 14-16
Thread: Black
Tail: Greenwell hackle fibres
Body: Pheasant tail fibres
Rib: Fine silver wire
Thorax: Mole fur, dyed olive
Thorax cover: Dark Nymph Skin
Hackle: Light Greenwell's cock

PHEASANT TAIL No 2
Position: Point fly
Hook: Kamasan B175 size 14-16
Thread: Black
Tail: Greenwell hackle fibres
Body: Pheasant tail fibres
Rib: Fine silver wire
Thorax: Pearl tinsel
Thorax cover: Dark Nymph Skin
Hackle: Light Greenwell's hen feather

PHEASANT TAIL No 3
Position: 2nd dropper
Hook: Kamasan B175 Size 14-16
Thread: Black
Tail: Badger cock hackle fibres
Body: Pheasant tail fibres
Rib: Fine silver wire
Thorax: Blue mole fur
Thorax cover: Dark Nymph Skin
Hackle: Badger hen

SILVER ROSS
Position: Point fly
Hook: Kamasan B100 size 14
Thread: Black
Tail: Black hackle fibres
Body: Flat silver tinsel
Rib: Fine silver wire
Thorax: Seal's fur, dyed crimson
Thorax cover: Dark Nymph Skin
Hackle: Black hen feather

ORANGE & BLACK
Position: 2nd dropper
Hook: Kamasan B100 size 14
Thread: Black
Tail: Black hackle fibres
Body: Orange floss with black tinsel over
Rib: Fine gold wire
Thorax: Mole fur, dyed black
Thorax cover: Dark Nymph Skin
Hackle: Black hen feather

COPPER BUG
Position: 2nd dropper
Hook: Kamasan B100 size 14
Thread: Brown
Tail: Natural red hackle fibres
Body: Fine copper wire
Thorax: Peacock herl
Thorax cover: Dark Nymph Skin
Hackle: Natural red hen feather

DARK GREENWELL'S
Position: 2nd dropper
Hook: Kamasan B100 size 14
Thread: Dark green
Tail: Greenwell's hackle fibres
Body: Green floss with pearl strip over
Rib: Fine gold wire
Thorax: Mole fur, dyed olive
Thorax cover: Dark Nymph Skin
Hackle: Greenwell hen feather

BADGER QUILL
Position: 2nd dropper
Hook: Kamasan B100 size 14-16
Thread: Black
Butt: Silver tinsel
Tail: Badger hackle fibres
Body: Stripped quill from peacock eye
Thorax: Grey fur
Thorax cover: Dark Nymph Skin
Hackle: Badger cock

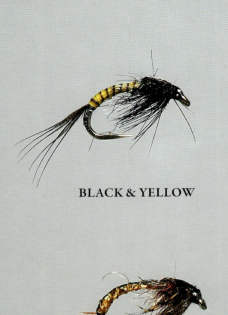

PHEASANT TAIL No 1

BLACK & YELLOW

ORANGE & BLACK

PHEASANT TAIL No 2

GOLD PARTRIDGE

COPPER BUG

PHEASANT TAIL No 3

BLACK SPINNER

DARK GREENWELL'S

SILVER ROSS

BLACK PARTRIDGE

BADGER QUILL

Some things never change

FISHING IN VARIOUS parts of the globe can be both different and the same. While this might appear a paradox, so many times an experience gained in one place translates almost perfectly to somewhere else, even when thousands of miles away. So my apologies then for choosing an Irish water as an example; I am confident that anglers can relate to these tales and cite similar occasions from fisheries that they have visited. In angling circles we're often guilty of dispensing far too quickly with tried and tested methods in exchange for the new. Some of these changes to techniques and fly patterns can simply be put down to adapting to developments in the fish's behaviour and feeding patterns. But, as I have often learned to my cost, substituting fads for hard earned experience is rarely successful.

THE RIVER SUIR

At times I am as guilty as anyone else for have a good old moan about the condition of the river. Given an audience, I will harp on about the good old days and trot out all of the reasons why I believe there has been such a decline in fish stocks, insect life and water quality in the river. But in the middle of these self-inflicted bouts of depression and accusation it is important to remember that, when it comes to fishing, things are not always as bad as they might first appear. Some of these allegedly negative trends are simply just cyclical changes and we need to recognise them as such. Spawning runs of salmon are a prime example. When I was a boy, the main spawning run on the Suir was in October. I often got into trouble by being late for school as I would became totally transfixed watching hundreds of salmon attempting to leap the weir in town to continue their journey upstream. Year after year the spawning runs would arrive later in the season. As a result, the spring runs were affected. But history tells us this has happened before. Would these delayed spawning runs still have happened anyway regardless of the strength of the stocks in the river? We will never know. Perhaps we are just going through another one of those cycles.

JULY ON THE RIVER

When it came to evening fishing on the river during the summer, we'd leave the house at around seven. But there was one brief period in the fishing calendar when my father would return home from work, wolf down his dinner and head for the river early. It was the first two weeks of July. For some reason, the trout back then would have two feeding flurries in the same evening. The first rise would happen at around 6.30pm and the other at the normal time, just after sunset. In these two weeks my father would often have the basket half full with trout as other anglers turned up for the evening's session. But father kept quiet about that golden fortnight; after all there was a supplementary income at stake.

Over the course of time, and my prolonged absence from the river, such important lessons were forgotten until, a few years ago, when I was back on the Suir in early July. I had been fishing most of the afternoon with very little to show for my efforts. I eventually arrived at Liamy's lane and was contemplating packing up with the intention of returning later for the evening fishing. Luckily for me I decided to stay. I sat down on the bank for a bite to eat and to smoke a cigarette. While enjoying my nicotine 'fix' I maintained a close observation of the pools across the river. I was beginning to regret my decision to stay when I noticed a couple of trout feeding in one of the pools under the far bank. This got me moving fairly swiftly. I waded in below the spot where I saw the trout rising and started fishing with the dry-fly. I began working my way slowly upstream towards the pool of feeding trout. As I cast the dry-fly over known lies, more trout came on the feed. An inspection of my waders indicated that Blue Winged Olives were starting to hatch in big numbers. On went two Blue Winged Olives and the action commenced. Trout after trout were either caught or lost in the next half hour. Then, just as I was really getting into the groove, the trout switched their feeding habits. Every rising trout I covered refused the Blue Winged Olives that had been taken so readily before. The rise form had changed. Instead of the previous, confident swirl, the trout were now quietly sipping down the natural insect. Fortunately I had been in this position before and recognised that, having returned to the water, the female insects had completed their egg-laying stage and had become 'spent' – falling to the water as they died. I quickly tied on two Sherry Spinners… a parachute-hackled fly on the dropper and the traditional Spinner on point. It was not long before I was back in among the trout again. I was working two pools roughly fifteen yards apart. Having taken a couple of trout from one of the pools, I would rest it and move to the other. For two hours I plied between the two pools and enjoyed some excellent dry-fly fishing. Then I noticed that, every so often, a very big trout would make an explosive rise in the upper pool.

This trout wasn't feeding as frequently as his smaller neighbours, but every time he came up he caught my attention. I decided to try for him. After I'd covered this trout from several different angles, he finally took the Spinner on the point and raced off downstream like a train. For some unknown reason, I had lost numerous trout in play that evening just as they came directly below me in the current. I later put it down to the small gape of the hooks I was using. I had the net out and ready to land the big trout. But just like several others that evening it shed the hook as I was drawing it towards the net. A beauty of around 2lb was lost. At around quarter to eight, the rise had finished and the river returned to its normal peaceful state.

Not long afterwards I could hear the sound of cars coming down the lane, announcing the arrival of the first anglers for the evening's fishing. By now, the trout had become dormant after the earlier banquet. I could easily distinguish from the voices I heard, and recognised the anglers that had arrived. Following a brief inspection of the water, I could hear their grumbling comments: "Nothing rising, as usual," was the gist. I had just enjoyed two wonderful hours' of dry-fly fishing. I had landed

A female, large dark olive. Good hatches of olives are still typical of the Suir

over a dozen trout and lost as many more at the net. The following day I returned to the same spot and, right on time, the trout came on the feed again. The same flies, same time and the same result. Right on cue, at 7.45, the boys turned up two hours too late and missed the rise again. This little tale has less to do with skill and is much more about good timing. In all the years that have passed since my departure from Ireland little had changed during those early weeks in July on the River Suir. Had I not stayed on that first afternoon I too would have missed the rise and would probably have been guilty of moaning about the river over a pint later that evening. The trade secrets my father had taught me all those years ago

127

SOME THINGS NEVER CHANGE

had not lost validity with time. It just suits us to think so at times. Perhaps we have become a little complacent over the years and may be guilty of not working as hard as perhaps my parent's generation had. Having cycled miles to get to a chosen spot in the river, my father had to stick by his decision. Making such decisions were not accidental, it required using the hard lessons learned to get the location and timing right. Today, it's a quick cast then jump in the car, if the fishing is slow, and race off to another spot. It becomes all too easy and, perhaps, opportunities are often missed as a result.

CARRIGATATA

Back on the River Suir, I was evening fishing again, this time with my brother Tommy, and I was about to get a harsh lesson in the perils of forgetfulness. Carrigatata (pronounced locally as Carrigatar) is at the extreme south of the waters controlled by the Cahir and District Angling Club. It is one of my favorite places in the whole river, especially when evening fishing for trout under a moonlit sky. Carrigatata is a renowned beat for salmon fishing. The upper stretch is deep and slow, with the water held back by the weir. Below the weir is a fast stream which is excellent for a salmon fly. The stream also holds a healthy stock of brown trout.

We tackled up just below the weir and I tied on the usual two dry-flies for that time of year – Pale Watery Spinner on the dropper and an August Dun on the point. I noticed a trout feeding in a pool just off the heavy current and, as Tommy was still tackling up, I decided to give it a cast. As the fly drifted slowly over the trout it rose, and confidently took my August Dun and was duly landed a couple of minutes later. Tommy enquired about the flies and then said: "Gimme one a dem yolks," which, roughly translated, means "Can I borrow one of your flies, please.?" When finally ready, Tommy crossed the river and started fishing close in by the old stone wall under the weir. I stayed in the spot where I had started and waited for something to happen.

Lesson one: I had known from experience that the trout always came on the feed first in the pools of heavy water on the far side of the river. After all, my father would always make a bee-line for that spot as soon as he had tackled up. Having mounted my rod first, I was still too slow to move and allowed my brother to end up in pole position. Armed with my two dry-flies he proceeded to give the trout on the far side a good pasting.

We fished on into the dark and I eventually moved upstream to the deeper water above the weir. Unfortunately, soon afterwards I snapped my cast of evening flies on a trout. Slightly annoyed with myself, I dismantled my rod and returned below the weir to wait for Tommy to re-cross the river. By now the rise of trout had petered out and he eventually made his way to my bank. I was in the mood for a pint and was anxious that I could make it to the pub before closing time. But I could not shift Tommy. I even offered to buy the round, which normally works, but on this night nothing would motivate him to move. So we sat down on the grass for a smoke and a chat. It was a beautiful evening; the moon was up in full with its brilliant light shimmering across the flowing water and the surrounding fields.

Lesson two: Remember what your father always taught you about fishing Carrigatata in a full moon. Tommy reminded me that, at this time of year when it appeared that the rise was over, the trout would eventually move out of the fast

Suir favourites: Sherry Spinners and the August Dun

water and feed again in by the rushes under our bank. We just had to be patient. We sat there and waited for what seemed like an eternity though in reality it was a mere twenty minutes. Sure enough, a trout came up for a sedge near a crop of tall rushes; not a splashy rise like those earlier, but a nice, quiet dimple under the surface. Within minutes several more trout joined in. It was not until the trout were feeding confidently that Tommy made his move, and again showed me the way. He finished the evening with more than twenty trout against my miserable half a dozen. We just barely made it to the pub before last orders and, to add to my misery, I had to listen to some gloating and a reminder of the mistakes I had made earlier that evening – several times over.

PERSISTENCE AND PATIENCE

It takes years of experience and watercraft to build up a detailed knowledge like this on any river or lake. Had I not been fishing with my brother that evening, I may well have gone home early. I had forgotten what had been drummed into me all those years before about how to fish Carrigatata in moonlight. Thirty years had passed, but the trout were still behaving in exactly in the same way. Most anglers would have reasonably packed up their gear and left the river once the rise was over. But it must have taken persistence and patience by the older generation of anglers to have discovered these little gems of information about the river and its moods.

As I get older it becomes increasingly difficult to remember everything learned over the years. This is exacerbated when returning to a fishery after a long absence, as I have experienced on the River Suir. Some type of *aide memoir* can prove useful at times. My son David now keeps a fishing diary and is able to recall dates, times, places and successful flies. He often refers to his little book when we venture out fishing these days. A useful and informative tool as the memory begins to fade, I feel. Maybe I just keep forgetting to keep it up to date...

We have become all too impatient these days and give up far too easily when things are not going our way. A poor day's fishing can often be rescued by applying a commonsense approach. What's required is good observational skills and putting in to action those hard-earned lessons we've received over the years. Fishing has always had a fair element of luck attached to it, but those anglers who are continuously successful have developed skills through hard work and by being observant. Success comes from the accumulation of knowledge and by being decisive when conditions change. In other words, good anglers generate their own luck. And one must never forget those hard-earned lessons because not everything changes with the passage of time. While I accept that most wild fisheries have declined over the years, it still becomes all too easy to wallow in negativity and lose sight of what is really going on under our very noses.

"The run at the other side of the bridge." Just below the town of Cahir

I discussed similar trends with a boatman on Lough Mask a few years ago. He told me that many anglers would happily arrive at the boat dock at the traditional time of 10am, just as he was returning from an excellent early morning's fishing. He was mystified why anglers appear never to change or try to adapt their approach, even if that means missing out on a dawn start, when fishing of every kind is often at its best.

I have witnessed a few early mornings in June on Lough Carra when the trout were feeding on caenis. It is little wonder that it can prove difficult to raise a trout during a normal morning's fishing – the fish have been gorging themselves for several hours before you arrived. Such lack of activity and dour fishing can often wrongly be prescribed to the fishery being out of sorts Then, as usuall happens, rumours start buzzing around and, before you know it, the lake or river is condemned for fishing badly. While some things never change, as I have already described we also have to accept that the behaviour of trout is continually altering as they adapt to climate change, which presumably affects the cycle of invertebrate life on which they depend. To be successful on a wild brown trout river or lake you must be prepared to be adaptable... and resolute. In this age of greater mobility, technology and information, we may have lost our perseverance and staying power.

Evening fishing

FOLLOWING MY EXODUS from Ireland I took the first few years of my absence from the River Suir very hard. I would lie awake, late into the night, looking out at a beautiful, clear, moonlit evening, dreaming of a bend in the river where I ought to be fishing.

River fishing can be very therapeutic at its best; it must be the sight and sound of running water that has such a calming effect on the mind. But river fishing in the late evening transcends even that pleasure, promoting an eerie feeling of remoteness yet a sense of being intimately close to nature. As the sun dips toward the horizon anticipation rises. Will the hatch come? Am I in the right area? Only sheer willpower prevents you from going anywhere near the pools into which, if left undisturbed, trout will congregate as the light fades.

The sounds of the day shift – the birdsong and the general clatter – subside and, as the cloak of darkness falls, the sound of running water seems amplified.

Deprived of much of your sight, your remaining senses heighten. You become even more alert, fishing by touch and sound. You can now hear trout rising; there... is that the sound of a trout sucking hatching sedges from the edge of the reeds?

It's not everyone's cup of tea, but I love the feeling of isolation that nightfall brings. And then there is the icing on the cake – fishing under a full moon.

BIG TROUT

There is no doubt that the best chance of catching one of the Suir's big trout on the fly is late at night. Some of these big trout can survive for nine or ten years in the river and have seen it all. Daylight fishing for them is next to useless. Yet, if you know where to find them, they will readily take a fly under the cover of darkness.

In the right conditions, big trout will move out of deep water where they have been holed up during the day and into the shallower pools late at night, to feed. It takes a few years to learn where these special pools are, and once put to memory, they remain a closely-guarded secret. As with all forms of fishing, to be successful late at night requires good instincts and some common sense.

A nice brace taken at dusk

THEY'RE BATS DEAR

The evening this photo (right) was taken, I eventually moved downstream of the golf course to where the water becomes deeper and the current slows a little. I was fishing in under the cover of some overhanging tree branches when my wife commented that she was surprised to see so many birds still flying around so late at night: "They're bats dear," I told her, and she took off like a rocket. She has never been seen on a riverbank at night again.

In my earlier days as a young boy on the river I would become nervous once darkness fell. I blame my father for this; he had a great passion for telling stories. He would spend the winter months telling us kid's yarns about the river. He had a particular flair for ghost stories. This was all very well until you found yourself on your own, in darkness, in one of places that he told us about. All those frightening visions from his tales would come flooding back. It was enough to make the hackles stand up on the back of your neck.

The river in darkness has a way of playing tricks on a young mind. It really hits home how dependent we are on our sight to make us feel comfortable and safe. Our nerves were made even more brittle knowing there were several pranksters about on the river at night. My uncle Liam was notorious for sneaking up on young anglers and frightening the lives out of them. He would hide in the bushes and just as the unsuspecting angler passed, would throw his landing net over their heads and pull them into the bushes. He carried a pencil torch which glowed red at night, his favourite trick was to hide and then switch on the torch just as you were passing him. He would position the torch under his chin to show off the one tooth left in his gob, all you would see is this glowing red face and a single fang sticking down.

You were very unfortunate indeed to stumble into the spot my uncle Tommy was fishing at night. He would let off such a roar that it would frighten the life out of you. Boy, could that man swear; to this day I have never heard anyone who could fit so many profanities into one sentence. If you recognised him in the river, the sensible thing was to give that area a wide berth or risk every evil in the universe being called down on your head. It was on one such evening that I allowed my father's tales to get the better of my imagination. I was very young at the time and on my own. I was fishing in a place called Armitage's. As darkness fell, I decided to move upriver to

Memory lane: An evening's fishing along the Golf Course

a spot called the Point Stream. The trout normally feed here long after the rise is over in the fast water below. To get there I had to bend down and crawl under some very low hanging branches of a large horse chestnut tree. This tree was huge and resembled the shape of a cone. I was about half way under the tree with my rod pointed behind me as I had been taught when I heard a very strange noise. It stopped me dead in my tracks. This was followed by an even louder noise. It sounded like a strange, loud cough.

My problem was I didn't know whether to go forwards or back the way I came as the distance to safety was just the same. My nerves were jangling and I began to slowly move backwards. But then all hell broke loose. There was a terrible sound and it felt like the tree had come alive. I dropped my rod and still don't know how I got out from under that tree so fast. I ran to the lane where I had left my bicycle earlier in the evening and shot off down the road as fast as I could pedal. I reckon if someone had timed me that night I would have broken some Olympic record. I kept looking behind to see if the monster was following me. Was I ever glad to see home. With panic subsiding the first task was to check my underwear for any 'accident' that might have been caused by the night's events.

The following morning, like it or not, I had no other choice but to cycle back to the place I had been fishing the previous evening. This was not false bravado nor was it an attempt on my behalf to exorcise some demons, I simply had to go back and find my rod. As I got near the horse chestnut tree my heart started pounding again, even in daylight...

But there was my rod lying on the ground under the tree where I had left it. As I crawled back under the tree, the whole nightmare started again. The tree came alive again; I grabbed my rod and got out of there as fast as I could. But curiosity got the better of me and I eventually got the nerve up and skirted around the tree for a look.

EVENING FISHING

A variety of Suir dry-flies, including the Badger Quill and Ginger Quill

I still cannot figure out how this could have occurred, but somehow a horse had gotten under the tree and, once inside, found itself trapped. When I stumbled across the unfortunate beast in the dark I must have frightened it, and it went ballistic. I don't know who was the more terrified that night, me, or the horse. To this day I am always nervous going under that tree in the hours of darkness.

BE DISCIPLINED

It may not always be possible, but attempt to position yourself on the river bank in a way that gives you the best view – perhaps looking back towards the night sky. The section of the Suir that flows through the town of Cahir runs from north to south so, on dark evenings, choosing the east bank of the river can make the difference between success and failure.

Be disciplined and shy away from pools favoured by the big fish later in the evening. As the main rise of the evening tails off, and it looks as if you've missed your chance, these trout will move into the best feeding pools. Many a night's fishing can be rescued by quietly approaching one of these pools from downstream and quickly picking off five or six trout with short, upstream casts. Trout will always conserve their energy, so look for pools away from any swift current, in the slacks where they can fin gently ready to grab any passing snack. This is where the trout will shoal up late at night on the look-out for easy pickings.

It goes without saying that ploughing around in the river causing all kinds of disturbance will achieve nothing except scaring the fish. Short-lining, even at night, is essential. It may be dark but trout can easily be put down by excessive long casting; always try to avoid alerting the trout to your presence.

During a hatch of sedges, the trout will often ignore the adult flies and go for the emerging pupae, so it pays at times to alter the angle of the cast and mix the flies on the leader. On countless occasions I have covered feeding fish and had every offering refused. Rest the area for a few minutes by working around the pool, then approach from a completely different angle to present the flies in a different manner. Sometimes the trout will only accept the fly if it is fished from above and allowed to skate over them in the current.

Even when the right pattern is being fished, trout will often prefer a fly presented a certain way to the exclusion of all others. The most productive approach to trout at night is from behind, fishing upstream with a floating line. The fly can then be allowed to float over the trout and recovered when it's out of the fish's line of sight. If a dead-drift fails, draw the line back in short pulls, making the flies skate across the surface, imitating the behaviour of the adult sedge. Colour is still very important at night, so be observant and always attempt to match the hatch. Getting the profile of the fly correct is also vital.

ALL ABOUT STEALLTH

The rise forms will provide an indication of the stage the trout are taking the natural insect or nymph, whether splashing on top for winged flies or swishing at the pupae just beneath the surface. Evening fishing is all about stealth so avoid torches shining on the water. Some of the huge lamps I see strapped to angler's heads today should be confined to the mines where they belong.

It is not uncommon for trout to switch their diet during a rise, so adapt the team of flies beforehand, as retying casts can be difficult in darkness. You can hedge your bets a little by greasing the top dropper fly, using a Spider pattern on the middle and a slim fly on the point. This will cater for those occasions when you're uncertain about what the trout are feeding on. The selection of flies can be altered for the following evening's fishing once you've worked out the trout's diet.

The bonus, years ago, of late evening fishing on the Suir was the possibility of hooking a salmon or grilse. I have been fortunate down the years to have landed quite a few grilse during evening fishing sessions. I was so lucky at one time, my brother Tommy reckoned if I cast the flies into a bucket I would find a salmon. The Marlodge is a top attractor pattern for grilse, if they are running the river in summer.

The usual late-evening routine on the Suir is to start in the fast water with a pair of size 14 dry-flies. This tradition has changed in recent years, with the dry-fly being replaced by small, bead-head nymphs if there are very few trout rising. Once the light begins to fade, a quick change is made to a ready-made team of size 12 flies, in preparation for the main rise. Finally, as the rise begins to peter out, abandon the fast water and move to where the current is much slower. From this time onwards most of the fishing will be confined to short-lining under the bank or behind reed beds.

FLY SELECTION

Evening fishing on the Suir gets fully underway in the month of June, or late May if the weather has been warm and settled. The first flies to fish at this time of year are the Alder and Black Sedge.

I was fishing the Suir some years ago in the first week of June and, over a few evenings' fishing, I quickly determined that the only fly which was working to any degree was the Alder. By the third evening, I was fishing three Alders on the cast.

I greased up the top dropper, had a standard pattern on the middle dropper, and I took the scissors to the point fly to remove most of the hackle. As the evening progressed, the trout would show a preference for the middle dropper and, when it got very late, they would take only the sunken fly on the point.

I caught some great bags of trout during that week in June and lost one of the biggest fish I ever hooked on the Suir. The trout took the Alder with a solid thump and – unusually for me – I played that fish off the reel as I knew it was very big. It ran me ragged up and down the river for half an hour and never once broke the surface. In the end the trout shed the hook. What I would have given for just one proper glimpse of that fish!

The Black Grouse is a great fly in June and again in September, while the Orange Grouse will fish well on the point during the first two weeks of July.

The Marlodge has to be the best performing 'silver' fly for the Suir, especially when the moon is up. In between moons the Silver and Gold Partridge will work well. The Silver Sedge is a great top dropper fly in July and August. When fished with the Balloon Caddis on the point (known locally as the Honda Fifty) the pairing makes a very effective combination. In general it pays to reduce the size of the Sedge patterns fished in September to ones tied quite skimpily on a size 14. The Cinnamon Sedge is well worth a try in August and September. A range of Sedges should always be carried in your fly box; the best body-colours are red, hare's ear and olive green.

The River Aherlow – a Suir tributary – generally fishes later into the evening than the main river. Years ago the strategy was to fish the main river first and, once the rise had finished, return to the Aherlow for at least another half an hour's fishing. Once we had crossed back to the Aherlow, my father would light up a cigar and send me off to one of the known hotspots. After he had enough of the cigar, or watching me losing endless trout, I would be ordered back and he would wade out into the same spot then proceed to show me how it was done. It was a blessed relief when he called me back, as I was always uncomfortable when he was standing watching me fishing; I just knew that I would perform badly.

Never fish the River Aherlow without having a Black Devil, Red Grouse and a Marlodge in your box or, preferably, on your leader. The Silver Sedge and Gold Sedge are terrific July and August patterns for this river. It also pays to try some lough flies at times; three of the best patterns that have worked for me in the past are the Peter Ross, Dunkeld and the Connemara Black; the latter working particularly well when black, grouse-wing sedges are on the water.

Finally, when fishing the slow, deeper water, the trout tend to feed in under the bank and quietly sip down passing or falling insects. This is when the range of Cul de Canard patterns, winged with buoyant CDC duck feather, will perform especially well.

A 4lb beauty, caught evening-fishing at The Park

Evening flies I

BLUE PENNELL
Hook: Kamasan B170 size 12-14
Thread: Blue
Tail: Golden pheasant tippets
Body: Blue floss
Rib: Fine flat silver tinsel
Wing: Single jungle cock feather
Hackle: Black cock

RED MARLODGE
Hook: Kamasan B170 size 10-14
Thread: Red
Tail: Golden pheasant crest
Body: Silver tinsel/red floss/silver tinsel
Rib: Oval silver tinsel
Throat hackles: No 1, Red cock - No 2, Guinea fowl
Wing: Bronze mallard
Cheeks: Jungle cock

RED GROUSE
Hook: Kamasan B170 size 12-14
Thread: Red
Tail: Golden pheasant tippets
Body: Red floss
Rib: Fine flat gold tinsel
Wing: Single jungle cock feather
Hackle: Grouse feather

ALDER
Hook: Kamasan B170 size 10-12
Thread: Black
Body: Peacock herl, dyed claret
Wing: Brown hen
Hackle: Black hen feather

BLACK DEVIL
Hook: Kamasan B170 size 10-14
Thread: Black
Tail: Golden pheasant tippets
Body: Black floss
Rib: Fine flat gold tinsel
Wing: Speckled grouse feather with red goose strip over
Hackle: Black cock feather
Cheeks: Jungle cock

ORANGE GROUSE
Hook: Kamasan B170 size 12-14
Thread: Orange
Tail: Golden pheasant tippets
Body: Orange seal's fur
Rib: Fine flat gold tinsel
Wing: Single jungle cock feather
Hackle: Grouse feather

BLACK GROUSE
Hook: Kamasan B170 size 12-14
Thread: Black
Tail: Golden pheasant tippets
Body: Pheasant tail fibres, dyed black
Rib: Flat gold tinsel
Wing: Single jungle cock feather
Hackle: Grouse feather

BUTCHER
Hook: Kamasan B170 size 12-14
Thread: Black
Tail: Goose fibres, dyed red
Body: Flat silver tinsel
Rib: Fine silver wire
Wing: Blue mallard feather
Hackle: Black cock

MARLODGE
Hook: Kamasan B170 size 10-14
Thread: Black
Tail: Golden pheasant crest
Body: Silver tinsel/black floss/silver tinsel
Rib: Oval silver tinsel
Throat hackle: Guinea fowl
Wing: Bronze mallard
Cheeks: Jungle cock

SILVER & GOLD PARTRIDGE
Hook: Kamasan B170 size 12-14
Thread: Black
Tail: Golden pheasant tippets
Body: Flat silver tinsel
Rib: Fine flat gold tinsel
Hackle: Brown partridge feather
Wing: Single jungle cock feather

BLUE PENNELL

ALDER

BUTCHER

RED MARLODGE

BLACK DEVIL

MARLODGE

RED GROUSE

ORANGE GROUSE

SILVER & GOLD PARTRIDGE

BLACK GROUSE

Evening flies II

BALLOON HARE'S EAR CADDIS
Hook: Light-wire sedge size 10-14
Thread: Brown
Body: Hare's ear fur
Wing: Deer hair fibres
Thorax: Hare's ear fur
Thorax cover: Yellow foam

ORANGE CDC
Hook: Kamasan B170 size 12-14
Thread: Orange
Body: Hare's ear fur, dyed orange
Wing: Natural CDC with strands of deer hair over
Hackle: Cree cock, underside trimmed

GOLD SEDGE
Hook: Light-wire sedge size 12-14
Thread: Brown
Body: Flat gold tinsel
Body hackle: Light Cree cock
Rib: Fine gold wire
Wing: Deer hair with CDC over
Shoulder hackle: Cree cock

SILVER SEDGE
Hook: Light-wire sedge size 10-14
Thread: Brown
Body: Flat silver tinsel
Body hackle: Light Cree cock hackle
Wing: Deer hair with natural CDC over
Shoulder hackle: Cree cock hackle
Horns: Stripped grizzle hackle stalks

RED CADDIS
Hook: Kamasan B170 size 10-14
Thread: Red
Body: Seal's fur, dyed red
Body hackle: Natural brown cock feather
Rib: Fine gold wire
Wing: Elk hair

CINNAMON SEDGE
Hook: Light-wire sedge size 12-14
Thread: Brown
Body: Tan coloured plastic strip
Wing: Deer hair fibres
Thorax: Seal's fur, dyed cinnamon
Hackle: Cinnamon cock feather

BLACK SEDGE
Hook: Light-wire sedge size 12-14
Thread: Black
Body: Black Mosaic dubbing
Wing: Black and natural deer hair mixed
Hackle: Grizzle, dyed brown

OLIVE CDC
Hook: Kamasan B170 size 12-14
Thread: Black
Body: Hare's ear, dyed olive
Rib: Fine gold wire
Wing: Natural CDC
Hackles: Grizzle, dyed golden olive

HARE'S EAR SEDGE
Hook: Light-wire sedge size 12-15
Thread: Brown
Body: Hare's ear fur
Rib: Pearl tinsel with fine gold wire over
Wing: Deer hair with natural CDC over
Thorax: Orange SLF
Hackle: Cree cock

BALLOON HARE'S EAR CADDIS

SILVER SEDGE

BLACK SEDGE

ORANGE CDC

RED CADDIS

OLIVE CDC

GOLD SEDGE

CINNAMON SEDGE

HARE'S EAR SEDGE

A beautiful springer

IT WAS THE 18th of March – the day after St. Patrick's Day – and I was flat broke. I decided to take my hangover for a day's salmon fishing on the Suir. The river was running high and spinning was the only method that might stand a reasonable chance of a fish.

To be honest, I had taken up salmon fishing only the previous year and still had an awful lot to learn. I wasn't particularly hopeful that I stood any chance of catching a salmon. Between the high water, my poor skills and the lack of a spring run, the prospects for the day were not encouraging. The hangover wasn't helping either.

I spent about half an hour fishing the weir in town before I bumped into my friend Ollie Hubbard. Ollie was also suffering from the night's celebrations and was out fishing to clear his head. He persuaded me to walk down to the Park and try for a salmon there. We arrived at the head of the Cottage Weir with Ollie fishing about 20 yards in front of me. He was casting a brown and gold Devon while I fished a blue and silver in order to present the salmon with a different coloured bait. A week earlier Ollie had taken a nice spring fish of around 10lb at the head of the Cottage Weir, so we gave that particular spot a good pasting with the spinners just in case the fish had left a buddy behind.

Thirty yards below the weir Ollie's bait hooked into the bottom and, as these things cost money, he was busily preparing an Otter device to send down the line and free up his Devon. So I passed Ollie and took up the lead position. What success I had enjoyed with spring salmon at that point in my career was with the brown and gold Devon so I immediately replaced the blue and silver. I was feeling a little more confident now, covering new ground first with my favourite Devon.

Within five minutes, my bait stopped dead in the water. I was convinced that I, too, had snagged the bottom. By this time Ollie had recovered his bait and was standing beside me. I gave the rod a few sharp tugs and nothing happened. Then I got the fright of my life as the rod arched and the line began to move slowly upstream. All of a sudden, the fish broke the water with his tail. The two of us went rigid; we guessed it was around the 20lb mark. The fish returned to his lie and nothing would move him for the next half-hour, including Ollie throwing big stones at where he thought the salmon was stationed. After almost an hour, my arms were aching and I gave the rod to Ollie to see if he could shift the stubborn salmon. Ollie tightened into the fish until the line was singing. I grabbed the rod back before we had a disaster. Experience told me to get below the fish and

The weir and salmon pass in Cahir town

turn his head but I was reluctant to do this as a lot of debris was lying just below me, under our bank. However, after fruitless wrestling with this fish I decided to bite the bullet, go below it and apply some real pressure. This got things moving fairly swiftly, the fish running upriver at speed, turning in an arc and throwing himself out of the water. This was our second sighting and brought a new estimate; not less than 25lb was our guess this time. My heart was pounding in my ears.

LIKE A ROCKET

I turned the fish for a second time and, on this run, he headed downstream. In seconds he'd emptied the spool and broken the drag on the Mitchell reel. But we now had him in shallow water and Ollie decided to wade out and try to gaff him. The salmon saw him and shot back up river like a rocket, with me running after him and the handle of the reel spinning like crazy. One and a half hours into the battle, we were right back where we started, the salmon in exactly the same spot as I had originally hooked it.

For the third time, I went below the fish and started applying side-strain and for the next hour, I played the fish cautiously, working my way down-river. The salmon made several attempts to smash the line with its tail and, after a further half-hour long battle, we had reached Ballyheron Weir. We were now almost a mile downstream from where I originally hooked the fish; I was very fortunate, indeed, to have clean banks in front of me.

But now came my moment of greatest despair. I had been playing the salmon for well over two hours. I was exhausted. Yet just as I hoped things might go my way, we watched the fish go over the weir, tail first, slowly feeling his way backwards in the torrent of water. If the salmon still had the strength to do this, what hope had I got?

MONSTER SALMON

I had only another twenty yards to go before I reached a line of tall poplar trees, on my bank. Ollie and I discussed the alternatives: if the fish should continue its journey downstream, Ollie was prepared to get into the river, rod in hand, and swim the fish down to where I could take the rod back and continue the fight. I doubt very much whether this plan would have succeeded owing to the depth of the water beneath us plus, of course, the strength of the current.

The salmon was now below us and I could proceed no

The Author with 32lb of monster salmon

further because of the trees. Then, as luck would have it, the monster salmon starting swimming towards me, right under our own bank. I suggested that Ollie lie on his belly and, if he got one chance go for it and gaff the salmon. Just as the salmon was swimming directly beneath us, Ollie reached out and struck it with the gaff just under the dorsal fin. When Ollie went to lift the huge fish while still lying down, the pressure on his belly resulted in what I can politely refer to as a massive explosion. I dived on top of the slightly deflated, though doubtless relieved, Ollie and helped him lift the salmon up onto the bank. I then ran a hundred yards into the field behind me before I dared lay the salmon down. It was a beauty around 30lb. Nothing on this scale had been seen in the river for years. After a couple of miles' hike up river, my first port of call was to my parents' house. Dutifully I listened to my father telling Ollie tales about the monsters he had lost over the years before, at last, he got the scales out. They 'maxed' on the 30lb mark, so we went to find some scales that went beyond 30lb. Finally, we succeeded in finding a rusty old set of scales in Ollie's house and this time they stopped at just over 32lb. The fish measured 42 inches long with a girth of over 18 inches.

In his time, my father caught over a thousand salmon from the Suir, and yet was never fortunate enough to break the 30lb barrier. I believe 29lb 8oz was his best fish. I was a very lucky young angler, indeed.

Chapter three: Loughs and lakes

Contents

Lough Carra	142-153
A memorable evening	154-161
Behaving like an idiot	162-163
Lough Carrowmore	164-169
Lough Lein	170-189

Lough Carra

THE SEASON ON Carra may start in chilly March, but I have to be honest I'm not very familiar with fishing the Lough in the early part of the season. I am more accustomed to being on the water during the warmer, summer months when there is usually plenty of insect activity. I did, however, manage a couple of days on the water in two successive Aprils with my friend Willie Burke. There was a reasonable hatch of duck fly – a type of midge – and a scattering of olives coming off when I visited. We had good fishing for the two days and caught some sizeable trout on the Silver Jungle Cock, Olive Emerger and Connemara Black.

The surprise came when I spooned a couple of my boat partner's trout. They were full of hog louse and very pale, almost white, freshwater shrimps. Since the decline of fly life on the lake – especially the mayfly – Carra trout appear to have become more dependent on bottom-living creatures like these to survive and grow.

Buzzers and Nymphs do not appear to work very well on this water, which is rather strange. I discussed this with my late friend Rod Tye on a number of occasions. He shared the same experience despite numerous attempts with various nymph selections over the years.

Carra is generally recognised as being the first of the

Moore Hall Bay in July

major western lakes to experience the mayfly hatch. The lake was once renowned for mayfly but, sadly, these hatches have declined massively over the last ten years. Carra is widely regarded as an environmentally unique water and as such the welfare of the lake appears to be the focus of many interested parties who recognise the need to reverse the recent decline in water quality. Let us all hope their endeavours are successful and can aid Carra's recovery.

CAENIS FEEDERS

I had some wonderful daytime fishing in June several years ago, fishing with wet and dry-flies. In more recent years I have tended to fish the lake early in the morning, returning again for the late evening fishing. On a calm June morning the hatch of caenis – a miniscule, pale upwinged fly – is tremendous and can form a blanket of insects over the surface of the water. The trout congregate very early in the morning, forming large shoals to gorge themselves on this tiny insect.

It is worth the experience of getting up at the crack of dawn just to witness these large gangs of trout in a feeding frenzy. The best places to find these caenis feeders are in sheltered bays or in calm areas around islands.

Fishing for caenis feeders very early in the morning is incredibly exciting. The trout shoal in the shallows and are very nervous; easily spooked by casting over their backs. The trick to catching them is to guess the direction the shoal is heading and have your imitations in position well in advance of its arrival.

At first, I attempted to match the hatch using tiny dry-flies tied to imitate this fragile little creature but this ended in failure. I was unable to differentiate my flies from the thousands of natural insects on the water.

With numerous trout feeding so intensely high in the water they tend to disturb the surface. Fishing tiny dry-flies, I was unable to detect a take in the ripples caused by the shoal. I often ended up putting the trout down by striking unnecessarily.

The best method is to fish a slightly bigger fly which is much easier to detect amongst the millions of caenis. The Grey Duster, a Black or Grey Shipman's or a Claret Bits dressed on a size 12 will work.

Motoring out past Connor Point

The other important piece of equipment for fishing a caenis hatch is an anchor. I have learned the hard way. Having discovered feeding fish, I frequently ruined my chances by inadvertently drifting on to the area I was hoping to avoid disturbing. Using an anchor, I can easily position myself off a chosen hotspot and ambush the trout as they cruise past the boat.

July, though, is my favourite time of the year on Carra. The Murrough, Green Peter, Sedge and Dry Buzzer fishing is at its peak. If we aren't up early for the caenis hatch, we tend to fish the lake from 9am until lunchtime and then pack up for the afternoon, returning again around 8.30pm for the evening rise.

Depending on conditions, the fishing on some mornings can be reasonably good using dry-flies. My favourite dry-flies for daytime fishing in July are the Fiery Brown Sedge, Claret Hopper, Claret Sedge, Black Hopper and a variation of the Grey Wulff.

For early evening dry-fly fishing, the Fiery Brown Sedge will work again, along with the Chocolate Brown Sedge and the Rusty Sedge. If everything goes to plan, the trout will come on the main feed shortly after 10pm, when a mix of dry Olive Buzzers on the droppers and a Claret Murrough on the point can work really well. I have also taken some big trout on the Silver Sedge late

LOUGH CARRA

A brace of wonderful Carra trout: Both fish took a sedge imitation

into the evening.

On occasion, the wet-fly will work both during the day and early evening provided there is a good wind on the water. Patterns such as the Claret Sedge, Connemara Black, Green Peter and the Golden Olive Bumble are all worth a go. If the occasional mayfly is hatching, then the Gorgeous George, Mattie's Mayfly and Cock Robin are some of my preferred wet mayfly patterns on Carra.

August, so often a balmy month, is still best in the evening. By then, slightly smaller sedges are commonplace and the Black and Red Sedge have performed particularly well for me in the early evening. Then it's back to fishing the dry Olive Buzzer later on in the evening.

The perfect summer evening for dry-fly sees a light ripple on the water. Many a good night's fishing was spoilt by a more significant wind getting up after sunset and temperatures dropping away. It can be very frustrating when this happens.

Should a light wind be constant all evening then the trout will normally feed after dark, but I despair when a cold breeze, however light, arrives after sunset. A late Guinness at the local is the only compensation.

By September, fishing on Lough Carra is typified by dapping live grasshoppers and daddy longlegs, using very long rods and a wind-blown floss line to carry baited hooks away from the boat. While I have never attempted this style of fishing, I enjoy watching others using this method. It appears to be such a relaxing and natural way to fish from a boat.

INTO THE HOURS OF DARKNESS

A number of Carra anglers use the dap throughout the summer months, fishing natural Green Peters and Murroughs late into the hours of darkness and catching some very big trout. It may not be everyone's cup of tea, but it's undeniably fly fishing...

Lough Carra was once noted for its tremendous mayfly hatch. Today, its reputation is that of an early-morning and late-evening brown trout fishery, the mayfly having lost its dominance.

The lake acquires most of its water through the numerous feeder streams that can be found along its shoreline. The most notable of these are Annie's River and the Ballintubber River. The lake is drained by the River Keel, which connects Carra with Lough Mask. Lough Carra is practically two areas, north and south, divided by the long narrow channel along Otter Point.

Carra is etched into a bed of limestone, the lakebed

A PASSION FOR TROUT

John Quirke with a 5lb Carra trout

situated approximately 9 miles from both Castlebar and Claremorris and is only 3 miles from Ballinrobe.

The lake covers a surface area of 4,000 acres with a shoreline which extends for 42 miles. The maximum depth of water is around 60 ft, located in an area known as Black Hole, south of Castle Carra. The lake is quite shallow in most areas, with an average depth of approximately 6 ft making it ideal for fly fishing.

itself being marl – a mix of mud and limestone – which gives it its unique, greenish appearance. But Carra is changing. Intensified farming methods have greatly contributed to pollution of the water. Carra was once nutrient poor but has now been reclassified as it contains high levels of nitrates and phosphates due to over-fertilization of the surrounding farmland. This is a sad but familiar story, affecting the majority of the Corrib catchment area and, indeed, many of Ireland's fisheries.

SUCCESSFUL ENHANCEMENT

The good news comes from a recent scientific survey of trout stocks on Lough Carra by the Central Fisheries Board. The survey indicated that the stock of wild brown trout is one of the largest and most balanced recorded on any trout lake in Ireland in the last 30 years.

The successful enhancement works to the spawning streams carried out by the local clubs and the Western Fisheries Board has boosted the stock of both mature and juvenile trout in the lake. This is very welcome news for both the local and visiting angler. For additional information on Lough Carra visit the dedicated website www.loughcarra.org – which has been developed by Chris and Lynda Huxley.

Three angling clubs regularly fish Carra. Lough Carra Angling Club was formed in 1934 and has around 80 members as I write. In addition, Partry Anglers Club and Belcarra Fishing Club also enjoy this wonderful lake. Other than holding competitions, the local clubs carry out some remedial works to the fishery and are improving the spawning streams on the lake each year.

ABOUT LOUGH CARRA

Lough Carra is situated in county Mayo, and is one of Ireland's premier brown trout fisheries. The Lough is

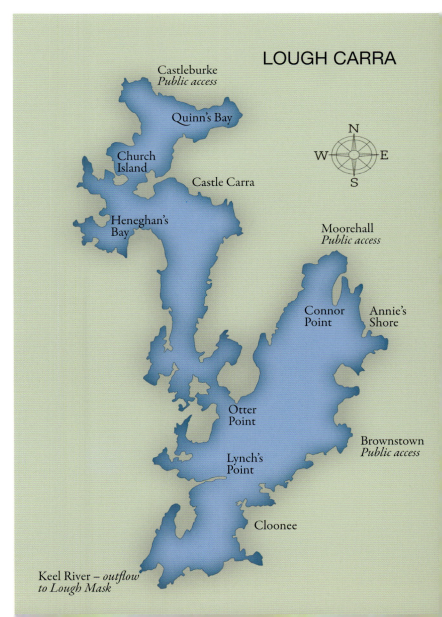

LOUGH CARRA

HOOKED ON CARRA

I was in the West of Ireland on one of my annual fishing trips with my family; if memory serves, I believe it was 2001. We were staying in a B&B just outside the town of Castlebar, in County Mayo. I'd fished Lough Carrowmore earlier in the week for a salmon and I was now on the hunt for some wild brown trout fishing.

The area was completely new to me and I had not yet established any local contacts. So, having had lunch one day in Castlebar with my wife and kids, I decided to patrol the streets to see if I could find a tackle shop. I located such a shop down one of the side streets in the town and this was where I had the pleasure of meeting Philip Cresham for the first time.

I enquired about the possibility of some trout fishing for the coming evening. Philip told me that Lough Mask was fishing well, but after a few searching questions, he quickly determined that Mask was no place for a novice boatman like me, especially for late-evening fishing.

Carra, on the other hand, is considered a very safe lake in comparison to Mask and Philip provided me with details on how to hire a boat and gave me directions to the lake.

I made my phone call, booked a boat, and at around 5pm headed off to find the water. Moore Hall is not the easiest place to find first time out. After several phone calls to James O'Reilly of Carra Boat Hire, I eventually found the correct location. This was to be the start of

My son David and John Quirke drifting on a soft, westerly breeze

This Carra beauty fell to a dry Buzzer

a great friendship with James who has been so helpful down through the years – for him nothing is ever too much trouble.

A LITTLE UNNERVING
We tackled up and at about 6pm set off into the unknown. The wind was southerly and James directed us to a spot called Rineen. So I started my first drift ever on Carra – a drift parallel to Annie's Shore towards Connor Point. The first thing that strikes you upon arrival on Carra is the greenish colour of the water, which is due to the light marl bottom. This is quite a contrast from the darker waters of Mask or Lough Lein. I admit, I found it a little unnerving at first.

David, my son, was my boat partner for the evening. We both started with a team of wet-flies mounted on the leader and fished on floating lines. We enjoyed a wonderful evening's fishing; I landed four trout and missed several more. David was not so lucky on this particular outing but we were both suitably impressed with the lough and the quality of the fishing. We packed up around 10 o'clock and headed for the shore. We could not help noticing that several boats had only just arrived out on the water as we were preparing to go in. It would be a full year before we discovered the reason why – and the excitement of late evening fishing on Carra.

We were so pleased with our first encounter on Lough Carra that we booked a boat for the following day and arrived early at Moore Hall. The wind had shifted to south-west and had increased in strength. Conditions were excellent for wet-fly fishing as we had a lovely, rolling wave.

I made a couple of changes to the cast from the night before, tying a Red-Arsed Green Peter on the top dropper, followed by a Killarney Black Sedge in the middle and my father's version of a Connemara Black on the point. Our first drift was parallel to Connor point and, with each subsequent drift, we worked our way towards Castle Island and beyond.

IGNORANT OF THE FORM
We had the Lough to ourselves. We were to discover later that at this time of year Carra had a reputation as an early morning and late evening fishery. I got the distinct impression that we were not expected to do well.

But trout have a wonderful tendency for not knowing the rules. Being ignorant of the 'form' of a fishery can sometimes be beneficial , as we were about to discover. I

An understandably cheerful Willie Burke

know of anglers who will not even venture out if conditions are 'wrong.' It is dangerous to fall into such traps at times. As it happened, our first full day's fishing on Carra was to be the best we ever encountered on this or any of the other great Western Loughs to the present day. The two of us boated 19 trout ranging between 1¼lb to 3½lb... a fantastic day's fishing on any wild brown trout fishery. We were moving trout for most of the day and I was especially pleased that all three flies on the leader were working well.

A WELL DESERVED GUINNESS

I just could not get over the fact that we had all of this quality fishing to ourselves – for the whole day. The action slowed later on in the afternoon and, by 6 o'clock, we were back on the shore and heading for a well-deserved pint of Guinness. But not before we had booked a boat for the next day.

The following morning we were greeted with a similar wind direction but a little brighter sky. With the same flies up, I started our first drift in the identical spot to the previous day and on my very first cast was in to a trout of about 2lb or so.

I landed two more trout by the time we had completed our first drift. David was not having such a good time at the other end of the boat. We were both fishing with similar flies and lines yet my luck was definitely in. He was starting to get a bit agitated, which always affects his fishing when he goes 'into one.' Nothing seems to be going right for him and there was a lot of grumbling on the bow of the boat. I know the feeling, to be fair; the water in front of you appears to be devoid of fish and yet your partner is moving trout after trout at the opposite end of the boat.

To take the pressure off David a little, I decided to experiment with some dry-flies and hoped that he would soon start meeting some cooperative trout. Not long afterwards he got into, and thankfully landed, his first fish of the day. Taking a break to celebrate, he cracked a can of Red Bull and ten minutes later was humming a tune. We now had a happy and smiley boat once more.

I continued fishing the dry-fly for an hour or so longer raising several fish but without connecting with any of them. By now David was moving fish with some regularity on the wet-flies and it was my turn to get frustrated. I took the decision to switch back to the wet-flies. It was a good call as shortly after we were both hitting the trout again. The fishing in the morning had been as good as before but, as the day wore on, the sun got stronger and brighter and the wind began to die. David decided to try a Buzzer nymph. Minutes later he was playing out the best fish of the day.

We ended with 17 top-quality trout. David's best fish was a beauty close to 4lb which rounded off yet another incredible session on Carra. In two days and one evening we had caught 40 trout. It was truly amazing fishing for wild brown trout – it would be quite a good tally on a stocked reservoir. Our achievements were all the more impressive as during summer months Lough Carra is not renowned for the quality of its daytime fishing.

RIDING ON TOP OF THE WAVE

As we slowly learned in ensuing trips, we had been fortunate to encounter perfect weather conditions for wet-fly-fishing on the lake. Carra trout like a big, rolling wave, particularly in a westerly breeze. It truly was a wonderful sight watching big brown trout, riding on top of the wave with their fins out of the water, chasing our team of wet-flies. We never really got past Castle Island on that trip, we didn't need to. However, Carra is a big lake and we decided there and then that on future visits we would devote at least one day to explore new areas of this beautiful fishery.

We spent the remainder of our holiday fishing Lough Carra and Carrowmore on alternate days. I was fortunate enough to land a couple of salmon on Carramore a few days later. If memory serves me correctly, our worst day on Carra after those initial first two days' fishing was nine trout landed between us. It was a remarkable fishing expedition and one which I shall never forget. We were well and truly hooked on the fishery and have returned to Carra every year since.

Three pounds weight – on the dry-fly

One to the Grey Wulff

The Silver Invicta. A great fly for Carra fry feeders

Carra wet-flies I

KATE MACLAREN
Hook: Heavy gauge size 10-12
Thread: Black
Butt: Glo-Brite No11
Tail: Golden crest feather
Body: Black seal's fur
Body hackle: Black cock
Rib: Oval silver tinsel
Shoulder hackle: Well-marked Greenwell's

MATTIE'S MAYFLY
Hook: Heavy gauge size 10-12
Thread: Red
Tail: Golden pheasant red rump feather
Body: Pale olive seal's fur
Body hackle: Pale olive cock
Rib: Gold oval tinsel
Wing: Golden pheasant tippets
Shoulder hackles: No1 – Partridge, dyed golden olive No2 – French partridge, dyed pale olive
Headband: Flat gold tinsel

WHITE SHRIMP
Hook: Kamasan B 100 size 10
Thread: White
Tail: Grey partridge hackle fibres
Body: White Mosaic dubbing
Shell back: Clear polythene
Rib: Fine silver wire
Antennae: Grey partridge hackle fibres

GREEN PETER (ROD TYE)
Hook: Long shank size 10
Body: Olive green seal's fur
Body hackle: Natural red cock
Rib: Fine gold wire
Wing: Hen pheasant dyed yellow
Head hackle: Golden pheasant rump feather

REVERSED RED MARLODGE
Hook: Heavy gauge size 10-12
Thread: Red
Tail: Golden pheasant crest
Body: Red floss/silver tinsel/red floss
Rib: Silver oval tinsel
Throat hackles: No1 – Red cock No2 – Guinea fowl
Wing: Bronze mallard feather
Cheeks: Jungle cock

GREEN PETER
Hook: Wide gape size 10-12
Thread: Olive
Body: Light olive seal's fur
Body hackle: Natural red cock
Rib: Gold oval tinsel
Wing: Hen pheasant
Head hackle: Natural red cock

CLARET SEDGE
Hook: Heavy gauge size 10-12
Thread: Claret
Body: Claret Mosaic dubbing
Body hackle: Furnace hen feather
Rib: Gold oval tinsel
Wing: Brown hen
Head hackle: Furnace hen feather

THE REBEL
Hook: Heavy gauge size 10-12
Thread: Black
Tail: Pheasant tail fibres
Tag: Purple Glo-Brite floss
Body: Black seal's fur
Body hackle: Black cock
Rib: Fine pearl tinsel
Head hackle: Grey partridge feather
Shoulder hackle: Bronze mallard strips
Cheeks: Jungle cock
Headband: Flat silver tinsel

HOGLOUSE
Hook: Heavy gauge size 12
Thread: Olive
Body: Hare's ear, olive and brown seal's fur
Legs: Partridge, dyed golden olive laid over the top of the body
Rib: Fine silver wire
Antennae: Partridge fibres dyed golden olive

GREEN PETER

CLARET SEDGE

KATE MACLAREN

REVERSED RED MARLODGE

THE REBEL

MATTIE'S MAYFLY

GREEN PETER

WHITE SHRIMP

HOGLOUSE

Carra wet-flies II

CONNEMARA BLACK
Hook: Heavy gauge size 10-12
Thread: Black
Butt: Flat silver tinsel
Tail: Golden pheasant crest
Body: Black seal's fur
Rib: Silver oval tinsel
Wing: Bronze mallard feather
Throat hackle: Blue jay
Shoulder hackle: Golden pheasant yellow rump feather
Cheeks: Jungle cock

GORGEOUS GEORGE
Hook: Heavy gauge size 10-12
Thread: Black
Butt: Glo-Brite No4
Tail: Glo-Brite No11
Body: Golden olive seal's fur
Body hackle: Golden olive cock
Rib: Gold oval tinsel
Throat hackle: Orange cock
Head hackle: Medium olive cock
Legs: Pheasant tail dyed red
Cheeks: Jungle cock

COCK ROBIN
Hook: Heavy gauge size 10-12
Thread: Red
Tail: Bronze mallard fibres with two Crystal Hair strands
Body: 1st half, golden olive seal's fur 2nd half, red seal's fur
Rib: Fine flat gold tinsel
Wing: Bronze mallard feather
Hackle: Natural red cock

GOLDEN OLIVE BUMBLE
Hook: Wide gape size 10-12
Thread: Red
Butt: Red seal fur
Tail: Golden pheasant crest dyed orange
Body: Golden olive seal's fur
Body hackle: Golden olive cock
Rib: Fine flat gold tinsel
Shoulder hackle: Blue jay

GOLD MUDDLER
Hook: Heavy gauge size 12
Thread: Grey
Body: Flat gold tinsel
Rib: Gold oval tinsel
Wing: Deer hair dyed orange
Head: Deer hair trimmed with some fibres left long

RED ARSED GREEN PETER
Hook: Sedge hook size 10-12
Thread: Dark olive
Butt: Red floss
Body: Green olive seal's fur
Body hackle: Natural red cock
Rib: Gold oval tinsel
Wing: Hen pheasant feather
Head hackle: Natural red cock

SOOTY OLIVE
Hook: Heavy gauge size 10-12
Thread: Black
Tail: Golden pheasant tippets
Body: Sooty olive seal's fur
Rib: Fine flat gold tinsel
Wing: Bronze mallard
Cheeks: Green goose biots
Hackle: Black hen

CLARET BUMBLE
Hook: Heavy gauge size 10-12
Thread: Claret
Tail: Golden pheasant tippets
Body: Medium claret seal's fur
Body hackle: Claret cock
Rib: Gold oval tinsel
Legs: Knotted pheasant tail fibres, dyed claret
Shoulder hackle: Blue jay
Cheeks: Jungle cock

DUNKELD
Hook: Heavy gauge size 10-12
Thread: Black
Tail: Golden pheasant crest
Body: Gold holographic tinsel
Body hackle: Orange cock
Rib: Gold oval tinsel
Throat hackle: Blue jay
Wing: Bronze mallard feather
Cheeks: Jungle cock

CONNEMARA BLACK

GOLDEN OLIVE BUMBLE

SOOTY OLIVE

GORGEOUS GEORGE

GOLD MUDDLER

CLARET BUMBLE

COCK ROBIN

RED ARSED GREEN PETER

DUNKELD

A memorable evening

IT WAS THE month of June and I was over in Ireland with my family for our annual summer holidays, which normally doubles up as a fishing trip. After an enjoyable lunch in Castlebar, my wife took off shopping in the town and I headed for Lough Carra with my son David for an afternoon's fishing. We launched the boat from Moore Hall armed with the usual team of wet-flies on the leader and dry-flies mounted on the spare rods.

Carra can be a very sulky lake during bright summer days and this particular afternoon was no exception, but previous experiences had taught us that daytime fishing can be quite brilliant in June. However timing is everything and this was not to be one of those occasions. After several hours' fishing with nothing to show for our efforts we swung the boat towards Castle Island for a bite to eat and a break. We decided to sit it out for a while and take in the beautiful scenery.

At around six, the wind dropped to a slight breeze and the sky clouded over. A light mist of rain drifted in the breeze and stayed with us for the remainder of the evening. Conditions were beginning to look more favourable for the coming evenings fishing. It was now time to get back on the water.

At around seven we were on a very slow drift past the front of Castle Island when I noticed several trout feeding, close to the shore in the flat calm. We had changed onto the dry-fly at this stage, as the wind was barely making a ripple on the water; I manoeuvred the boat in closer so that we could cover these fish.

David was fishing his favourite Fiery Brown Sedge on the dropper and a small size 14 Grey Wulff on the point.

We both cast at the rising fish, and shortly afterwards, a trout sipped down David's Wulff. He reacted with one of his normal lightning-fast strikes and missed the fish.

CONSTANT BADGERING

Despite my constant badgering, I was having one hell of a job to get him to slow down when striking on the dry-fly. The message still hadn't sunk in; two more takes came but his arm shot up like a rocket ending in the same result. Both fish gone! Worse still, the disturbance had scared off the remaining trout or, at the least, had put them down, so I decided to change position and set up a new drift along Annie's shore, close to one of the tall reed beds.

We were now drifting along very slowly as the misty-rain was coming down a little heavier and the surface of the lake had become almost flat calm.

We had been fishing our dry-flies along the edge of the reed beds for about ten minutes when I witnessed a Carra phenomenon for the first time; without any disturbance to surface of the water at all, David's Grey Wulff dry-fly just simply disappeared. We both looked at the spot where his fly had been. Then he struck and all hell broke loose.

The fly had been sucked down by a huge trout and, because he was that second late bringing up the rod David actually hooked the fish this time.

The trout shot across the front of the boat, rolled on its flank, and with one splash of its massive tail dived beneath the boat and out the other side – all within a split second. David was now leaning over the side, the tip of his rod arching over the gunnels and into the water.

The fish continued its powerful surge and, with most of David's rod now under the boat there was very little he could do to get things under control. It was almost inevitable; the trout shed the hook not long afterwards and the line fell slack. It's difficult to accurately gauge a

The Murrough – a top Carra Sedge pattern

A PASSION FOR TROUT

Under attack from a late-night sedge hatch

fish you haven't fully seen, but I estimated its weight at not less than 8lb. Once it dawned on David what had just happened, his evening was destroyed. It was a wild brown trout of a lifetime, lost forever. Despite David losing the big brownie, we fished on making the most of the exceptional evening, though I'm not sure my son's heart was truly in it.

On every subsequent visit to Carra, the tale of this big trout will inevitably come up, when we are having a pint and sharing stories. It's lucky I am always around to ensure that the fish does not grow any bigger with the dual effects of time and alcohol.

THE LIGHT BEGAN TO FADE

We had already decided earlier in the day that this, our first evening, would be the one in which we would stay late. It had already been quite eventful up to now.

We had become quite inquisitive when observing other boats venturing out on to the water when we would normally be packing up our gear and heading for the shore. There had to be a reason.

At around ten, as the evening light began to fade we had our first indication that something spectacular was about to happen. Gulls began to appear in number, dive bombing the surface, swooping low and snapping at emerging winged insects. Then, shortly after the gulls had appeared, we caught sight of our first Murrough skittering across the water.

I had been told about the evening Murrough fishing on Carra and, in the event that I might one day get the opportunity to fish a hatch, I had tied a monstrous fly on a longshank, low-water salmon hook. I suppose the fly could be best described as an overgrown Sedge, bushy and bristling with deer hair – a Murrough Sedgehog, if you like.

It was tied with claret seal's fur and buoyant deer hair, added at intervals across the top of the body. Its giant absurdity was completed with a long wing of brown turkey, a dense furnace hackle at the head and two long fibres of pheasant tail to imitate its antennae.

In the right conditions, the hatch of sedge and buzzer late at night on Carra can be phenomenal. These were such conditions, and both insects were out in force.

The sun had long since dipped below the horizon

and, in the deepening gloom, I could hear, more than see, several trout feeding in the vicinity of the boat. The trout were taking the Murrough in a violent fashion. The activity began to increase as the main rise of the evening got underway. I remember similar feeding frenzies on the River Suir on warm summer evenings. Even though the heart is pounding fast, this is a time for the angler to remain calm while the trout get ever more excited.

For some unknown reason, David and I started speaking in whispers to each other, as though we thought the trout could hear not just our voices, but exactly what we were saying. Perhaps it is one of those inexplicable traits of night fishing!

A DIFFERENT TACTIC

Although the fly I was fishing was very big, I could no longer make out its shape in the darkness. I did not want to take the risk of making fresh thin-air strikes into imagined takes and scaring off the fish, so I decided to adopt a different tactic. I dressed the fly in Gink, made a short cast, and then started a very slow figure-of-eight retrieve.

On that very first cast I got a strong pull and a few minutes later, landed a beauty over 2lb. Was this luck I wondered? I was surprised that a wild brown trout could be fooled into taking such a huge Sedgehog, but then the natural murrough is not exactly a small insect. After a couple of more casts I had another good take and was into my second large fish.

By now, the trout were rising all over Carra. One fish, in particular, was splashing wildly at the fly at about five minute intervals. The explosive rise of this trout stood out, amongst the rest; he was definitely a big fish. A

The reed beds where David lost his big trout

couple of pulls on the oars, and I was able to make a cast to where I thought he was feeding, but I had no take despite my best attempts.

Eventually the boat would drift slowly away from this trout's territory. I continued to catch trout for the next hour or so, wherever we drifted, but each time the big trout would rise and I would oar the boat back to have another cast for him. The monster trout was like a magnet tempting me back as it burst through the water's surface. I never did fool that fish into taking my Murrough Sedgehog, but I did land eleven other trout and lost several more at the back of the boat, falling foul of my usual bad habit of playing fish far too hard, in my anxiety to cast again.

Most of the trout I caught that evening ranged between 2lb and 3lb 8oz. It was a glorious night's dry-fly fishing and one I shall never forget. We stopped fishing some time after midnight. The main rise was over by then, but plenty of trout were still rising as we were leaving, particularly in the shelter of the reed beds. I was surprised how long the fish fed that night. On the River Suir and on some English stillwater's, the main rise to sedges lasts for about half an hour then, as if a switch had been thrown, and majority of fish stop feeding and go down. On Carra that evening, there was a slow build up to the main rise then the frenzy, followed by a slow cooling off period. I got the impression we could have stayed out, fishing for much longer, and still caught trout. It was obviously the perfect evening for the dry-fly, and we happened to be there to enjoy it.

A LONG JOURNEY

I could not have written the script better for our first late evening's fishing on Lough Carra. True, David had no luck at all that evening and lost an eight-pounder, but he has made up for it on evenings since. It was the start of a long journey.

Since that first year we have learned a considerable amount about fishing late evenings on Lough Carra and I continue to develop new flies behind the vice, especially various Olive Dry Buzzer patterns. Every time I think I have it cracked, we encounter a different insect on each visit to the lake. But that's all part of the fun and excitement of fishing Carra.

I've returned to fish Carra every summer since then with my son David. We link up with our four friends from Tipperary and enjoy a long weekend's fishing... along with the *craic* at the pub.

We stay at a superb guesthouse on the lakeshore near Moore Hall which is run by Anne and Tommy MacGovern. Anne and Tommy specialise in looking after fishermen. They are used to crazy anglers getting up in the middle of the night in order to be on the water for the crack of dawn. Breakfast time at the MacGoverns' is always a good laugh, and you get a wonderful reception no matter what hour you return to the guesthouse from the lake.

This year a couple of us plan to stay out on the lake all night and fish into the dawn, it could be very exciting if we stumble on the perfect evening again.

Richie Rowe fishing dry-fly on a perfect moonlit evening

Carra dry-flies I

RUSTY BROWN SEDGE
Hook: Light wire size 12
Thread: Brown
Body: Hares ear & brown seal's fur mixed
Wing: Pale deer hair
Post: Pale deer hair
Thorax: Fiery brown seal's fur
Hackle: Natural red cock

WELSHMAN'S BUTTON No1
Hook: Light wire size 12
Thread: Black
Body: Chocolate brown seal's fur
Wing: Dark brown deer hair
Post: Dark brown deer hair
Thorax: Dirty yellow seal's fur
Hackle: Black cock

OLIVE SHUTTLECOCK
Hook: Light buzzer wire, size 12
Thread: Light olive
Body: Heron herl
Rib: Olive Flexi floss
Thorax: Hares ear & olive seal's fur mixed
Wing: CDC dyed olive

MIXED CLARET MURROUGH
Hook: Longshank size 10
Thread: Claret
Tail: Deer hair fibres
Body: Claret Mosaic dubbing
Rib: Gold oval tinsel
Wing over body: Deer hair/sedgehog style
Main wing: Brown turkey strips
Hackle: Furnace cock, underside trimmed
Horns: Pheasant tail fibres

OLIVE BUZZER BALL
Hook: Light wire, wide gape size 12
Thread: Black
Rib: Fine silver wire
Body hackles: No1: Light olive, No2: Cree, No3: Grizzle

GREY DUSTER
Hook: Light wire size 12
Thread: Black
Body: Grey Mosaic dubbing
Hackle: Badger cock

RED SEDGE
Hook: Light wire size 12
Thread: Red
Body: Red seal's fur mixed with pearl strips
Wing: Natural deer hair
Thorax: Red seal's fur
Hackle: Brown/black grizzle cock

BLACK SEDGE
Hook: Light wire size 12
Thread: Black
Body: Black Mosaic dubbing
Wing: Natural deer hair
Thorax: Red seal's fur
Hackle: Black/brown grizzle cock

PARACHUTE OLIVE
Hook: Light wire size 12
Thread: Olive
Body: Heron herl
Rib: Olive Flexi Floss
Post: Grey EPS fibres
Hackle: Light olive grizzle cock

Carra dry-flies II

CLARET HOPPER
Hook: Light wire size 12
Thread: Black
Body: Claret Mosaic dubbing
Legs: Knotted pheasant tail fibres
Wing: Natural CDC
Hackle: Natural red

OLIVE SHIPMAN'S
Hook: Light wire size 12
Thread: Light olive
Breathers: EPS fibres
Body: Light olive seal's fur
Rib: Fine pearl tinsel
Body hackle: Grizzle cock, reversed

ORANGE & BLACK HOPPER
Hook: Light wire size 12
Thread: Black
Butt: Deep orange seal's fur
Body: Black Mosaic dubbing
Legs: Knotted pheasant tail fibres, dyed black
Wing: Natural CDC
Hackle: Natural red, underside trimmed

EMERALD HOPPER
Hook: Light wire size 12
Thread: Medium olive
Body: Olive Mosaic dubbing
Rib: Hot orange Ultra wire
Legs: Knotted pheasant tail
Wing: CDC, dyed olive
Hackle: Medium olive cock

ORANGE HOPPER
Hook: Light wire size 12
Thread: Black
Body: Deep orange seal's fur
Rib: Fine pearl tinsel
Legs: Knotted pheasant tail fibres
Wing: Natural CDC with pearl strips over
Hackle: Well-marked Greenwell's cock

GREY WULFF VARIANT
Hook: Light wire size 12
Thread: Black
Tail: Deer hair fibres/crystal hair
Body: Grey fur
Wing: Natural deer hair, tied upright
Hackles: No1-Natural red cock, No2-Grey cock

MICK'S BLACK HOPPER
Hook: Light wire size 12
Thread: Black
Body: Black seal's fur
Rib: Red Ultra wire
Wing: Natural CDC
Legs: Knotted pheasant tail dyed red
Hackle: Black cock, underside trimmed

YELLOW HEAD BUZZER
Hook: Buzzer hook size 12-14
Thread: Olive
Body: Light olive seal's fur
Rib: Fine gold wire
Body: Olive grizzle cock
Wing: Grey DNA fibres
Cheeks: Jungle cock, dyed yellow
Thorax: Yellow seal's fur
Breather: Grey DNA fibres

WELSHMAN'S BUTTON No2
Hook: Light wire size 12
Thread: Black
Body: Dark brown seal's fur
Flanks: Pale deer hair fibres
Wing: Dark brown deer hair
Hackle: Black cock, underside trimmed

CLARET HOPPER   **EMERALD HOPPER**   **MICK'S BLACK HOPPER**

OLIVE SHIPMAN'S   **ORANGE HOPPER**   **YELLOW HEAD BUZZER MOF**

ORANGE & BLACK HOPPER   **GREY WULFF VARIANT**   **WELSHMAN'S BUTTON No2**

Behaving like an idiot

HAVING SPENT THE whole of my working life in the construction industry – namely house building – one would assume I had a clear understanding of Health & Safety practises and the fundamentals of good risk management.

Unfortunately, in my blind passion for angling, some of that training went out of the window a few years ago.

I'd just gone through the financial year-end, in which it is not unusual for us to complete 20% of our total business in the last six weeks of the financial calendar. To drive some stress out of my system, I had the car packed and was ready for a week's fishing in the West of Ireland. We were heading for Carra.

The fishing on Lough Carra had been exceptional the previous year. I could not get there fast enough to do some fishing. I'd had the boat booked weeks before I left England and, as soon as the family arrived in Castlebar, I set off for Carra.

Along with my sons Daniel and David, I arrived on the shore at Moore Hall to be greeted by a storm blowing up from the south. Daniel was nominated gillie for the day. We'd usually keep him sweet by offering one euro for every trout he netted for us. On a slow day, he would get bored and upwardly renegotiate the rate – one which was bordering on extortion.

WHITE HORSES

Danny was quite young at the time; probably around ten years old. I had always taken my three sons out fishing with me from an early age, partly because I wanted to teach them how to fish and enjoy their company, but also to get them out from under their mother's feet. David, by this time, was well on the way to becoming a competent boat angler and I had high hopes for Danny. My other son, Michael, would far rather watch paint dry than go fishing. You can't win them all…

We arrived only to see the wind howling up the lake, stirring the waves into a sea of white horses. We decided to tackle up anyway and play a waiting game. It was while tackling up, that our first disaster struck.

David had leant his rod on the inside of the car door to keep it upright while he tied on the cast of flies. A gust of wind hit the car and the door slammed shut, smashing it to pieces. The omens were not good.

I determined straight away that it was too dangerous to launch the boat so we decided to sit it out in the car for a few hours in the hope the wind would subside a little. It was incredibly frustrating, I had waited twelve months for this week to arrive, and here I was looking out at the water unable to get out fishing and already had a broken rod in the boot.

Boredom set in after a couple of hours and I decided to take a drive around the shoreline and see if conditions were any better at the southern end of the lake. I figured there might be some shelter from the land mass at the far end without thinking, of course, how I was going to get there in a boat.

Conditions were just as ugly at the southern end of the lough so I returned to Moore Hall for another session waiting in the car. The sensible thing to have done would have been to keep going and head for home, or to the pub for an early pint of Guinness.

ONLY TWO LIFEJACKETS

A year's waiting and frustration was eating away at me like a cancer and, eventually, my desire to go fishing got the better of me. Through staring at the water long enough, I had convinced myself that the wind had subsided a little so I decided to launch the boat. We had only two life jackets between us, for David and Danny. To make our prospects worse, I have the swimming skills of a large granite boulder.

We headed out from the jetty at Moore Hall with the intention of making for Castle Island. I knew that if we could make it to the back of the Island we would have some shelter from the wind and high waves. We could then fish a few short drifts and hope the wind would eventually die down.

As I motored into the wind, the height of the waves and the level of spray coming over the point of the boat significantly reduced my visibility. The boys were growing increasingly uncomfortable and I could sense there was fear in the boat.

Close to Connor point there are groups of boulders or skerries, which rise up from the depths to the surface. Over hundreds of years, they have become encrusted with a coating of marl giving them a soft exterior several inches thick. They are unique to Lough Carra.

The boys' trepidation only became worse when I beached the boat on top of a cluster of these boulders; luckily for me, their soft coating of marl prevented any damage being done to the boat. We lurched dangerously sideways in the wind and almost turned completely over several times. I shall never forget the look of sheer horror on Danny's face as I attempted to get the boat released from those rocks.

Not being a competent boatman at the time, I admit I panicked a little and my nervousness transmited itself to the boys as I was shouting at David to grab an oar and help me get the boat under control and off the rocks. I eventually freed the boat with David's help, turned around and headed for the jetty, and safety, as quickly as conditions allowed – to the intense relief of both boys.

I'd put all our lives at risk just so I could satisfy my desire to cast a line. Because of that incident, Danny has never gone out on Carra with us again despite my every attempt and bribe. I did persuade him to come out on a boat with me one day afterwards on Elinor in England, though the lake on that occasion was flat calm. Mum set out a picnic on the shore which is the only reason I reckoned he turned up; he does like his grub.

After that day on Elinor, Danny never came fishing with me again. He denies that the Carra incident is the reason why, but I cannot help feeling that there is an underlying fear there, and one that may never go away thanks to my irresponsibility.

TEMPTING FATE

Maybe one day, when his best football days are behind him, Danny will return to fly fishing and ease my guilty conscience. I behaved like an idiot that day on Carra, but thankfully, have learned my lesson about life's priorities.

It is always very sad when we hear accounts of fellow anglers losing their lives whilst out fishing. I often reflect on that day on Lough Carra and how so, very easily a day's pleasure fishing can turn into a disaster. Accidents can and will happen, but there is no excuse for acting irresponsibly and tempting fate as I did.

Carra can be a dangerous place in a big wind.

Lough Carrowmore

AT ONE TIME Carrowmore was known as the Black Lake – a place almost devoid of fish. That it now has substantial runs of both salmon and sea-trout is entirely thanks to the decision, some years ago, to build a weir which raised the water levels in the lake by around one meter. The North Western Regional Fisheries Board also did their bit to ensure the unhindered passage of salmon and sea-trout up the Munhin River and on into the Lough.

Situated near the village of Bangor in north-west Mayo, Carrowmore is now considered one of Ireland's premier salmon and sea-trout fisheries. It is 4½ miles long and 3 miles wide, covering an area of approximately 2,500 acres. And it is very shallow throughout; a recent survey indicated that large areas of the lough are between three and six feet deep. Because Carrowmore is so shallow, its water is prone to muddiness following strong winds. The cloudy water usually makes for poor fishing, as I have personally experienced several times. Fortunately, the lake soon settles down again and, in the meantime, there is the alternative of some salmon fly-fishing on the Owenmore river or, if you prefer, brown trout fishing on Loughs Conn and Carra.

On one occasion I did fish the lake when the water was quite cloudy and lost two salmon in the first couple of hours. The next day the water was clear and I could not raise a fish, so don't entirely discount Carrowmore when the waters are murky.

Carrowmore is drained by a single river, the Munhin, which is how the salmon and sea-trout enter the lake. The major nursery and spawning rivers are the Glencullin, Glenturk and Bellanboy, with two lesser streams, the Muingerroon and Cloontakilla also acting as potential nurseries for salmon and sea-trout. Brown trout are also resident in the lake but these tend to be very small in size and are not considered worth fishing for.

DOMINANT COLOURS

The salmon season opens on the lake on the January 1, the Owenmore River a month later, on February 1. The season ends on both lake and river on September 30.

Salmon run into Lough Carrowmore all year round, but it is in the spring and early summer that the lake enjoys the biggest and best runs of fish. June 16 – the opening of the UK's river coarse fishing season – is known locally as Gael Day and traditionally associated with the peak of the sea-trout migration into Carrowmore.

I prefer the lake to the river, as I enjoy fishing from a boat more and more these days. It is the ease with which I can travel and the feeling of freedom on the open water that I enjoy so much.

The dominant colours for successful fly patterns on

Carrowmore on a beautiful, clear spring day

the lake are Claret, Black, Yellow/Golden Olive and Orange, while I find a fly with red in it, like the Soldier Palmer, can work extremely well at times.

I generally fish a claret fly, such as the Clan Chief or a Claret Bumble, on the top dropper. A yellowish fly like the Octopus, Golden Olive Bumble and the Yellow Ordie are some of the best flies to occupy the middle dropper position. If the sea-trout are running the lake, then the Pretender Bumble fished on a size 10 has taken its fair share of trout for me in the middle dropper position. A small Shrimp Fly with black and orange in the tying fished on the point can be very good, but I tend to start with the Soldier Palmer as it has been a really lucky fly for me on Carrowmore.

DRIFTS

The eastern side of the lake is the most productive for salmon and sea-trout, the three main spawning rivers being situated on that shore. If fishing the water for the first time, I recommend the local ghillies as they will clearly know the best drifts to suit the prevailing conditions. Once you are familiar with these drifts, then you can venture out on your own; Carrowmore is considered a very safe lake to fish.

The normal route is Bog Bay first, the Black Banks followed by Paradise Bay. Then moving north to the point where the shoreline cuts in to the mouth of the Glencullin River. The shoreline cuts in again slightly further north and this leads to a large bay outside the Glenturk and Bellanboy rivers. A northerly or southerly wind will allow a drift tight along the shoreline for a considerable distance over some very productive water.

I first fished Lough Carrowmore some ten years ago and fell in love with the place so much that I built a house in the area.

Perversely, an Irish friend of my living in Cambridge, Frank Lindsay, introduced me to Carrowmore. Frank originated from Mount Jubilee, just outside the village of Bangor, and was always raving about the Lough and the Owenmore River. He eventually persuaded me to give the fishing a go by booking a boat for me and my son David. Our outing was in early June.

My ghillie on that first day on the lake was Kenneth Cosgrove, son of John Cosgrove. John met us on the shore, inspected our equipment, particularly the flies we

A bright, early-season Carrowmore grilse

had tied on. We made some quick adjustments following John's advice and headed out to fish Bog Bay. Kenneth was under instructions from his dad not to move up the lake until we had at least given Bog Bay one drift. We were fishing only ten minutes when I hooked and boated a sea-trout of about 1¾lb.

We motored up the lake to take up a drift tight in along the northern shore, outside Paradise Bay. We were not long into the drift when David hooked a salmon around 12lb. This was to be the first of many lost fish on Carrowmore for David over the next few years.

His average was to be an incredible two fish lost per visit after that. Being a typical trout angler, he strikes first and asks questions later. The salmon had taken a Soldier Palmer – one that my father had tied. God only knows why he chose to pick that particular fly, but it was fortuitous that he did. We soon discovered that the salmon on Carrowmore have a liking for this pattern.

David tied a new cast, then we decided to move further up the lake towards Glencullin. As the wind was northerly, we decided try a longer drift by the shore back towards Paradise Bay. An hour or so later, David hooked another salmon and again got smashed up by striking too hard and fast. This second salmon also showed a preference for the Soldier Palmer.

I continued to catch and release small sea-trout. It was not until late into the afternoon before I moved my first grilse. We were fishing a drift in Paradise Bay when the fish rolled over my top dropper but missed the fly. A short time later a second grilse came out of the water just

LOUGH CARROWMORE

A Carrowmore hotspot: Drifting along the edge of the White Shore

A PASSION FOR TROUT

as I was lifting off but, again, missed the fly. Even though we had both been beaten by the salmon – David having lost his two fish and I having merely seen fish – we had a great day and vowed to return the following year.

I was back on Carrowmore the following June with Gerry Deane as our boatman. We had a brilliant day with Gerry raising six salmon. David proved his consistency as a trout angler and got broken on two salmon... yet again. I moved four salmon, landing two; one of 8lb to the Claret Clan Chief on the top dropper and the other 5½ lb to the Soldier Palmer on the point. We also caught many sea-trout, retaining two good-sized fish.

Subsequent visits to the lake coincided with an algae bloom. Run-off of agricultural fertiliser from the surrounding land appears to be one of the major causes of water enrichment. This problem is always exacerbated when water temperatures increase during the summer which, unfortunately, was the only time that my work schedule would permit a visit.

In more recent years the algae blooms have abated. The hue and cry appears to have resulted in co-operation from the surrounding landowners. As a result of this focus the lake is less prone to 'soup up' in the summer. This was evident when I visited the lake in July 2008 and enjoyed some excellent sea trout fishing. Carrowmore saw a much-improved run of sea-trout in 2008; some lucky anglers timed this run to perfection and had some truly fantastic fishing. I arrived a week or so later with my friend Willie Burke for a couple of very good days' fishing. I missed one salmon but the sea-trout were hopping off the flies for most of the two days. It was great sport: we caught and released loads of trout, with even the resident brownies much more active than usual.

PERMITS

Bangor Angling Club controls and manages the fishing on Carrowmore along with 1.8 miles of both banks on a section of the Owenmore River. Fishing on the river is always fly-only now. Spinning is permitted on the Lake up until the end of March after which it, too, becomes fly-only.

Permits can be obtained from the fisheries manager, Seamus Henry who can be found in the West End Bar, situated on the main road running through Bangor. It's not that he's a heavy drinker, I should point out, but because he's actually based there. So, if you do fancy a pint after a day's fishing this is *the* place where anglers go to socialise and swap the odd tale or two.

The club has more than 150 members, mostly local anglers but Lough Carrowmore and the River Owenmore are popular destinations for anglers from all over the world. It is estimated that between 2,500 and 3,000 bed-nights in the local community are generated each season due in no small part to the club's efforts in popularising the fishery. There is a community spirit about the way the club functions. Committee members also work closely with the Regional Fisheries Board to ensure full cooperation on all environmental and fishing matters. And that's something we can all endorse by trying the fishing for ourselves.

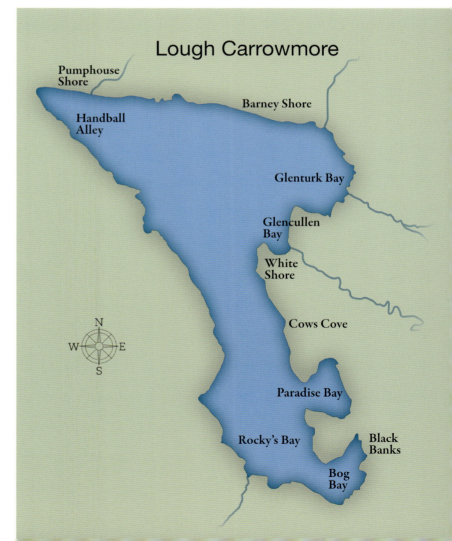

Carrowmore wet-flies

COCK ROBIN
Hook: Heavy gauge size 8-12
Thread: Black or red
Tail: Pheasant tail fibres
Body: 1st half, golden olive seal's fur
2nd half, red seal's fur
Rib: Gold oval tinsel
Legs: Knotted pheasant tail fibres
Wing: Bronze mallard
Hackle: Natural red cock

OCTOPUS
Hook: Heavy gauge size 8-12
Thread: Red
Butt: Flat gold tinsel
Tail: Glo-Brite floss No11
Body: Light olive SLF
Rib: Gold oval tinsel
Body hackle: Medium olive
Shoulder hackle: Golden pheasant yellow rump feather
Headband: Flat gold tinsel

BLACK JUNGLE COCK
Hook: Heavy gauge size 8-12
Thread: Black
Tail: Golden pheasant tippets
Body: Black seal's fur
Rib: Fine flat silver tinsel
Throat hackle: Red cock
Shoulder hackle: Black cock
Wing: Jungle cock

CLARET BUMBLE
Hook: Heavy gauge size 8-12
Thread: Claret
Tail: Golden pheasant tippets
Body: Medium claret seal's fur
Body hackle: Claret cock
Rib: Fine flat gold tinsel
Shoulder hackle: Blue jay
Cheeks: Jungle cock

GOLDEN OLIVE BUMBLE
Hook: Heavy gauge size 8-12
Thread: Red
Butt: Flat gold tinsel
Tail: Golden pheasant crest, dyed orange
Body: Golden olive seal's fur
Body hackle: Golden olive
Rib: Fine flat gold tinsel
Shoulder hackle: Blue jay

YELLOW ORDIE
Hook: Heavy gauge size 8-12
Thread: Black
Butt: Flat silver tinsel
Tail: Pheasant tail fibres
Body hackles: 1st-black, 2nd-dark olive, 3rd-medium olive, 4th-golden olive, 5th-golden ginger, 6th-pale ginger, 7th-white, 8th-yellow
Wing: Bronze mallard strips

CLARET CLAN CHIEF
Hook: Heavy gauge size 8-12
Thread: Black
Butt: Flat silver tinsel
Tail: Glo-Brite floss No's 11 & 8
Body: Black seal's fur
Body hackle: Claret cock
Rib: Gold oval tinsel
Head hackle: Golden pheasant blue neck feather
Cheeks: Jungle cock

KINGSMILL
Hook: Heavy gauge size 8-12
Thread: Black
Butt: Blue floss
Tail: Golden pheasant crest
Body: Black ostrich herl
Rib: Silver oval tinsel
Wing: Crow feather/GP crest feather
Cheeks: Jungle cock

GREEN PETER
Hook: Heavy gauge size 8-12
Thread: Medium olive
Butt: Red Straggle
Body: Olive green seal's fur
Body hackle: Natural red
Rib: Gold oval tinsel
Wing: Hen pheasant feather, dyed yellow
Shoulder hackle: Partridge dyed golden olive

SOLDIER PALMER
Hook: Heavy gauge size 8-12
Thread: Red
Butt: Pearl tinsel
Tail: Red floss
Body: Crimson seal's fur
Body hackle: Dark red cock
Rib: No1, pearl tinsel
No2, gold oval tinsel
Head hackle: Dark red cock tied long

BIBIO
Hook: Heavy gauge size 8-12
Thread: Black
Butt: Flat silver tinsel
Body: Black/orange/black seal's fur
Body hackle: Black cock
Rib: Silver oval tinsel
Shoulder hackle: Black hen tied long
Cheeks: Jungle cock

PRETENDER BUMBLE
Hook: Heavy gauge size 8-12
Thread: Black
Butt: Flat silver tinsel
Tail: Golden pheasant tippets
Body: Black seal's fur
Body hackles: No1, red cock
No2, black cock
Rib: Silver oval tinsel
Shoulder hackle: Blue jay
Cheeks: Jungle cock

Lough Lein

THE LAKES OF Killarney, in Co Kerry, is an area of outstanding beauty and a renowned scenic attraction for tourists from all over the world. Lough Lein, or Leane in some spellings, is also known as the lower lake. It's an expansive water covering 5,000 acres, and is the largest in a system of three lakes. Lein, with its dark peat stained waters, holds some special memories for me as it was my first experience of fishing from a boat. Even after some thirty years of fishing this wonderful lake I still feel that childlike excitement every time I return.

The lake is principally known for salmon, brown trout and, to a lesser degree, sea trout. There are no pike in any of the three lakes. Other notable species of fish in Lough Lein are the twaite shad, on which the large, ferox trout feed. There are also char, tench and perch. The deepest area of the lake runs to almost 200 feet – a trough situated along the shore below the Purple Mountain.

THE BASICS

The salmon season opens on January 17. The middle lake, Muckross Lake, tends to be the first of the three to fish well, followed by the upper lake and, finally, Lough Lein really gets going from around March 17 onwards. Fishing for brown trout gets underway on February 15. Towards the end of March and into early April, the duckfly (a large chironomid, or buzzer) appears on the water, followed by the hawthorn fly and then the alder fly. The lake is renowned for fishing best for trout in the last week of May to mid-June. The mayfly tends to be smaller in size and the hatch a bit sporadic compared to other Irish lakes. Lough Carra is renowned for its early hatch of mayfly whilst Lein is the reverse and is usually the last to appear. During the summer months the sedge will dominate the trout's attention. Just like the mayfly, these are usually quite small in size and mainly dark in colour. On calmer days and early evenings, the hatch of

A magnificent view of the Black Valley

midge can be quite prolific.

We know from the salmon anglers that Lein holds plenty of big trout, and some massive specimens are taken while trolling each year including the record brown trout, which weighed 21lb.

Lein receives the majority of its water from the numerous rivers that enter the lake along 22 miles of beautiful shoreline. The main rivers used by trout and salmon for spawning include the Rivers Flesk, Loe, Deenagh, Finnow, Cool, Crinagh, Cotteners, Gaddagh and the Gweestin. In contrast, only one river flows out of the lake – the Laune, located on the western shore. Trolling is the preferred salmon fishing method for the local anglers, the record Lein salmon weighed 49lb. Conversely, many salmon and grilse are also caught on trout flies throughout the season.

FISHERY MANAGEMENT

Fishing on the lakes and rivers of Killarney is managed by the South Western Regional Fisheries whose website address is www.swrfb.ie. Should you wish to find out more about the locality and fishing, there is another informative tourist oriented website at www.killarney.ie.

The surrounding woodlands and parks are managed by the National Parks and Wildlife Services.

There are two angling clubs on the lake – Killarney Salmon & Trout Angling Club, formed in 1982 has a membership of over 100 anglers; and Lough Lein Anglers, founded around 1940, has more than 150 members. With such prolific fishing in the area there are a total of six clubs spread across the whole system of lakes and rivers with a membership of almost 1,000 anglers. To their credit, the local clubs are actively engaged in the environmental management of their waters and in addition, carry out spawning stream enhancement works on a regular basis.

Like most fisheries in Ireland Lein's water quality has declined over the years through enrichment by phosphates from forestry and agricultural farming. It is believed that progress in some areas in the reduction of phosphates entering the water system is now being achieved. Unfortunately, this pollution has caused insect

DJ O'Riordan with three brown trout and a salmon caught on the troll. The trout weighed 15lb 8oz, 11.lb 8oz, 8lb 8oz and the salmon 9lb

life to diminish significantly in the last ten years.

The growing number of cormorants on the lakes is high on the agenda of concerns for the angling clubs. So, too, is the management of the perch in Lough Lein. Some years ago, almost three-quarters of a million perch were removed from the fishery, but their numbers are on the increase again.

You don't need a trout rod licence in Ireland; the right to fish these great lakes for free was fought over for many years by Irish anglers. You will require a licence only if you fish for salmon and sea trout, and this comes with tags to prove the fishes' provenance. The size limit for takeable trout was increased in 2008 to 10 inches from the nose to the fork of the tail. This is now the standard for all competitions on this water, unless fished on a catch-and-release basis.

BOAT HIRE

From what was once a thriving industry in the town, there are now very few professional boatmen left on the lake. Most anglers today either own boats or hire one, self-driven. It is true that Lough Lein is generally considered a safe water when compared to the likes of Mask or Corrib but, like any lake of its size, it can blow up very badly and quickly. That's why I'd recommend a boatman if you are at all unfamiliar with any large water and, if you should choose not to, then ensure that you obtain an accurate weather forecast before venturing on to the water. There are hidden hazards, too. Rocky patches – skerries – rise to the surface in many areas of the lake. Most are well-marked with posts and buoys but some aren't, so keep a sharp lookout when motoring across the lake. In low-water conditions, areas like the Heron Stones and Fossa Shore require particular attention. You must also be careful of the sandbars that lie off several of Lein's thirty islands.

The sandbar off Brown Island can be quite deceptive, as it stretches out in the lake for an incredible distance. Quite a number of boats have been beached on this submerged expanse of sand, with the engine's water intake sucking in debris, the propeller shearing its pins and the further possibility of capsizing. My brother Tommy knows this particular sand bar all too intimately...

WHERE TO FISH

If you are fishing the lake early in the season, Bog Bay, the area just out from Ross Castle can fish very well. This is one of the best bays in the lake for nymph fishing. The shallow bays of Victoria and Goreen, are renowned early season hotspots. You will see most of the boats congregating in and around these bays in May and June.

David with two "yellow bellies" around 1lb each. May 2007

From late May onwards, fishing in Bog Bay is sometimes destroyed with a blanket of pond weed. These weeds are not native to the water – African, I am told, and a phenomenon of the last three or four years. I believe Lough Corrib is also suffering from a similar problem.

Later in the season, most boats head back west to the mouth of the River Laune and Sweeney's Shore. Brown Island can also fish well at this time of the year. I particularly enjoy fishing around the area known as the Wash; both in the shallows and out near the salmon runs. These areas, and out from Mahoney's Point, can be very productive when the fish 'switch on' in a westerly wind. It would be foolish to pass by the Heron Stones at any time of year. The pockets at the back of Innisfallen Island can provide great fishing, but not once the water level gets low. These are also some of my favourite areas for dry-fly fishing.

A west-wind will provide an excellent, long drift from the mouth of the River Laune all the way along the Fossa shore; this is all productive trout water. I am not as familiar with the east side of the lake as I would like; the west dominates my attention. The Hen and Chickens was one of my father's favourite drifts on this area of the lake. The mouth of the River Flesk is also a known hotspot. A south east wind will provide a good, long drift from the lake hotel towards the mouth of the river, and on towards an expansive area of shallow water known as the Sand Bank. Other areas worthy of a drift are the Muckross Shore, Rough Island and the Copper Mines.

It is worth a trip over to the Eastern side of the lough just to fish against some of the most stunning scenery that Ireland has to offer. And, if you are lucky, you may even catch sight of a white-tailed sea eagle. These birds of prey were reintroduced into Kerry after an absence of over 100 years. I hope they do well as they are magnificent birds. If you want to try for a salmon with trout flies, it is worth putting up a few size 10s on the leader. Patterns such as the Black Jungle Cock, Dunkeld, Bibio Variant and Thunder & Lightning can be very successful. Any fly dressed with a mixture of black and blue seal's fur in the body is also well worth a try. The most productive areas are around the mouths of rivers especially where deep water meets shallow. The salmon tend to lay up off these shelves, waiting for the rivers to go into flood so they can carry on their journey upstream to spawn.

METHODS

I have no doubt in my mind that the wet-fly is by far the most productive method of catching trout on Lough Lein. My preferred way of fishing wet-flies is with a

Sunset over Bog Bay

floating line; I rarely use anything else, even on slow days. I have experimented quite a lot in the past five or six years with nymphs and dry-flies, discovering that nymphs can work well in shallow waters. If the trout are up in the water in a good wave then, the wet-fly is king. The trout on Lein generally like the fly to be moved, sometimes at speed. They will take the fly at any time during the retrieve but, noticeably, just after the flies have landed in the water. You need to be prepared for this eventuality or many opportunities will be missed. Short-lining is often the solution to these lightening-fast takes.

Like most Lough fishing, if the take does not come soon after starting the retrieve, the trout will often follow the fly back to the boat. At the moment the top dropper breaks the surface, they then make a last, desperate lunge in an effort to catch the fly before it disappears. I cannot speak for others but I find that, all too frustratingly, I miss the vast majority of these takes on Lein. The secret is not to lift the bob fly out of the water too quickly. Instead, raise the rod early towards the end of the retrieve and skate the bob fly just under or in the surface film to induce the take. Skating the bob fly on top of the surface will simply attract lots of attention but very few hook ups. Killarney trout are definitely not boat shy, so there is no real need to cast a long line. On the worst of days, you will always rise trout with the wet-fly on the Killarney lakes, which is the exciting bit. But I have to say that nymphs and especially dry-flies seem to sift the bigger trout from the bunch. I tend to fish with four flies on a leader, each spaced 4ft apart. My overall leader length is approximately 17ft long. If the wind is boxing, then I will reduce to three. I normally fish with a fluorocarbon leader of about 6lb breaking strain, going down to 5lb when fishing dry-flies. My preferred rod, is a seven-weight 10ft 6in Sage.

The trout on Lein are generally small when compared to those encountered in the great, western lakes of Mask and Carra, but they are numerous. They also have a tendency to spin like crazy when hooked, which is why you need what might seem a disproportionally strong leader. Always keep the fish high in the water when playing them or else you'll end up with a beautiful bird's nest every time.

The size of fly normally fished on Lein is a 12 or 14. Lein trout definitely prefer a pattern with black in the dressing. On a slow day, I often put a well-dressed size 10 on the top dropper to get a reaction and it works for me regularly. The trout here are very fast, in fact the fastest

LOUGH LEIN

A beautifully marked Lein brown trout

I have ever known on any Lough. So don't despair: you will rise and lose a lot of trout throughout the course of the day. While you will not meet as many trout on nymphs, the conversion rate of takes to fish boated improves dramatically.

I have noticed, in the last couple of years, the average size of Lein trout has increased. Catching a trout around the one pound mark and slightly above has become much more common these days. I recently hooked a lovely trout of around 2½lb on a nymph. Twice I had him to the rim of the net but I lost him in the end. In the same few days' fishing, I hooked and lost an even bigger one of about 4lb while drifting off Sweeney's Shore. These would be considered exceptional trout for Lein, but that's the magic of fishing this water, you never know what might turn up next. And there is always the chance of a salmon; this can be a regular occurrence, especially in the summer months when grilse are running.

I have never fished Lough Lein into darkness but this is definitely on my "To Do" list. I am told the fishing can be superb. September and early October can also provide excellent fishing; the trout are shoaling at this time of year as their spawning instincts have kicked in. The trouble then is finding the shoals but, once located, the fishing for a short period can be frenetic. The trick here is to use the oars to edge the boat in and out rather than straight-line drifting. This way you stand a better chance of locating the fish. The action ceases pretty swiftly once you have drifted passed the shoal, so start the engine; give the area in which you had the takes a wide berth and come around again for a second drift.

There is a common perception amongst anglers on Lein that if the lake level is rising, the trout fishing is going to be useless. In August last year I fished the Lough for four days. Each day the water levels rose on average about two inches, which is an incredible amount of rainfall for a lough the size of Lein.

I experienced some of the most wonderful fishing I have ever had in Killarney, catching and releasing literally hundreds of trout over the four days, with some lovely sea trout among them. I had a similar experience again in September. It only proves that there are no hard and fast rules when it comes to fishing.

FLIES

Black is the dominant colour for flies used on Lough Lein, but red, blue, dark olive, orange and claret all have a use. Pale-coloured flies do not generally perform well on Lein. Having said that, I have had far too many good days with the Invicta and Octopus to discount any colour on this lake.

Some flies will perform well here all season long, patterns such as the Bibio Variant, Watson's Fancy Watson Bumble and the Black Jungle Cock. In May, the Sooty Olive fishes well, along with the Alder and small, black Sedge imitations.

The Invicta, Kate Maclaren, and McGorman are excellent flies when brown sedges are on the water. The Connemara Black and Killarney Black Sedge are effective patterns when darker sedges are about, though these are flies that also can perform well throughout the season. A silver fly such as the Marlodge works well when fished late into a summer's evening.

In September, small snail imitating patterns such as the

Black & Peacock Spider and the Coch-y-Bondhu work well. This is also the time of year when claret flies come into their own. Flies such as the Claret Bumble, Claret Rebel and the UV Claret Dabbler are all good back-end-of-season patterns to try out.

Attractor flies such as Thunder & Lightning and Dunkeld will always catch trout on Lein. I had some great days' fishing in August 2008 with the Thunder & Lightning and, of course, it's not just the trout that are attracted to these patterns; the occasional salmon has been caught on these two brightly coloured wet-flies, over the years. Other patterns preferred by some of the local anglers would include old favourites such as the Johnston and the Kingsmill, the latter also being a good sea trout fly. A Black Jungle Cock with a red butt and blue pearl in the body, the Zulu, Blae & Black and a Black Spider with small Jungle Cock eyes will be found in their fly boxes.

A NEW RANGE OF EMERGERS

During the European Championships, I covered quite a few rising fish with both wet and dry-flies and, unusually for Lein trout, my offers were mostly refused. We did not encounter the normal wet and windy conditions associated with Killarney at this time of year. In the calmer conditions the trout were rising all over the lake but were very fussy and not easy to catch. Even though I had reduced the size of my dry-flies to skimpy size 14s and attracted lots of rises, I still managed very few hook-ups. This set me thinking. On my return to England I sat down to complete a new range of Emergers which I was convinced would be the solution to the problem. I tied these flies in various sizes down to tiny 16s using some previously effective blends and colours. On my next visit to Lein some of these new patterns worked brilliantly, particularly the AK47.

While black is king on Lein, the other dominant colour to emerge during the Championships was olive/green. The Green Peter and Stimulator variant accounted for their fair share of fish. Before we all headed for home I spent a pleasure day's fishing with the Dutch squad sharing a boat with team member Bram Kwak. I gave Bram some Emergers and a Green Stimulator for the top dropper. He landed quite a few trout that day and even managed to get broken up in a salmon that hit him near the Heron Stones. The fish took the Stimulator; it was all over in a split second!

My personal favourite is a fly I invented over 20 years ago – the Black&Copper Partridge. From May onwards, this fly will almost always occupy the top dropper position on the leader as my starting point. I tie several versions of this highly successful pattern.

A body tied with bushy seal's fur is normally reserved for the top dropper position. If the trout are really on this fly I will often combine it with the spider version on the point. Interestingly, the popularity of silver-coloured flies has waned over time. Some years ago it would have been considered madness to go out on the water without a Silver Jungle Cock on the point, but the brilliance of this fly has dulled, for reasons only trout would know.

On bright days I very often fish a Red Marlodge on the point, to good effect. It's also not a bad fry imitator, most effective as the season breathes its last. The fact is, a huge variety of wet-flies will work on Lough Lein, and many anglers have personal favourites. Always carry a good selection of patterns for this fishery, as the trout will often as not show a preference for a particular colour and shape of fly... to the exclusion of most others.

RING THE CHANGES

The Munster Championship, held in May each year, has been a success story for me. I have not finished outside of the top ten in the last four years, winning it twice... but never with the same flies in successive years. There is simply no consistency, with ever-changing weather patterns which may be related to climate change. There are waters where you could fish all day with six patterns but not Lough Lein. Ring the changes from the admittedly long list I have presented and you may enjoy the same success I have had.

The Black&Copper Partridge

Lough Lein wet-flies I

CLARET ROCKET
Hook: Kamasan B 100 size 12-14
Thread: Claret
Body: Claret Mosaic dubbing
Rib: Fine pearl tinsel
Body hackle: Furnace cock
Legs: Knotted pheasant tail fibres dyed claret
Head hackle: Medium claret cock
Cheeks: Jungle cock dyed orange

MICK'S BLACK & COPPER
Hook: Kamasan B 100 size 12-14
Thread: Black
Body: Black seal's fur
Rib: Medium flat copper tinsel
Thorax: Black/blue seal's fur mixed
Thorax cheeks: Red holographic tinsel
Hackle: Partridge brown neck feather
Cheeks: Jungle cock dyed yellow

GOLDEN OLIVE DABBLER
Hook: Kamasan B 175 size 12-14
Thread: Red
Tail: Bronze mallard fibres, strands of Crystal Hair
Body: Golden olive seal's fur
Rib: Gold oval tinsel
Body hackle: Golden olive cock
Shoulder hackle: Bronze mallard strips

MICK'S SOOTY OLIVE
Hook: Kamasan B 175 size 12-14
Thread: Black
Tail: Bronze mallard fibres
Body: Dark sooty olive seal's fur
Rib: Hot orange Ultra wire
Wing: Mallard, pale wing feather
Hackle: Black hen
Cheeks: Jungle cock dyed yellow

REVERSED RED MARLODGE
Hook: Kamasan B 175 size 12-14
Thread: Red
Tail: Golden olive crest
Body: Silver tinsel/red floss/silver tinsel
Rib: Fine silver wire
Wing: Bronze mallard feather
Hackles: No1, guinea fowl – No2, red cock hackle
Cheeks: Jungle cock

BIBIO VARIANT
Hook: Kamasan B 100 size 12-14
Thread: Black
Tail: Golden pheasant tippets
Body: Black/red/black seal's fur
Ribs: No1, pearl tinsel – No2, fine silver wire
Body hackle: Black cock
Shoulder hackle: Partridge brown neck feather
Cheeks: Jungle cock

THUNDER & LIGHTNING
Hook: Kamasan B 175 size 12-14
Thread: Black
Tail: Golden pheasant crest dyed orange
Body: Black seal's fur
Rib: Gold oval tinsel
Body hackle: Orange cock feather
Throat hackle: Blue jay
Wing: Bronze mallard
Cheeks: Jungle cock dyed yellow

UV CLARET BUMBLE
Hook: Kamasan B 175 size 12-14
Thread: Claret
Tail: Golden pheasant tippets
Body: Claret UV Straggle
Rib: Fine gold wire
Body hackle: Claret cock
Legs: Knotted pheasant tail, dyed claret
Shoulder hackle: Blue jay
Cheeks: Jungle cock

UV BLACK & COPPER
Hook: Kamasan B 100 size 12-14
Thread: Black
Body: Black UV Straggle
Rib: Medium flat copper tinsel
Thorax: Red UV Straggle
Hackle: Partridge brown neck feather
Cheeks: Jungle cock dyed orange

BLACK DABBLER
Hook: Kamasan B 175 size 12-14
Thread: Black
Butt: Flat silver tinsel
Tail: Bronze mallard fibres
Body: Black seal's fur
Rib: Red holographic tinsel
Body hackle: Black cock
Shoulder hackle: Bronze mallard strips
Cheeks: Jungle cock dyed yellow

BLAE & GREEN
Hook: Kamasan B 175 size 12-14
Thread: Black
Tail: Black hackle fibres
Body: Veniard's green floss
Rib: Fine flat gold tinsel
Wing: Mallard, pale wing feather
Hackle: Black hen
Cheeks: Jungle cock

Lough Lein wet-flies II

CONNEMARA BLACK VARIANT
Hook: Kamasan B 175 size 12-14
Thread: Black
Butt: Pearl tinsel
Tail: Golden pheasant crest
Body: Black seal's fur
Rib: Silver oval tinsel
Wing: Bronze mallard
Hackles: No1, orange cock -No 2, blue jay
Cheeks: Jungle cock

WATSON'S FANCY
Hook: Kamasan B 175 size 12-14
Thread: Black
Butt: Flat silver tinsel
Tail: Golden pheasant tippets
Body: 1st half, red seal's fur – 2nd half, black seal's fur
Rib: Silver oval tinsel
Wing: Crow feather
Hackle: Black cock
Cheeks: Jungle cock

BLACK & PEACOCK VARIANT
Hook: Kamasan B 100 size 12-14
Thread: Black
Butt: Flat silver tinsel
Body: Black Ice Yarn
Hackle: Black hen, one turn
Cheeks: Jungle cock

BLAE & BLACK
Hook: Kamasan B 175 size 12-14
Thread: Black
Tail: Golden pheasant tippets
Body: Black tinsel or floss
Rib: Fine silver wire
Thorax: Black SLF
Hackle: Black hen
Wing: Mallard, pale wing feather

CLARET CLAN CHIEF
Hook: Kamasan B 175 size 12-14
Thread: Claret
Tail: Glo-Brite No's 11 & 7
Body: Black seal's fur
Rib: Gold oval tinsel
Body hackle: Claret cock
Shoulder hackle: Furnace hen
Cheeks: Jungle cock

DUNKELD
Hook: Kamasan B 175 size 12-14
Thread: Black
Tail: Golden pheasant crest
Body: Flat gold tinsel
Rib: Fine gold wire
Body hackle: Orange cock
Throat hackle: Blue jay
Wing: Bronze mallard
Cheeks: Jungle cock

KATE MACLAREN VARIANT
Hook: Kamasan B 175 size 12-14
Thread: Black
Tail: Golden pheasant crest
Body: Black seal's fur
Rib: Fine pearl tinsel
Body hackle: Black cock
Shoulder hackles: No1, orange hen No 2, natural red cock

JOHNSTON
Hook: Kamasan B 175 size 12-14
Thread: Black
Butt: Orange seal's fur
Tail: Golden pheasant crest
Body: Medium olive seal's fur
Rib: Gold oval tinsel
Wing: Bronze mallard
Hackle: Black hen

KINGSMILL VARIANT
Hook: Kamasan B 175 size 12-14
Thread: Black
Butt: Blue tinsel
Tail: Golden pheasant crest
Body: Ostrich herl dyed black
Rib: Silver oval tinsel
Wing: Crow feather, golden crest dyed orange
Hackle: Black hen
Cheeks: Jungle cock

BLACK SPIDER
Hook: Kamasan B 175 size 12-14
Thread: Black
Butt: Flat silver tinsel
Body: Ostrich herl dyed black
Rib: Fine red holographic tinsel
Hackle: Black hen
Cheeks: Jungle cock

BUTCHER VARIANT
Hook: Kamasan B 175 size 12-14
Thread: Black
Tail: Goose feather dyed red
Body: Flat silver tinsel
Rib: Fine silver wire
Thorax: Red holographic tinsel
Wing: Mallard blue feather
Hackle: Black hen

CONNEMARA BLACK VARIANT   **JOHNSTON**

CLARET CLAN CHIEF

WATSON'S FANCY   **KINGSMILL VARIANT**

DUNKELD

BLACK & PEACOCK VARIANT   **BLACK SPIDER**

KATE MACLAREN VARIANT

BLAE & BLACK   **BUTCHER VARIANT**

Lough Lein wet-flies III

HARE'S EAR & CLARET
Hook: Kamasan B170 size 12-14
Thread: Black
Tail: Bronze mallard fibres
Body: Hare's ear fur
Rib: Fine flat gold tinsel
Wing: Woodcock feather
Cheeks: Jungle cock
Hackle: Claret cock

BLACK JUNGLE COCK No1
Hook: Kamasan B170 size 12-14
Thread: Black
Butt: Flat silver tinsel
Tail: Golden pheasant tippets
Body: Black seal's fur
Rib: Oval silver tinsel
Wing: Jungle cock feathers
Hackles: 1st, Red cock – 2nd, Black cock

CLARET REBEL
Hook: Kamasan B170 size 12-14
Thread: Bright claret
Butt: Silver tinsel
Tail: Purple floss
Body: Claret seal's fur
Rib: Pearl tinsel with gold oval tinsel over
Body hackle: Claret cock
Shoulder hackle: Bronze mallard strips
Cheeks: Jungle cock

BIBIO VARIANT No2
Hook: Kamasan B100 size 14
Thread: Black
Butt: Glo-Brite floss No7
Tail: Golden pheasant tippets
Body: Black seal's fur
Thorax: Orange seal's fur
Rib: Fine pearl tinsel
Body hackle: Black cock
Legs: Knotted pheasant tail, dyed red
Cheeks: Jungle cock

BLACK SEDGE
Hook: Kamasan B170 size 12-14
Thread: Black
Body: Black seal's fur
Rib: Gold oval tinsel
Body hackle: Furnace cock
Wing: Crow feather
Head hackle: Furnace hen

SILVER JUNGLE COCK
Hook: Kamasan B170 size 12-14
Thread: Fire orange
Tail: Golden pheasant tippets
Body: Silver holographic tinsel
Rib: Fine silver wire
Wings: Jungle cock feathers
Hackle: Black hen feather

INVICTA
Hook: Kamasan B170 size 12-14
Thread: Orange
Butt: Glo-Brite floss No10
Tail: Golden pheasant crest
Body: Yellow seal's fur
Rib: Gold oval tinsel
Body hackle: Deep natural red cock
Wing: Hen pheasant, dyed golden olive
Throat hackle: Blue jay

BLACK JUNGLE COCK No3
Hook: Kamasan B170 size 12-14
Thread: Black
Butt: Flat silver tinsel
Tail: Red floss
Body: Black & blue seal's fur, mixed
Rib: Fine flat silver tinsel
Wing: Jungle cock feathers, dyed yellow
Hackle: Black cock

McGORMAN
Hook: Kamasan B170 size 12-14
Thread: Black
Butt: Bright blue floss
Tail: Mallard flank feather fibres
Body: Peacock herl
Body hackle: Natural brown cock
Rib: Fine copper wire
Wing: Hen pheasant, dyed olive brown

BLACK JUNGLE COCK No2
Hook: Kamasan B170 size 12-14
Thread: Black
Butt: Flat silver tinsel
Tail: Golden pheasant tippets
Body: Black & blue seal's fur, mixed
Rib: Fine flat silver tinsel
Wing: Jungle cock feathers, dyed yellow
Hackle: Black cock

WATSON'S BUMBLE
Hook: Kamasan B170 size 12-14
Thread: Black
Tail: Golden pheasant crest feather
Body: 1st quarter, red seal's fur remainder, black seal's fur
Body hackle: Black cock
Rib: Silver oval tinsel
Head hackle: Blue jay
Cheeks: Jungle cock

COCH-Y-BONDHU
Hook: Kamasan B100 size 12-14
Thread: Brown
Butt: Flat gold tinsel
Body: Peacock herl
Hackle: Furnace hen, one turn
Cheeks: Jungle cock

HARE'S EAR & CLARET

BLACK SEDGE

McGORMAN

BLACK JUNGLE COCK No1

BLACK JUNGLE COCK No2

SILVER JUNGLE COCK

CLARET REBEL

INVICTA

WATSON'S BUMBLE

BIBIO VARIANT No2

BLACK JUNGLE COCK No3

COCH-Y-BONDHU

Drifting Bog Bay, with a splendid view of Ross Castle

NYMPHS AND DRY-FLIES

We have already established that Lough Lein is the province of the wet-fly. At least, that's its tradition. For me, tradition has plenty of value but my innovator instincts always want to create the exceptions that disprove the rule. And so I have dabbled with both nymph and dry-fly fishing on Lein. At one time, this would have been easy. Now, I live in England, making ad hoc experimentation a sporadic affair. That said, I am now very confident that nymphs are effective on Lein, and to a lesser extent, depending on wind strength, dry-flies will also work. I have discovered through trial and error that shallow bays and island shores are the most productive areas with the nymphs, and open, deep water less so. The difficulty with presenting nymphs in deep water is that these open areas are often exposed to the full force of the wind, and in a strong wind, the boat drifts too quickly for the method to be truly effective. There is, in any case, no necessity to fish these areas, for Lough Lein offers many sheltered bays which suit the use of nymphs and dry-flies.

BUZZERS ON THE LOUGH

For nymph fishing, I tend to fish my usual long leader of 18 feet of fluorocarbon with a Hackled Buzzer or Emerger pattern on the top dropper and middle droppers, and a heavier, size 12 Buzzer on the point. Depending on wind speed, I normally fish a fairly fast figure of eight retrieve. In my experience on Lein, and in a similar vein to wet-fly fishing, the majority of the takes normally come early in the retrieve. When I first started fishing Buzzers on this lake the conversion rate of takes to fish boated was somewhere in the region of 90 per cent. The trout really took the nymph with confidence. Latterly, with many anglers competent in fishing the method, the trout have become more exposed to this style of fishing and seem to have 'wised up.'

I dress almost all of my Buzzers on B100 Kamasan hooks, which are exceedingly strong plus their heavy gauge wire adds essential weight to the fly. I tend to fish Buzzers on size 12 and 14 hooks as I have found both these sizes are sufficient to cover all my needs on this water. The top dropper position is fairly critical on Lein, whatever method the angler is using. A Spider-type Buzzer pattern with a sparse collar hackle, or an Emerger, is a must as far as I am concerned.

Buzzer fishing on Lein usually gets under way with the appearance of a tiny lime-green buzzer followed by black then on to bottle-green and finally, brown. The most successful patterns for me in recent years have been the Red Holo Buzzer, the AK47 Emerger and a hackled Pheasant Tail. Black and brown Buzzers will continue to fish well throughout the remainder of the season. The Pheasant Tail in both hackled and nymph-style is very good in the middle dropper position along with a sparsely dressed Hare's Ear. The green buzzer will again put in an appearance in September, albeit much smaller in size.

If the trout are near the surface, a hackled fly on the top dropper is essential. Black is always a favourite colour in this position but in May, I have found the Pale Green Emerger even better. For those in the know, Bog Bay is probably the best bay for Buzzer fishing on Lein. Other notable areas are the Metal Man, The Wash, Victoria and Gaureen. I have yet to explore the east of the lake with this style of fishing but I'm confident that the Sand Bank and mouth of the Flesk River are ideal areas given the right conditions.

DIAWL BACHS

In recent years I have been successful with the Diawl Bach on Lein, often in preference to Buzzers. I feel the Buzzer method's success is often limited to particular shallow bays whereas the Diawl Bach appears to have more universal trout appeal. The most productive size of fly is a 14. Black is again the dominant colour; however, a

Diawl Bach with a lime-green butt and green holographic cheeks is a favourite of mine during the early part of the season. The touch of lime green obviously attracts the trout when a similarly-coloured insect is on the water.

The original Diawl Bach is well worth a go at any time while May and June are great months for the olive variants. The Sooty Diawl Bach and a lighter olive version work best in June. My Favourite Diawl Bach is one with blue pearl in the body. Blue mixed with black or claret herl is a recurring theme on this water. My other favourite is the gold-ribbed Diawl Bach.

DRY-FLIES

The trout on Lough Lein are not as free-rising as they are on other loughs. The water does not enjoy the prolific sedge hatches that I have seen elsewhere in Ireland, and which draw the fish to feed regularly at the surface. I was fortunate enough in 2008 to get a few extra days' fishing on Lein and decided to devote a bit more time to the dry-fly. It was an enjoyable experience and I landed several bigger-than-average trout on the Bibio and small Black Hoppers.

The areas of the Lough that I found the dry-fly fished best were around the Metal Man, the Heron Stones and Lamb Island. If there was one area I would expect to find surface-feeding trout it would be Sweeney's Shore and the Metal Man – especially late in the season. I had a similar experience the following year when fishing the dry-fly on shallow bays in the East and again caught some quality trout. I suspect that the dry-fly would perform best when fished late in the summer evenings when the lake has calmed and the bigger trout come on the feed to some prolific hatches of midge.

Size is a critical factor with the dry-fly on Lein. Black and olive patterns dressed on a size 14 hook work best. Bigger flies seem to attract a lot of splashy rises but very little contact. In some seasons, Lein can experience a fall of ants around July, which is why I have included a couple of Foam Ants in my selection. Fishing small flies requires light tackle and top quality leaders – 4lb fluorocarbon works best for me.

Dutch team-member Bram Kwak, in action in Victoria Bay

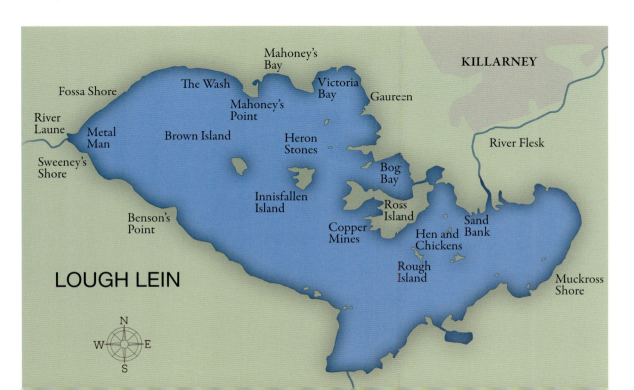

Lough Lein I
nymphs and dry-flies

BLACK & COPPER BUZZER
Hook: Kamasan B 100 size 12-14
Thread: Black
Body: Pheasant tail dyed black
Rib: Fine flat copper tinsel
Thorax: Seal's fur dyed black
Cheeks: Red holographic tinsel

EMERGING BLACK BUZZER
Hook: Kamasan B 100 size 12-14
Thread: Black
Body: Black tinsel or floss
Rib: Fine silver wire
Thorax: Red Micro Brite
Wing: White EPS fibres
Hackle: Black cock
Cheeks: Jungle cock

FIERY BROWN SEDGE
Hook: Light wire size 12-14
Thread: Brown
Body: Fiery brown seal's fur
Wing: Pale deer hair
Hackle: Fiery brown cock, tied parachute style
Horns: Deer hair fibres

HARE'S EAR
Hook: Heavy gauge size 12-14
Thread: Fire orange
Butt: Gold holographic tinsel
Body: Hare's ear fur
Rib: Fine gold wire
Cheeks: Gold holographic tinsel

PHEASANT TAIL BUZZER
Hook: Kamasan B 100 size 12-14
Thread: Black
Body: Pheasant tail fibres
Rib: Bright copper wire
Thorax: Black floss, varnished over
Cheeks: Fine flat silver tinsel

F FLY
Hook: Light wire size 12-14
Thread: Medium olive
Body: Medium olive SLF
Wing: Natural CDC
Hackle: Light blue dun, underside trimmed

CRUNCHER
Hook: Heavy gauge size 12-14
Thread: Black
Tail: Brown hackle fibres
Body: Pheasant tail fibres
Rib: Fine gold wire
Thorax: Peacock herl
Cheeks: Fine flat gold holographic tinsel
Hackle: Greenwell's hen

BLACK BUZZER No2
Hook: Kamasan B 100 Size 12-14
Thread: Black
Body: Black tinsel or floss
Rib: Fine silver wire
Thorax: Black floss, varnished over
Cheeks: Red holographic tinsel

SOOTY OLIVE SPIDER
Hook: Kamasan B 100 size 12-14
Thread: Black
Butt: Glo-Brite floss No 6
Body: Pheasant tail fibres, dyed dark olive
Rib: Fine silver wire
Thorax: Sooty olive seal's fur
Cheeks: Fine flat silver tinsel
Hackle: Black hen
Cheeks: Jungle cock

BLACK CDC
Hook: Light wire size 14
Thread: Black
Body: Red/black seal's fur mixed
Wing: Dyed red CDC with red DNA strands over

BLUE HOLO DIAWL BACH
Hook: Heavy gauge size 12-14
Thread: Black
Tail: Black hackle fibres
Body: Black floss
Rib: Blue pearl tinsel
Throat hackle: Black hen fibres
Cheeks: Jungle cock

BLACK & COPPER BUZZER

BLACK BUZZER No2

PHEASANT TAIL BUZZER

EMERGING BLACK BUZZER

SOOTY OLIVE SPIDER

F FLY

FIERY BROWN SEDGE

BLACK CDC

CRUNCHER

HARE'S EAR

BLUE HOLO DIAWL BACH

Lough Lein
nymphs and dry-flies II

BLACK BUZZER No1
Hook: Kamasan B 100 12-14
Thread: Black
Tail: Black hackle fibres
Body: Pheasant tail fibres, dyed black
Rib: Fine flat silver tinsel
Thorax: Black Ice Yarn
Thorax cover: Dark Nymph Skin
Hackle: Black hen

BLACK ANT
Hook: Light wire size 14
Thread: Black
Body: Foam ant body, black
Hackle: Black cock

ADULT BLACK BUZZER
Hook: Buzzer size 14
Thread: Black
Body: Black tinsel
Rib: Fine silver wire
Wing: White EPS fibres
Thorax: Red Micro Brite
Hackle: Black cock

PARACHUTE BLACK BUZZER
Hook: Light wire size 14
Thread: Black
Body: Black seal's fur
Tail: Grizzle hackle fibres
Post: White DNA fibres
Thorax: Black SLF
Hackle: Grizzle cock

BLACK SNAIL
Hook: Kamasan B 100 size 12-14
Thread: Black
Butt: Flat silver tinsel
Body: Black Ice Yarn, over lead wire
Hackle: Black hen, one turn
Cheeks: Jungle cock

SOOTY OLIVE CRUNCHER
Hook: Light wire size 12-14
Thread: Black
Butt: Glo-Brite No 6
Tail: Golden pheasant yellow rump feather
Body: Pheasant tail fibres, dyed dark olive
Thorax: Sooty olive seal's fur
Hackle: Black hen
Cheeks: Jungle cock

PHEASANT TAIL EMERGER
Hook: Kamasan B 100 size 12-14
Thread: Orange
Body: Pheasant tail fibres
Rib: Fine silver wire
Thorax: Rusty brown Micro Brite
Hackle: Cree cock, one turn

CONNEMARA NYMPH
Hook: Heavy Gauge size 12-14
Thread: Black
Tail: Golden pheasant yellow rump feather
Body: Pheasant tail, dyed black
Rib: Fine silver wire
Thorax: Black seal's fur
Thorax cover: Bronze mallard fibres
Throat hackle: Blue jay

BROWN ANT
Hook: Light wire size 14
Thread: Brown
Body: Foam ant body, brown
Hackle: Brown cock

BLUE HOLO SPIDER
Hook: Kamasan B 100 size 12-14
Thread: Black
Body: Pheasant tail fibres, dyed black
Rib: Blue pearl tinsel
Thorax: Black seal's fur
Thorax cover: Red holographic tinsel
Hackle: Black hen

SHIPMAN'S BLACK BUZZER
Hook: Light wire size 14
Thread: Black
Breathers: White EPS fibres
Butt: Glo-Brite No 7
Body: Black seal's fur
Rib: Fine pearl tinsel
Hackle: Grizzle cock, reversed

BLACK BUZZER No1

BLACK SNAIL

CONNEMARA NYMPH

BLACK ANT

SOOTY OLIVE CRUNCHER

BROWN ANT

ADULT BLACK BUZZER

PHEASANT TAIL EMERGER

BLUE HOLO SPIDER

PARACHUTE BLACK BUZZER

SHIPMAN'S BLACK BUZZER

Lough Lein
nymphs and dry-flies III

DARK OLIVE SPIDER
Hook: Kamasan B 100 size 12-14
Thread: Medium olive
Body: Pheasant tail fibres, dyed dark olive
Rib: Fine gold wire
Thorax: Orange seal's fur & hare's ear
Hackle: Rusty brown badger cock
Cheeks: Jungle cock

BIBIO VARIANT No 2
Hook: Light wire size 14
Thread: Black
Body: Black/orange seal's fur
Rib: Fine pearl tinsel
Legs: Pheasant tail fibres, dyed orang
Hackle: Black cock, underside trimmed

GOLD RIBBED DIAWL BACH
Hook: Heavy gauge size 12-14
Thread: Fire orange
Tail: Golden pheasant red rump feather
Body: Peacock herl, dyed orange
Rib: Fine flat gold tinsel
Throat hackle: Golden pheasant red rump fibres
Cheeks: Jungle cock

PALE GREEN EMERGER
Hook: Kamasan B 100 size 12-14
Thread: Medium olive
Body: Pale olive Ultra wire
Thorax: Bright olive SLF
Wings: White DNA fibres split into V
Hackle: Light grey dun

BLACK CRUNCHER
Hook: Heavy gauge size 12-14
Thread: Black
Tail: Black hen hackle fibres
Body: Pheasant tail fibres, dyed red
Rib: Hot orange Ultra wire
Thorax: Black SLF
Hackle: Greenwell's cock
Cheeks: Jungle cock

GREEN DEVIL
Hook: Light wire size 12-14
Thread: Fire red
Tail: Black hackle fibres
Body: Veniard's green floss
Rib: Fine flat gold holographic tinsel
Thorax: Brown/grey SLF
Hackle: Black hen
Cheeks: Jungle cock

BLACK DIAWL BACH
Hook: Heavy gauge size 12-14
Thread: Black
Tail: Black hackle fibres
Body: Black Flexi Floss
Throat: Black hen
Cheeks: Jungle cock

OLIVE DIAWL BACH
Hook: Heavy gauge size 12-14
Thread: Medium olive
Tail: Medium olive hackle fibres
Body: Medium olive Flexi floss
Thorax: Grey SLF
Throat hackle: Medium olive hen
Cheeks: Jungle cock dyed yellow

BIBIO VARIANT No 1
Hook: Light wire size 14
Thread: Black
Body: Black seal's fur
Rib: Fine red holographic tinsel
Legs: Pheasant tail fibres, dyed red
Hackle: Black cock

RED HOLO DIAWL BACH
Hook: Heavy gauge size 12-14
Thread: Red
Butt: Glo-Brite No3
Tail: Brown hackle fibres
Body: Peacock herl
Rib: Fine copper wire
Cheeks: Red holographic tinsel
Throat hackle: Brown hackle fibres

PALE OLIVE SPIDER
Hook: Light wire size 14
Thread: Medium olive
Body: Pale olive SLF
Wing: Grey DNA fibres, split into a V
Thorax: Lime green SLF
Hackle: Light grey dun, underside trimmed

Chapter Four: Casting off

Contents

Flies and fly-tying	192-203
Competition fishing	204-213
Catch-and-release	214-219
The future	220-225

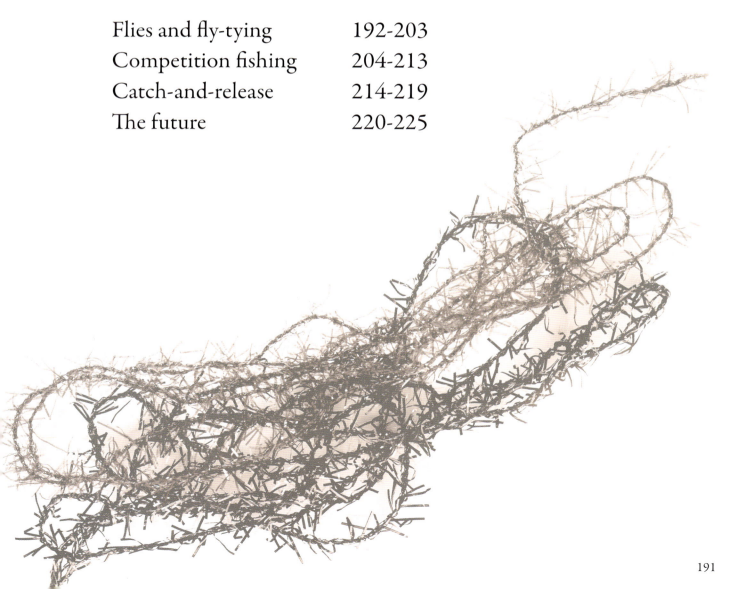

Flies and fly-tying

FLY-TYING IS one of the great passions in my life; my world as an angler would not be complete without it.

The book that has provided me the most inspiration and information is John Veniard's Fly Dressing Guide. In over 30 years' of fly-tying, I've often referred to this book. It is, in my opinion, one of the finest fly-pattern books ever published. Another great source of information on modern materials and flies are the game fishing magazines. Whenever I read something of interest I cut it out and, after years of collecting, have now built up a huge file I can refer to. Often before visiting a new fishery I will open my file of cuttings and see if there is any useful information pertaining to that particular water. However, one thing I have often noticed is discrepancies between the photo of a fly and its tying recipe. For the fly tyer, this inconsistency can cause real problems and because of this I have striven to be as accurate as I can be when listing the materials for each fly. However, nothing is ever that simple and, to ensure that I am not having a similar effect on fellow fly tyers, the descriptions given earlier should be read in conjunction with the following overview of materials.

HOOKS

In almost every pattern shown, Kamasan hooks have been used. Since switching to these hooks, I have encountered very few problems with either hooking or holding fish, even with the light-wire models which were

Favourite hooks: (clockwise from top left) Kamasan B175 (10 and 14) B100 and B170

once the bane of angler's lives. The heavy gauge B175s and the B100 Grub Hooks could tow a bus, the latter being excellent for tying heavy Buzzers. The B175 is my preferred choice for wet-flies and nymphs such as Diawl Bachs and longshank Buzzers. I also tie many of my small river wet-flies on these hooks making use of the critical weight in the design. The B100 is shy on shank, and generous in gape so lends itself to tying round the bend, providing the fly tyer with options to adjust the fly's body length. For my lake and stillwater dry-flies I now tie all my patterns on B170s. This particular hook has excellent strength and holding ability – so necessary when a trout takes off on a violent run.

THREADS

I was fortunate enough, some years ago, to have purchased a quantity of real silk threads and flosses. Wherever possible I have used Pearsall's Gossamer silk as the tying thread and Pearsall's Naples floss for the bodies. Colours such as waxed Primrose Gossamer and Green Naples are required to replicate the exact hue of the bodies for the Greenwell's patterns illustrated in the book. I realise that these materials are difficult to acquire today but, fortunately, the majority of the colours used for floss bodies are black and green, for which there are suitable substitutes. I have also used Glo Brite fluorescent floss in some patterns. The range of colours is excellent for adding a distinctive butt on a variety of patterns.

A colourful array of traditional silk threads and flosses

A wonderful range of dyed seal's furs

DUBBING

I use Mosaic Dubbing on a variety of dry-fly and wet-fly patterns. The fur comes blended with tiny strands of holographic tinsels and is excellent for dry-fly and sedge imitations. When prescribing seal's fur, the colours come from the extensive range by Frankie McPhillips. His blend of seal's fur colours is simply magnificent. I have also blended a number of furs myself; the colours are described in the tying recipes, but it's almost impossible for me to quantify the mix. When combining seal's fur with hare's fur, as in the Stone Fly, the mix is usually 60/40 in favour of seal's fur. Strategically placed but not overdone, UV dubbing can have a dramatic effect on a fly's performance.

For the bodies of small, river dry-flies I have extensively used Davy Wotton's SLF Masterclass Blends. Orvis Ice Dubbing is my preferred choice for the thorax of many nymphs and Emerger patterns. I have also used Micro Brite for the thorax of numerous small wet-fly patterns; these colours come from Veniard's extra-fine range. I have also replaced peacock herl in the thorax of my patterns with Micro Brite, simply because of its superior light-reflective qualities.

WINGS AND WIRES

For the wings of river dry-flies and stillwater Emergers, EPS fibres and DNA strands are my favourite materials. Both of these new products have excellent light-reflective qualities. For the winging on some wet-fly dressings I have used dyed hen pheasant wings in yellow and golden olive. These, and all of the dyed jungle cock feathers, were supplied by the late Rod Tye. From the range of dyed jungle cock feathers available, the most productive colour, in my opinion, is yellow. When I've added yellow jungle cock to patterns such as the Black Jungle Cock and Sooty Olive my catch rate has increased noticeably.

Dyed jungle cock, employed in the cheeks of some Diawl Bachs and Crunchers, can also be effective, yellow again is quite distinctive but so too is orange. I also purchased a number of dyed, grizzle saddle capes from Rod, particularly those used in the tying of dry sedge patterns. Rod certainly had an excellent eye for colour. UNI-French is my preferred choice when tinsels are required. Unlike a number of other products on the market that quickly become tarnished with time, this brand of materials holds its original sheen after considerable use.

REFLECTION

Undoubtedly, my inspiration for tying flies came from my father and my tying style from the River Suir. On reflection, creating imitative patterns for the river was a great place to start - such influences are still an integral part of my fly-tying psyche. I am always looking to create that perfect fly – if it exists – and I take failure to heart,

Effective colours of UV Straggle

DNA strands: A superb winging material for many dry-flies and Emergers

particularly when my creations aren't as effective as I'd hoped. After a bit of sulking, I soon bounce back eager to return to the vice to make those vital corrections. Having worked in the construction industry all my life I am essentially a production man at heart and never recognised that fly-tying offered a means of expressing my creativity. I'm pleased, then, that even after 40 years at the vice I still have plenty of ideas and creating new patterns is just something that comes naturally to me. There's no doubt that fishing on UK reservoirs has left its mark. The exciting thing about stillwater fly-fishing is that nothing stands still, creating limitless opportunities to experiment with flies and methods.

COLOUR AND FORM

I frequently have to discipline myself to tie a range of sizes of a particular pattern. I suffer from a low boredom threshold and my instinct is to endlessly tie something different. This has a big drawback, as I have often had cause on the water to regret not tying a couple more of a particular fly, in different sizes. Now, I aim to have at least four samples of my most successful patterns at all times.

The last ten years have been a particularly interesting period in fly-tying, with new materials coming on to the market every season. The speed of change is quite surprising but also exciting. The correct colour and shape are elements every tyer should strive to achieve in their flies; however, just when you think you have found the perfect combination a new material turns up and sets off another chain of events. My fly-tying errs towards the imitative-style these days. It is not because I think new materials are ineffective... quite the opposite. It's simply a matter of achieving the right balance. I enjoy blending the new with the old, my tendency being to tone things down a little by using more subtle colours. An example of this is when dubbing seal's fur on to UV Straggle. While Straggle is a superb modern material there are times when its glittery effect is just a little overpowering. Over-dubbing with fur remedies the situation beautifully. The result has been hugely successful allowing me to create patterns such as the UV Claret Dabbler and UV Bibio Hopper.

Another example of combining new with old is in the Emergers I tie. I like the bodies to look realistic and to achieve this I often use Flexi Floss ribbed over a loosely-dubbed body of seal's fur. Both materials are available in a huge range of colours, so the opportunities to mix-and-match are endless.

I have a fondness for mixing colours and materials, which I attribute to my love of Irish lough-style flies. I enjoy blending different colours of seal's fur to create new and interesting effects. Many of my most successful Hoppers have two colours in the body. The idea is not to diminish the main body colour; the second colour is simply employed as a trigger point, either in the butt or the thorax. For dry or wet-flies my objective is either to imitate or stimulate – sometimes both. I prefer the bodies of my dry-flies tied loosely; in this way they add translucency and to achieve this I mostly use seal's fur in the dressings. The majority of stillwater fly-fishing methods require some form of retrieve to trigger a reaction, not so with the dry-fly. A cruising trout has plenty of time to examine your imitation so it's important to get it right especially in flat calm conditions. In the crystal clear waters of Lough Carra I found it fascinating to watch trout examining my dry-fly, the disappointing bit is when it gently turned away having detected danger. Tightly compressed bodies, particularly on dry-flies are

All manner of tinsels and wires

Dyed jungle cock: Deadly on both nymphs and wet-flies

lifeless, they also reduce buoyancy. For this reason I also avoid ribbing a fly's body, wherever I can.

In addition to seal's fur, I use two other materials to impart life to a dry-fly; they are CDC and deer hair. Adding just a few strands of deer hair under a CDC feather creates that speckled look in the wing, which is particularly effective in Emerger, and Sedge patterns.

KEEPING IT SIMPLE

Many of the flies today are far too busy and overdressed. 'Keep it simple' is a motto that should remain uppermost in fly tyers' minds. After all, why do minimalist patterns such as the Diawl Bach and the Shipman's Buzzer work so well? The cost of fly-tying materials today is also an issue and if your budget is sensitive, there are ways to be creative without breaking the bank. A few years ago, while out Christmas shopping, I ventured into a craft shop. It was like entering Aladdin's cave. I was amazed to discover all sorts of threads, beads and embellishments, all of which could be put to use in the vice at a fraction of the cost of similar fly-tying products. Indeed, much of what we use comes from handicraft hobbies. Christmas is a very productive time for the scavenging fly tyer; all those coloured tinsels on display are far too good an opportunity to miss. Some years ago, I even cut the gold holographic strands of hair from my daughter's Barbie Doll, long before any such material came on the fly-tying market. There are many ways to reduce costs for the imaginative and inventive mind. One of my most effective Mayfly bodies came from strips cut from a baby's plastic training nappy which I coloured with a permanent marker pen.

I am as guilty as most of having far too many flies in my box. Like so many other anglers I have my personal favourites for each fishery which I rely on as my starting point. But every now and then, just for the hell of it, I tie some wild inventions on the leader and give them a go. It was such experimentation that led to the discovery of the Black and Copper Partridge for Lough Lein, and the excellent AK47 Emerger and UV Claret Dabbler on stillwaters. Then there's the Silver Sedge, which works just about everywhere. These four patterns employ tying methods that may be used to create a wide range of other flies, so I have included a tying sequence on each to illustrate the key techniques.

My quiet place - at the vice

Black & Copper Partridge

THE BLACK & COPPER Partridge was my first effort at attempting to imitate an emerging black sedge. I devised the pattern over 20 years ago with Lough Lein specifically in mind. Over the years I have tinkered around the edges of the design, but this I feel, is the final version. Originally intended for the middle dropper position, the Black & Copper has since proven a great success on the top dropper and that is where I now find it fishes best. An excellent pattern and one to try when small black sedges are on the wing.

Recipe

Hook: Grub hook size 10-12
Thread: Black
Rib: Flat copper tinsel
Body: Mixed black and blue seal's fur
Wing buds: Red, holographic tinsel
Thorax: Mixed black and blue seal's fur
Wing: Black bucktail
Hackle: Brown partridge
Cheeks: Jungle cock

When the fur has been taken far enough to cover three-quarters of the hook, take hold of the copper tinsel and wind it over the body in well-spaced turns.

Secure the loose end of the copper tinsel with tying thread, then trim off the excess. Next, using a needle-tip, thoroughly tease out the fur.

Run on the thread then catch in a length of copper tinsel well round the bend. Dub on the fur-mix then wind it along the shank in close turns.

Catch in a strand of red holographic tinsel either side of the body. Dub on another pinch of the fur mix, then wind it on to form the thorax.

A PASSION FOR TROUT

With the thorax in place, pull the strands of holographic forward, so they sit along either side, and secure the loose ends just behind the eye.

Trim off the waste ends of the holographic tinsel, then take a small pinch of dyed black bucktail. Catch in the bucktail so that it sits quite upright.

Secure the bucktail with tight thread wraps and trim off the waste. Next, catch in a brown, partridge body feather, by its tip.

Take hold of the partridge feather, by its base, and wind on three full turns. Stroke the fibres at each turn so that they sweep back over the body.

Secure the hackle, then trim off the excess stem and tip. Prepare two small jungle cock feathers and catch them in either side of the thorax.

Position the jungle cock feathers so that they expose the red holographic cheeks. Finally, build the head and cast off with a whip finish.

AK47 Emerger

The AK47 was invented as a top dropper pattern with adult, black buzzers in mind. I went through a period in my fly-tying mixing Flexi Floss with fur and feathers, combining different colours. Grey Flexi floss spun over the top of black seal's fur creates the two-tone effect seen in the body of many natural insects. For the collar I use what I can only describe as a "dirty" badger cock hackle, which is very close to a light Furnace. The hackle's off-white coloured fibres and dark centre give the fly a very natural look. This is an excellent, early-season pattern for when the trout start looking to the surface for food.

Recipe

Hook: Sedge hook size 10-12
Thread: Black
Rib: Grey Flexi Floss
Body: Black
Wing buds: Red goose biots
Thorax: Black seal's fur and blue Ice Yarn, mixed
Wing: White DNA fibres
Hackle: Furnace cock hackle

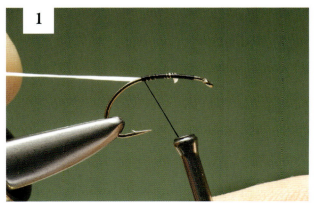

Fix the hook in the vice and run on the tying thread just behind the eye. Catch in a length of grey Flexi Floss and secure it to the shank.

Using a finger-and-thumb twist, dub the fur on to the thread to form a thin rope. Wind the fur rope in close turns along the shank, to form a slim body.

Once the fur has covered three-quarters of the shank take hold of the Flexi Floss. Stretch the floss and wind it over the body, in evenly-spaced turns.

Secure the end of the floss with thread, then remove the excess. Select two, dyed red goose biots. Shape the ends and catch them in either side of the body.

Take a mixed pinch of seal's fur and Ice Yarn and dub it on to the thread. Wind the fur from the base of the goose biots to a point just short of the eye, to form the thorax.

Take hold of the hackle by its tip, using a pair of hackle pliers. Wind on two or three full turns, working toward the eye.

Take a slim bunch of white DNA fibres. Catch them in at the eye with tight thread-turns. Position the DNA fibres at a 45-degree angle in front of the thorax.

Secure the hackle tip with tying thread before removing it with scissors. At the same time, trim away the waste end of the hackle stem.

Prepare a Furnace cock hackle by removing any soft or broken fibres from its base. Catch it in by a its bare stem immediately in front of the DNA fibres.

Stroke the hackle fibres so that they sweep back slightly over the body. Finally, build a small head with tying thread and cast off with a whip finish.

Silver Sedge

THIS IS AN old River Suir wet-fly, designed for late-evening fishing. I have made quite a few changes to what was, initially, a relatively simple fly. By adding horns of stripped hackle stems and a CDC wing, the pattern became very buoyant and can now be fished wet or dry. The further addition of deer hair strands in the wing, provides that speckled look seen in the natural sedge. When fished as part of a team of wet-flies, the Silver Sedge is an excellent top dropper pattern; the CDC wing creates a wake in the water that definitely excites the trout.

Recipe

Hook: Sedge hook size 10-12
Thread: Black or brown
Rib: Fine, silver wire
Body: Flat, silver tinsel
Body hackle: Cree cock hackle
Under wing: Natural deer hair
Wing: Natural CDC and Mirror Flash
Horns: Stripped grizzle hackle stems
Collar hackle: Cree cock hackle

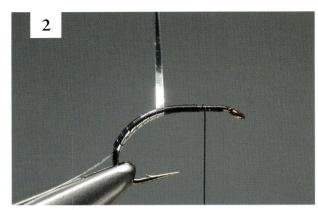

Take the thread back up the shank to a position close to the eye. Wind the flat, silver tinsel in touching-turns, to form a slim, even body, with no gaps.

Secure the loose end of the tinsel with thread and remove the excess. Next, prepare and catch in a well-marked Cree cock hackle where the body begins.

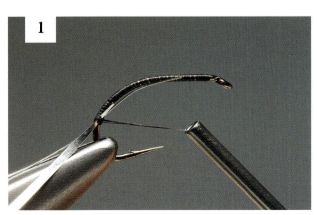

Fix the hook in the vice and run the tying thread well round the bend. Catch in a length of fine silver wire and then one of flat, silver tinsel.

Take hold of the hackle, by its tip, using a pair of hackle pliers. Wind the hackle along the body in open, evenly spaced turns.

A PASSION FOR TROUT

5 When the hackle-turns have reached the end of the body, wind the silver wire up through them. Use evenly spaced turns of wire to lock the hackle stem to the body.

6 Secure the end of the wire and remove the excess plus the hackle-tip. Take a few fibres of deer hair and catch them in so their tips project past the bend.

7 Secure the deer hair firmly then catch in a pair of natural, grey CdC plumes over the top to form the main wing. Add a couple of strands of Mirror Flash and trim away the excess CDC.

8 Catch in two stripped grizzle hackle stems, to form the horns then select a second Cree cock hackle. Remove the fibres from the hackle's base and catch it in just behind the eye.

9 Take hold of the hackle by its tip, using a pair of hackle pliers. Starting from the wing-base, apply fiver or six turns, working toward the eye.

10 Secure the hackle-tip with tight thread-turns then remove the excess. Build a small head, then cast off the tying thread with a whip finish.

201

UV Claret Dabbler

A PATTERN INITIALLY devised for stillwater wet-fly fishing, which has proven itself on wild fisheries as well. Through trial and error, I ended up mixing Mosaic dubbing with UV Straggle, thus losing that artificial, glitzy-look and ending up with a more toned-down body colour. Claret is an underused colour on reservoir flies, and I have to say, I have been surprised at just how well this pattern works for rainbows. During the summer, I tend to fish a sedge pattern on the top dropper and vary the middle dropper from time to time, but the UV Claret Dabbler will always occupy the point.

Recipe

Hook: Kamasan B175 size 10-12
Thread: Black
Tail: Dyed red pheasant tail and Mirror Flash
Rib: Fine, flat gold tinsel
Body: Claret UV Straggle and claret Mosaic
Body hackle: Claret cock hackle
Shoulder hackle: Natural red cock
Collar hackle: Bronze mallard
Cheeks: Dyed red goose biots

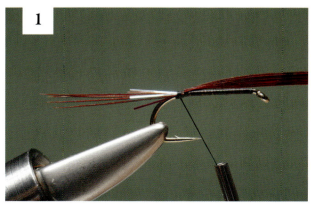

Fix the hook in the vice and run on the tying thread down to the bend. There, catch in a few strands of dyed red pheasant tail, plus short strands of Mirror Flash.

Catch in a length of fine, flat gold tinsel at the base of the tail. At exactly the same point, also catch in a couple of inches of claret UV Straggle.

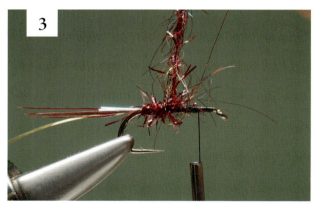

Use close-turns of tying thread to lock the waste ends of the tail, rib, and Straggle along the hook shank. That done, take a pinch of claret Mosaic and dub it on to the Straggle.

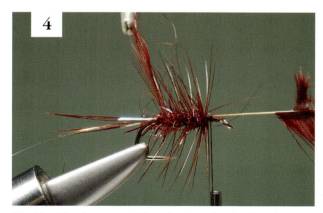

Wind the Mosaic-covered Straggle along the shank, to form the body. Next, catch in a dyed claret cock hackle and wind it down to the tail in open, evenly spaced turns..

Keeping tension on the hackle-tip so the turns of hackle remain in position, wind the gold tinsel up through them. The turns of tinsel should also be open and evenly spaced.

Secure the end of the tinsel and remove the excess, plus the hackle-tip. Catch in a natural brown cock hackle and apply three turns, to form the shoulder hackle.

Remove the excess hackle, then select two slips of bronze mallard. Catch them in both above and below the body gently easing the fibres around the sides.

If a gap is still left along either side of the body, after the bronze mallard fibres have been positioned, simply add a few extra to form a continuous collar.

Secure the bronze mallard fibres with tight thread-turns then trim off the waste. Shape the ends of two dyed red goose biots and use them to form cheeks.

Fix the biots firmly in place before trimming off the waste ends. Build a small head with tying thread, before casting off with a whip finish.

Competition fishing

I FIRST ENTERED a major competition when I was just 17 years old, awarded a place on the club team to fish the Munster Lake Championships on Lough Lein in Killarney.

Being essentially a river angler, I knew very little about lake fishing and was finding it a new and difficult experience. The night before the big competition I was out on the town and was so late getting home I decided not to risk a front door entry and instead opted for a more stealthy approach.

I climbed up on the back wall then on to the roof of the single-storey extension, and in through my bedroom window. I was about to get undressed when I heard my father shuffling about in the adjacent room. I dived into the bed fully-clothed just before the door opened and my father told me it was time to get up!

I survived the long car journey down to Killarney and even the first few hours' of fishing but, eventually, tiredness and the rocking motion of the boat took its toll. I managed to land a qualifying trout on my very first cast but after that it was a tale of woe. I became so tired that I went into automatic pilot; I continued casting as if I were fully awake but lost every trout I brought to the flies. I had no idea how many trout I had moved or hooked during the day but, unbeknown to me, the boatman had been keeping a tally. Unfortunately, he was also on chatting terms with my father and, after the competition, wasted no time in seeking him out. Seven trout won the competition that day and I had apparently missed over eighty takes!

I certainly knew I had risen loads of fish and, as my father frequently reminded me, I had thrown away a great chance to become the youngest ever Munster Champion. I still somehow managed to qualify for the Interprovincial Final at my very first attempt but, unfortunately, as my finances at the time were unable to stretch as far as the entry fee, I never did get to fish in that final. Not long after that competition, I set off for England to work, stayed for eleven months, and returned to Ireland after a serious bout of home-sickness (her name was Rosie!).

THRIVING ON COMPETITION

On my return to England two years later, despite being approached on a number of occasions, I neglected the invitation to join one of the local angling club teams. I now regret being a shrinking violet.

In those early years in England I did manage to qualify for, and fish, a couple of Troutmaster Finals, but these were considered more fun days rather than serious competition. While some anglers don't like competition fishing, I've since discovered that I thrive on it. In my opinion, competition fishing sharpens angling skills and improves your overall knowledge of techniques and flies.

For some 20 years in the UK, my fishing had been, perhaps, too leisurely; you might call it 'pleasure fishing' though, as I discovered later, competitions can also bring plenty of pleasure. I still believe I would have been a much sharper angler had I started fishing trout matches a good deal earlier.

In 1995, things got a little more interesting. My brother Tommy had qualified to fish for the Ireland A Team in the European Championships to be held on

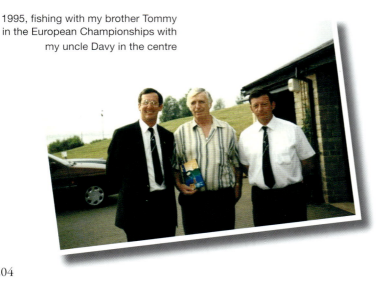

1995, fishing with my brother Tommy in the European Championships with my uncle Davy in the centre

55 years on, Munster Lake Champion 2005 & 2006

My father, on the right, being presented with the Mangan Cup after winning the Munster Lake Championship in 1950

Rutland Water. I joined up with the team at Rutland and stayed with them for a few days. Some of the team had little or no experience of fishing for rainbow trout on stillwaters; my time in England had, at least, afforded me some knowledge of the subject.

So I gave them whatever advice and assistance I could. My flies must have been of some use to the guys, as my boxes were practically emptied. 'Cleaned out' is, I think, the correct expression.

The evening before the competition I received a bombshell of a call from the manager of the team: "How would you like to represent your country?" he asked. Ireland had travelled to the UK with three reserves, and the organisers allowed Ireland to enter a C team with very little notice. I made up the final place in the team of four. A sleepless night followed!

If you're not acquainted with boat-fishing matches, this is how it works on most of them. The boat's big enough for only two anglers. So, by way of fair play, angling pairs are drawn from opposing teams, each to monitor the other's honesty.

My fishing partner for the day was a chap from Belgium; unfortunately, the competition was halted half way through the afternoon due to a dangerous thunderstorm hanging over the reservoir and, allegedly, striking one member of the English team. Shortly before the steward's fast boat rounded us up and sent us back to harbour – with bolts of lightning streaking across the sky – I caught my only trout of the day and saved myself from a dreaded 'blank.' The Ireland A team, meanwhile, finished with the bronze medals, behind England, while France took the gold.

It was my first taste of a major international competition and I thoroughly enjoyed the whole experience. Great friendships are made during these Internationals, some of which are for life.

RECENT TIMES

It has been only in the last seven years that I have got back into serious competition fishing again. In the intervening years, I would meet up with various Irish teams whenever major competitions were staged in the UK, helping them out with flies and stillwater techniques. It would be 2003 before I'd again be in a position to fish a major competition and attempt qualification into the national team through the competition route in Ireland.

In 2003, I fished the Munster Lake Championships in Killarney. It had been an absence of over 20 years and I was rusty; I finished just outside the top 20. I certainly had enough chances that day to have done a lot better.

I also had an unfortunate incident that year; I inadvertently left my fishing partner for the day on the shore. The number of the boat we were using was printed in the programme, so, having tackled up, I headed off to where the boat was moored, assuming my partner would automatically do the same. Neither I nor my boatman that day, Malcolm O'Brien were made aware of our responsibilities to find my fishing partner. So we waited for him as long as possible, and after a 'no show', we headed out into Bog Bay to join the rest of the boats for the start of the competition. I wrongly thought that my partner had not turned up; with over 200 anglers competing on the day, it is not unreasonable to assume a few might fall by the wayside. Unfortunately, on this day my partner was there, lost among the milling crowd.

Since that day, I have always made it a priority to find my partner as early as possible on the morning of a competition. To the partner I didn't find that year, my sincere apologies. It is as unacceptable to be left on the shore as it was unintentional.

THE VERY SAME TROPHY

Two years later, 2005 proved to be a great year for me as I won the Munster Lake Championship by catching 11 trout. Collecting the trophy was also quite an emotional moment for deeply personal reasons. Up until that year, my father had been the only member of our fishing club to win the Lake Championship, in 1950. Fifty five years on, I was to become the second O'Farrell whose name was on the cup. It was quite surreal to be holding the very same trophy my father had held in his hands all those years before.

My club also had one of its most successful years in 2005; two other anglers, Richie Rowe and Willie Burke, finished in second and ninth places to complete one of our best years in the Lake Championships.

I captained Munster in 2005 for the Interprovincial finals in September. The team went on to win both Interprovincial finals on Loughs Lein and Mask. I finished in sixth place overall on Lough Lein which I was pleased about; but it was not good enough to make the national team that year. 2006 was to prove to be an even better year; I went on to win the Munster Lake Championship in May for the second year running.

Having fished on various drifts throughout the day, it was getting close to three o'clock and I had nothing to show for my efforts. A black cloud was hanging over my head and I couldn't help feeling the dreaded blank was looming. The thought of going from Hero to Zero in just one year, was almost too much to bear. Then as we approached the mouth of Bog bay I caught two trout fairly quickly and lost several more.

For some inexplicable reason, the water in the lower end of Bog Bay was very dirty and clouded so we stayed outside of it, near the mouth of the bay. I then had an unusual experience; while drifting slowly past the point of an island I was able to make six casts into a difficult inlet between some rocks. Each cast resulted in a take. I landed five out of the six trout I hooked in a matter of minutes. I caught two more trout after that, one from the

Ireland's Autumn International team that fished Mentieth in September 2007

same spot again and another in the next drift before the competition ended. I finished up with nine trout which was just good enough to take first place again.

I captained Munster once more that year. We did not do so well when we fished the TAFI Interprovincial in September on Lough Owel, but one week later we went on to win the ITFFA Championship held on Lough Lene near Collinstown for the second year in a row. I finished in sixth place overall and qualified to fish the Autumn International which was due to be held in Scotland in 2007. I was going for three in a row when I fished the Munster Lake Championship in May 2007, a feat which had never previously been achieved. I came close by finishing sixth.

But for a little bad luck near the end it might have been a different story. With 15 minutes to go, I hooked and lost a trout which I estimated to be around 2lb, but I suppose everyone has hard luck stories on the day.

I had again qualified to fish on the Munster team, and in September of that year we won the ITFFA Interprovincial on Lough Lein, making it three wins in a row, which was a fantastic achievement for the team.

HOME INTERNATIONALS

Fishing for Ireland in the Home Internationals was a great experience and one that I would love to repeat. I thoroughly enjoyed the whole event.

Robert Reilly was a first-class team captain, having represented his country eight times and won the coveted Brown Bowl. He had all the experience required to lead the team. No surprise that Robert has now taken on the role of International team coach. Michael Callaghan looked after the team very well and provided for our every need. He even managed to keep us away from the bar after each practice day.

Michael's 'up and at them' war speech the evening before the match is one I shall never forget. I made some great friends during the International and have remained in contact with some of the guys ever since.

I fished my first National Angling Championships in 2008 on Lough Conn in April and, along with a hundred or so other anglers, drew a blank. Conn seemed to set the scene for the year with difficult conditions on the day of major competitions. The day was very bright with little wind in the afternoon. Although I had qualified for the previous three National Finals I did not fish them,

as several of these events were staged the day before the Munster Lake Championship in Killarney. It was simply not feasible to fish this competition and then face a marathon car journey back down south that evening and do justice to the Munster Championships the following day. It was also not fair on the Munster lads; some of them attempted to fish both competitions back to back, and were worn out at the end of it.

I was shocked to discover later, contrary to what I'd been told, that there were qualifying places for the Ireland team to be won in the National Final. It just goes to show how much I needed to learn about the competition scene in Ireland. Had I not been misinformed or been so ignorant I might have made a greater effort to fish this competition more often. I missed my chances.

The Munster Lakes competition came again in May, on another flat-calm day. I finished in seventh place overall and, for the fourth year in succession, retained my place in the Munster team. The TAFI Interprovincial was fished in September on Lough Lein. Munster won the final and I finished in eight place overall, earning myself a qualifying place on the Ireland team sheet to fish the European Championships in 2009. We were not so lucky the following week on Lough Leane in the ITFFA final. Munster were going for four wins in a row but we ended up finishing in third spot. I did not help the team any by having a shocker of a day.

THE WORLD CUP

The World Cup on Lough Mask is a wonderful competition, as I discovered the first time I entered it.

The inaugural competition was staged on Mask in 1953, and now attracts anglers from all over the world, as befits its name. The list of winners since 1953 contain some famous names in Irish angling circles, including my good friend Dick Willis. Dick likes to remind me about his World Cup victory every time we meet.

Mask is an enormous expanse of water covering an area of 20,431 acres and is a daunting lake when first encountered. The event is staged over five days; the first four are qualifying heats, with the final normally fished on the August Bank Holiday Monday.

It is a credit to the organisers that they can manage hundreds of anglers arriving on the shore each day for their heats, and get them out safely on to the lake on time and without incident. Yes, it's a great competition, but

COMPETITION FISHING

World Cup 2009. Kevin Rowe being presented with the trophy for heaviest trout of the whole competition

for many of us it also manages to be a major social event, spread over five days. For the small town of Ballinrobe, it provides a commercial windfall, too, with hundreds of anglers and their friend's descending on the area seeking lodgings, food and a pint!

I fished my heat on the second day of the competition and qualified for the final on Monday. Having created some spare time, I packed my gear and immediately headed off down the road for an evening's fishing on Lough Carra. James, whom I hire my boat from on Lough Carra, thought I was mad to be going fishing again after being on Mask all day. I suppose fishing like this could be considered a form of madness by some, but when your days are limited as mine, you pack in every bit of fishing you can. I caught a couple of superb trout that evening on the dry Black Sedge, and my fishing appetite was, finally, sated.

I got off to a great start on the morning of the final. I had a trout in the boat after only fifteen minutes and lost an even bigger one minutes later. Billy Graham, the winner of this competition in 1999, was our boatman for the day so we were in good hands. The time speeds by quickly when with a knowledgeable angler like Billy.

As seemed to happen on all the major competitions in 2008, the wind died to nothing after a few hours and we spent most of the rest of the day fishing in a millpond. Without a ripple, fishing gets tough, but I raised two more trout, and missed both takes, finishing up just outside the top 20. Not a bad effort for my first attempt, I thought. I once again headed off to Carra for the evening. James insisted I eat before going fishing. We sat in front of his bungalow on the shoreline on a lovely summer's evening looking out across the water and having a good old chat. It was a conversation I'm glad I had because it was to prove my last with him. James passed away a few months later.

One of our club members, Kevin Rowe, fared the best of all of us, winning the prize for the heaviest trout with a fish of 4lb 7oz. His prize for catching this impressive brown trout wasn't bad, either; a brand-new lake boat. By coincidence, another member of our club, John Purtil, had caught the heaviest fish the year before and also won a boat. If this keeps up, we will have to dig a marina in Tipperary to accommodate the club flotilla.

The crowds that gather on the final day of the World Cup to see the boats off in the morning – and greet them on their return in the evening – are amazing. I had never previously encountered such tremendous local support for any fishing competition.

I visited the late Rod Tye several times over the course of the competition for help and advice; I was not very familiar with Lough Mask. Rod was a brilliant angler and a mine of information about flies and tactics. We also chewed the fat about Lough Carra, sharing different experiences and trading fly patterns. I met up with Rod again in early 2009 to discuss this book and he had kindly agreed to write a section in it relating to my fly-tying and choice of patterns.

A DIFFICULT YEAR

Rod sadly passed away later that year. Never one to give up or complain, he fought his illness right to the very end. The sport of angling is a poorer place without him but his legacy lives on through the many fishing articles he has written down the years.

What a difficult year 2009 turned out to be. It may have been the loss of my job in the recession or something else, but I couldn't help feeling that the bad-luck cloud was forever suspended above my head.

My first major competition of the New Year was the Munster Lake Championships held on Lough Lein in May. I boated over 20 trout that day but only one big enough to count. How frustrating. The competition was won by my good friend Mick Linehan with seven trout. I also lost my place on the Munster team, after four consecutive years of being in it, which didn't go down too well in my psyche.

Next up was the National Final in June on Lough

Owel. My son David also qualified for this, his first major final, and enjoyed a great day partnered with Pat Foley. I believe the *craic* in the boat that day was excellent. The temperature on the day of the final dropped significantly and, within an hour of the start, the heavens opened and a bitter cold rain fell like a waterfall.

Unfortunately for me, my jacket leaked. For the first time ever I had to abandon a competition before the end as I had become so cold and wet that I no longer had any feeling in my hands. I could not even remove the fly from the one trout I did land. The jacket is, belatedly, in the bin.

David boated two trout in the final, one of which measured long enought to count, but he was unlucky to lose half a dozen more. I would have been delighted had he won a place on the Ireland team. Next time, maybe! For me, one of the highlights of competition was the night before the final. I ran into my good friends from the Ireland team who'd fished with me on Mentieth; Eddie Harte and Robert Reilly. John Quirke travelled over from Dublin and was in good form and, when John is on form, a great night will always be had by all...

LEXUS EUROPEAN CHAMPIONSHIPS

As a landmark, 2009 was the first year I entered a major competition in the UK. I chose the Lexus European Fly Fishing Championship, superbly managed by England International angler John Horsey.

It's a competition that attracts fly fishers from all over Europe. I chose a qualifying heat on Pitsford Water in July and finished in second place, landing 16 trout, and qualified at the final on Chew Valley in September.

The final was fished on September 1, following a week of strong winds. My boat partner for the day was Czech angler Milan Hladik. It was fun, and we have remained in contact ever since, but my bad luck continued. I landed three trout on my trusty Dabblers but lost 11 others. Five trout won the competition. I could have cried.

Squeezed in between the Lexus qualifier and final, I again managed to fish the World Cup on Lough Mask. Against the flow, I was feeling pretty good for my qualifying heat on Mask, as I had landed ten trout on Lough Carra in the previous couple of days' outings. Despite the lake being whipped by storm-force winds during the heats, I managed to qualify for the final with two trout caught on a Daddy Longlegs.

The final was fished in good weather but Mask, like so many other large waters, is all about being in the right place at the right time and taking your chances. I managed only one trout and missed several others. Once I realised I had no real chance of winning, the tension in the boat lifted and I had a great laugh with our boatman David Hall. David made the mistake of telling us a tale about his superb boating skills and I didn't stop ribbing him for the rest of the day.

EUROPEAN CHAMPIONSHIPS-KILLARNEY

Boy, was I looking forward to the European Championships in Killarney. Although I have lived in the UK for more than 25 years, I consider Lough Lein my home water.

The other venues used in the championship – which tests anglers' skills by moving them from one water to the next – were Lough Carragh and the River Blackwater. I had never fished Carragh but understood that the tactics for this lake were not dissimilar to Lough Lein. Overall, I felt I had a reasonable chance of doing well for my country, and my confidence only improved after winning the first session on Lough Lein.

I headed off to my second session, on the river, that afternoon feeling very buoyant. Then it all went pear-shaped. Unfortunately, I blanked which is the one thing that had to

A nearly day: The 2009 Lexus final on Chew

Elinor's Ed Foster, casting a long line on Rutland

be avoided at all cost. The penalty points which a blank attracts are terminally damaging in this competition.

I tipped two trout and actually lost three more as I played them on the river session but that's how it goes sometimes, I told myself with an uncharacteristic positivity. I won the fourth session, on Lough Carragh, but had not achieved the consistency I so badly needed. Both Irish teams were very disappointed with their final placings in the championships, especially as we were fishing on home ground. I returned to England pondering the whole thing, more than a little disillusioned. France won the championship, followed by the Czech Republic in silver medal place and Poland picking up the bronze.

I never enter anything unless I feel I can win. I can just about cope with losing provided I have given it my all. But I remember thinking afterwards that, if Irish teams of the future want to compete and not just make up the numbers in the European and World Championships, a serious rethink is required. The strength of any team is its structure. Everything should be about team structure, and nothing else. I believe that, if we are to compete as a country, we need to understand how the most successful countries get it so right, and mirror their structure, planning and tactics.

Ireland is not short of angling talent. It continues to produce many fine anglers who are more than capable of beating any opposition on their day. Dave Donavan was a case in point at the European Championship. He took the individual bronze medal and was never out of the top section of the results from Day One, proving his skills and consistency over all five sessions. Ireland needs a team of similar, consistent anglers (which, on this evidence, possibly counts me out!) but it needs more than that; we must harness these individual qualities and turn them into a strong unit with an overriding hunger and desire to win.

UK COMPETITIONS

Since taking up competition fishing several years ago, I have adjusted my fishing methods in England. With the exception of Elinor, which I love fishing early in the season, I now tend to veer away from fishing the smaller waters and concentrate more on the likes of Draycote, Pitsford and Grafham.

The difficulties most anglers face when arriving on a large water is to locate the fish and ascertain the depth they are holding at. On smaller waters, locating the fish is less of a challenge; these fisheries tend to be reasonably well stocked and do not run to any great depths. In a day, or sometimes in a morning, you can fish the entire bank or cover most areas by boat.

To be successful on the bigger waters you generally have to work a little harder at finding and catching the fish. I restrict myself in my choice of flies these days. I now rarely fish with beaded or weighted flies on stillwaters, in an attempt to condition myself to competition rules which don't allow them.

I may be restricting myself at times but, by raising the bar for myself, I get greater pleasure from my fishing. Each to his own, but I would rather take up golf than spend my day casting a two-inch lure and waiting for a fish to pull.

LAKE OF MENTEITH

Located in Scotland's lowland region not far from Stirling, Menteith is a beautiful lake and a superb fishery; the quality of the rainbows there are simply outstanding.

It was the venue for the 2007 Home International. I was fishing the competiton, and the team had practiced hard every day on the lead up to the competition. I was paired with Scottish angler Gus Shepherd. Menteith is home waters for Gus and he had high expectations on the day, but sadly for him it was not to be. I finished up with three trout, catching a couple on the dry-fly. I had

A great dry-fly water – the beautiful Lake of Menteith

HEATHER FLY

OLIVE & ORANGE HOPPER

UV BIBIO

some success on the practice days fishing with dry-flies.

I had tied a Bibio using black and red UV Straggle that trout seem to like. I also got a glimpse of an insect that hatches on Menteith in August. As soon as I got back to the vice I tied up some imitations, which I think represent the adult insect quite well.

Menteith was also my first encounter with blue trout. These trout look more like salmon than rainbows and they are powerfully built. The scrap from one of these wonderful fish was simply amazing and it got even better when I hooked several of them on the dry-fly.

Apart from the beautiful scenery, what I enjoyed most about Menteith was being able to fish the dry-fly in shallow water along the banks of rushes; it reminded me so much of Lough Carra. There was a great sense of anticipation every time I popped the fly in tight along the edge of the reeds. On more than one occasion that anticipation was rewarded with a cracking trout.

On the big day, Ireland collected the wooden spoon and Wales won the event. But I fell in love with Menteith. One day, I'll be back there.

Menteith Hoppers

HEATHER FLY
Hook: Light wire size 12
Thread: Black
Body: Black UV Straggle
Wing: CDC, dyed red
Legs: Pheasant tail, dyed red
Hackle: Grizzle dyed fiery brown

OLIVE & ORANGE HOPPER
Hook: Kamasan B 175 size 12
Thread: Olive or black
Body: Olive Mosaic dubbing
Rib: Hot orange Ultra wire
Thorax: Orange Mosaic dubbing
Wing: CDC, dyed olive
Legs: Pheasant tail, dyed orange
Hackle: Grizzle, dyed fiery brown

UV BIBIO
Hook: Light wire size 12
Thread: Black
Body: UV Straggle-black/red/black
Wing: Natural CDC
Legs: Pheasant tail, dyed red
Hackle: Black cock hackle

A cracking Menteith blue

THE LENGTHS YOU GO TO

Living in England while simultaneously using the route to national qualification in Ireland is not easy and, more to the point, very expensive. For every major competition in Ireland I have to build two extra days into my plans to accommodate the flights. This has proved so difficult with work commitments, I sometimes fly into Ireland the evening before a competition and back the day after, allowing no time for practice.

A prime example of just one of those weeks went something like this: Got up early on Friday morning and said goodbye to my wife and kids. Attended a board meeting that morning then rushed off to Stansted Airport to catch the afternoon flight to Knock. I met up with my friend Willie Burke that evening; Willie had kindly driven up from Tipperary with most of my fishing gear.

The next morning I was out on Mask to fish the Interprovincial Final. My boat partner for the day was Basil Shields from Lough Corrib, a man with a reputation as an exceptional angler and, as it turned out, a gentleman to boot. After a good trouncing from Basil in the final, I went on to fish Lough Carra the following morning before heading off on a four-hour car journey south to Tipperary to see my family. Yes. It really is a long way to Tipperary – even from Mayo. The following day I caught a flight from Cork Airport to Edinburgh to join up with the Irish team. A friend picked me up at the airport and drove me to the hotel near Sterling where the team was staying. Tuesday was our first practice session, I enjoyed a great day's fishing with Eddie Harte but had to leave early to catch another flight down south to attend a board meeting the following day. So, on Wednesday morning I attended a main board meeting and straight afterwards shot off to Luton for my return flight to Scotland to catch up with the team for the evening's debrief meeting and fly-tying session. Thursday, up early, for a practice day followed by another team meeting and more fly-tying . We finished up at around 12pm that night.

Friday, we fished the International match and after the evening meal, had a few scoops and a singsong with the boys until the wee hours of the morning.

Saturday, up early to catch my flight to Luton and prove to my family that their father actually existed.

Monday morning, it was up at 5am to catch a flight to Glasgow. I was the Director appointed to present the Group's results to our two companies in Scotland. Monday night, I slept like a baby. However, it wasn't long before I was back in Ireland, on Lough Lein, to fish the club qualifier for the following year's Munster team. Who ever said fishing is relaxing?

Catch-and-release

THE CATCH-AND-RELEASE movement continues to grow. Each year its mantra reaches out to increasing numbers of fishermen, throughout the world. The practise of catching and then returning game fish, rather than killing them, has its roots in North America and was aimed at conserving their declining stocks.

In Europe, salmon anglers have also had to face this same issue. For many, the mental barrier of releasing a hard-won salmon, even though it was doing the right thing for the future of the fishery, was difficult to overcome. Thankfully, what was initially seen as draconian legislation has begun to change the mindset of many salmon anglers and those who also fish for wild trout.

It's increasingly noticeable that some authors of trout- or salmon-fishing articles feel compelled to record the number of fish released. But this change in attitudes is not a perfectly smooth process and while these articles may be helpful in spreading the gospel, I doubt very much whether mere political correctness and moral debate will be enough to alter some deeply entrenched attitudes. To bring about a cultural change in anything always takes time. Taking fish home for the table, especially in rural areas, was once a necessity. But fly fishing is now more of a leisure activity and, with stocks of wild fish in decline, concern for the environment should trump mere greed.

Perhaps the greatest resistance to change is tradition. 'This is how we have always done things' is an attitude that pervades much of life but is not an adequate defence for not trying something different. The injured party feels they are being denied a right; something is being taken away from them. That's understandable, but the world is a changing place.

THE SUIR IN DAYS GONE BY

In my father's day, fish supplemented wages and provided food. Fishing back then could best be described as a necessity rather than sport – or maybe a bit of both. One of nine children, I was brought up on a diet of salmon and trout. Religious doctrines at the time dictated that no meat could be eaten on a Friday. So, hail, rain or shine, my father's job every Thursday during the season was to provide a fish for the following day's table. Agricultural methods were not as intensive or advanced as they are today, and human pollution – in a country so sparsely populated – was not a major problem. The river was in excellent health, and so was the aquatic insect life, with prolific hatches of olives and sedges.

Stocks of wild brown trout in the Suir were simply astounding. There is an area just below the bridge in The Swiss Cottage on the river known as Heavey's Lawn. It is a gap of little more than ten yards between the bridge and a tall tree. It is a well-known hotspot for trout. I often watched a couple of anglers as they worked both banks with the dry-fly and, in a matter of hours, took 20 or 30 trout from this one small section in the river.

As if by magic, the pools would refill with trout within days. This was true of all good trout pools in the river, as the biggest trout will aggressively move in to the most productive feeding areas. Yet even the older generation of anglers recognised the penalties of over-fishing, despite excellent stocks of trout in the river. My father would seldom return to an area he'd fished for several days, sometimes 'resting' it for more than a week. New trout would then, inevitably, colonise the prime pools that had recently been vacated.

DRIVEN TO DISTRACTION

The wet-fly angler would be driven to total distraction early in the season by catching unwanted salmon parr. I watched massive shoals of parr build up in front of the weir in Cahir, waiting for the right water conditions to allow them to swim towards the sea.

Then time moved on. Until there is sufficient and sustained change, such sights will be confined to history books and anecdote. The returning salmon have fared no better. They were once so plentiful on the Suir, my father could afford to choose which fish he would target. Paticular lies in the river, known as salmon 'stands' to

Carefully releasing a nicely-conditioned brown trout

local anglers, would be renowned for producing many fish. Other stands would have a reputation for holding bigger-than-average salmon. It was on these particular spots that my father would concentrate his efforts, usually ignoring the rest.

This is a far cry from how things are today. The river's spring and summer runs of salmon have shrunk pitifully. The Suir flows for 114 miles and, as such, is the second longest river in Ireland. Yet, despite the serious decline in salmon stocks and the efforts of the clubs on the Suir, no support or assistance can be found to fund a hatchery to aid recovery. This is at a time when a number of the major spawning streams have become polluted, or silted up, and cormorant predation is at its peak.

INFORMED DECISIONS

In 2007, the Suir was designated a catch-and-release fishery by the Regional Fishery Board. Some salmon anglers on the Suir feel that the measures introduced by the authorities are Draconian. I cannot help feeling that this decision was reached in some part on the basis of scant catch records returned by salmon anglers at the end of each season to the Fisheries Board. The Board can make informed decisions based only on statistics.

If catch returns were suppressed or neglected, to puposely suggest that the fishing had been poor, a decision had to be made. If, year on year, catch statistics indicated diminishing stock, the Fishery Board had to act. So the law now states that fishing for salmon on the River Suir is confined to the use of a single, barbless hook and that all salmon must be safely returned.

A wild salmon and brown trout fishery that restocks itself through nature is a wonderful gift. We are here as individuals for only a short time and, as custodians of the river, clubs and individuals have a duty of care to ensure that those who come after us do not look back and blame this generation for doing nothing to save the river; or even worse, accuse us of having contributed to its destruction.

There can be no justification whatsoever for killing salmon illegally. The simple fact remains that a dead salmon cannot spawn. Given that the commercial nets which scooped out thousands of fish have finally been removed, we now have the greatest opportunity in years to allow the salmon time to recover. The long view is required here and the thinking is not rocket science. The more salmon that are allowed to swim upstream to spawn the quicker the stocks will recover. We have witnessed what over-fishing has done to the Ocean's cod and herring stocks. Today, we are seeing mass media attention directed at the devastation of the blue fin tuna. To my mind, a combination of education, common sense and properly enforced legislation is the only way to combat this overriding need to kill everything.

An alternative solution which the authorities may have considered is the introduction of a limited number of fish tags to each salmon angler, attached to every fish that is killed. Should these be used up, the individual could then resort to catch-and-release. Personally I would only be in favour of this when salmon stocks show significant signs of recovery. The idea is that a bag check would reveal any un-tagged salmon but such measures still require the honesty and integrity of each angler and the support of club members in enforcing the law. Still, all of these attitudes are not confined to anglers and clubs on the Suir.

The same debates, offering up the same excuses, have been and will continue to be used by others across the world. For those that require scientific evidence of the benefits of catch-and-release, the case studies already exist from North America and Russia.

GLORY FOR SOME

Some clubs on the Suir introduced trout bag limits several years ago. Others have increased the size limit for takeable trout. These are all positive moves towards conservation and I applaud all of them. Bragging rites and boasting still play a very important but negative part in the world of fishing today. I suppose killing small trout just adds to the body count and the glory for some.

We all like to recall those exceptional fishing days; it's what anglers tend to do when they meet on social occasions. Fortunately, the displaying of baskets of dead trout in these modern times is generally frowned upon on most fisheries.

MODERN COMMUNICATIONS

Oddly enough I feel mobile phones are also having a

Allowing a rainbow time to recover

detrimental effect on trout and salmon stocks. In my father's time, every catch was kept secret. If a particular area of the river was fishing well, I would be warned under pain of death not to disclose it to anyone. After all, income and dinner for the family was at stake.

Today, people can't wait to get on their mobile phone to boast about a good day's fishing. The bush telegraph was always healthy in fishing circles, but in these modern times, information moves, literally, at the speed of light.

A good example of this phenomenon occurred one July evening when I was fishing on the Suir. I started with the dry-fly in Liamy's lane and ended up at the head of the island opposite Walter Nolan's house. I had one of the best night's fishing on the river in memory. The trout were feeding all evening and I was steadily picking them off with the Sherry Spinner.

Unbelievably I had the river to myself and, as it grew dark, a good hatch of sedge came off and the trout went berserk for about 45 minutes. At times I did not know where to place the team of flies next, as there were so many trout feeding intensely around me. I did not keep count of the number of trout I caught but I estimated it to be between 50 and 60. I retained a few of the better fish for my Uncle Sean, who was over from England on holiday with his family. The rest were released.

I met my brother Tommy a little later for a pint and recounted my wonderful evening's fishing at Walter Nolan's. The next evening I headed for the same spot full of confidence, only to be greeted by five other anglers lined up where I'd been, and a chorus of 'I heard you had a great night's fishing here last night.' One angler told me that this was his first outing of the season and would not have bothered until he had heard about my catch from the previous evening. The power of the mobile phone is great indeed. Unfortunately, as I discovered, you're never certain that the information you send only stays with the people you want it to.

I got out of there in disgust and headed back up to Liamy's lane where I had another great evening's fishing. It was, perhaps, poetic justice that the trout didn't rise that evening at Walter Nolan's, so the gang of unhappy anglers headed home disbelieving and grumbling.

Many anglers today will not even venture out on the river unless they get word that the fishing is good. Before the scourge of the mobile phone it was still possible for sections of the river to remain safe from heavy angling pressure. It seems that modern technology has even impacted upon the conservative world of fly-fishing.

KILLING WAS COMPULSORY
On the UK's 'put and take' stillwaters, it would once have been deemed cheating to release a fish back into the

John Cosgrove with a tagged, Carrowmore spring salmon

water. The killing of all fish caught was, quite literally, compulsory on most fisheries; releasing trout suggested that the angler was attempting to select only the bigger fish. Things changed when fishery owners on both small stillwaters and reservoirs began to realise that by operating a system of catch-and-release they could keep their better anglers (those who could easily catch their limit) happy and possibly have to stock fewer fish. Both of these outcomes made commercial sense.

The result was also an easing among many anglers of the desire to catch and kill a limit bag. Additionally, with a combination of catch-and-release and a time bonus the sight of huge numbers of dead trout after a competition weigh-in became a thing of the past.

Personally, I think it comes as a great relief to no longer have to kill a fish simply because the rules say so. My wife used to get heartily sick of the sight of bags of rainbow trout in the kitchen sink, and the subsequent chore of cleaning them then finding someone to eat them. Fortunately, we lived near an old people's home for a few years; grateful recipients of a bag of trout every now and then. But there were also bad times when these fish went to waste – a criminal waste, to my mind.

I suppose it goes without saying that, over time, trout caught and released will be become more difficult to

CATCH-AND-RELEASE

Jimmy Docherty releasing a salmon on Lough Carrowmore

catch. But surely that can only add to the challenge of fly fishing? We are sportsmen, not fishmongers, aren't we? It may be inevitable that, now and then, we find a shoal of recently-stocked trout that have never seen an artificial fly before. These uneducated fish will take a fly – almost any fly – freely. Anyone new to the sport can revel in those moments, and there's nothing wrong with some easy sport to recharge the enthusiasm. But with a little more experience, surely we will relish a challenge?

It's certainly true for me. Because of the change in rules to catch-and-release, I'm now able to enjoy my fishing on stillwaters even more. I can now take a couple of fish for a friend who really appreciates them, whereas I once had to find someone – anyone – who would take unwanted dead trout off my hands.

In the UK competition-scene there has been the same groundswell against waste. The attitude and forward thinking of people like John Horsey, who organises the Lexus team and individual competitions, deserves some credit. I fished the Lexus final on Grafham in 2010 along with ninety-nine other anglers. On the day, the normal bag limit of eight fish was reduced to four and, if you were lucky to catch your four fish, you were obliged to go catch-and-release using barbless hooks. Three hundred and nineteen fish were released that day. It's hard to believe that there was once a time when those fish would be carted off in fertiliser sacks.

There is a potential downside to catch-and-release which is sometimes – though rarely in my experience – revealed in the heat of competition. Rainbow trout fight so hard, they need both care and patience if they are to recover fully. Many of today's major UK competitions are run on a time bonus basis; catch your limit and then stop fishing. And that's fine. Other competitions are fished up to a bag limit, then become catch-and-release. In such competitions, the ticking clock is the enemy. Time-saving is sometimes incompatible with the patient and successful release of a fish. We should always bear this in mind.

On a more local level, I have fished several competitions with my club, the Mid Northants Trout Fishers Association. In one of those competitions the bag limit is just two fish. The twist is that you must retain the first fish you catch and, if fortunate enough to land a few more, you then select just one of them. Once that second fish is in the boat you can continue fishing but every trout must be released. If you happen to land a really big fish after you have already taken your two, then tough luck – back it goes, unweighed. The idea behind this initiative is to give every angler a chance of winning the competition, including the beginners. It also puts the fun back into fishing, and we should all applaud that.

LOUGHS AND WILD FISH

While the idea of catch-and-release quickly became part of the UK's stillwater competition scene, it was not so quick to be adopted in Ireland. The stakes, though, were much higher. In the UK's stocked stillwaters, fish caught can be replaced. But Ireland's fish are wild, and the reason fisheries have moved to catch-and-release is environmental rather than financial. The Interprovincial final several years ago on Lough Mask was one of the first catch-and-release competitions I fished in Ireland. My numbers may be a bit shaky but, if I remember correctly, several hundred trout were caught and released on the day. Not everyone agreed with the concept but I, and many others like me, thought that it was a great step forward for competition fishing in Ireland.

When the TAFI inter-provincial final took place on Lough Lein, even bigger numbers of trout were caught and released. In these two days alone, there were around a thousand wild brown trout released for others to fish for later. Bigger, perhaps and maybe wiser fish, too.

Years ago, when oars were the sole method of boat propulsion, vast areas of the big loughs were safe from even the most energetic boat anglers. Today, with the common use of high-powered outboard motors, all areas of the lake are accessible. Historically-safe enclaves on the lake are now open to angling pressure throughout the whole season. Combine this with modern methods of fishing plus issues of pollution and the only conclusion one can draw is an ultimate decline in the stocks of this beautiful, wild fish.

In 2007, a bag limit of four trout was imposed on the Corrib/Mask catchment area. I suspect that, over time, similar bag limits will be introduced on all wild brown trout fisheries in Ireland. Many of the clubs and associations in Ireland are driving through these changes, as they fully appreciate the effects that pollution and over-fishing are having on their fisheries and environments.

Let's hope that change will not come too late for some others. Given sufficient time, people will get used to anything and the new will eventually become the norm, which I suspect is the case on many rivers in North America. But I also believe that the numbers of environmentally-aware anglers and organisations who care about their local fishery and its future will eventually out-grow their opposites and bring about enlightenment.

Catch-and-release is now becoming the norm, along with bag limits and the increasing of the size that wild fish can be legally taken. It makes sense not to kill fish that have not yet spawned. We must also look to the future through our youth programmes to continue this momentum of cultural change. Young anglers coming through the ranks of progressive clubs are being taught to respect the environment and treat catch-and-release as standard behaviour. All of this is good news for the long-term sustainability of wild fisheries. And attitudes are changing; I hope the momentum of this change is growing and cannot be reversed.

Sadly, the gains from anglers returning fish are just a skirmish; the bigger battle is against pollution, alien species which have been introduced and to combat predation problems such as the influx of cormorants inland. In tandem with other conservation initiatives already in place, we must continue to drive through the reversal in the decline of our wonderful wild fisheries.

The late Rod Tye, releasing a beautiful Lough Mask trout

CASTING OFF

The future

I WAS MULLING over what I was going to write for the final chapter in this book for some time when, following a telephone conversation with Robert Reilly I had one of those eureka moments.

What better way to end the book than to discuss the future and specifically the work than is being done by angling clubs and associations to promote our sport and to develop our young anglers?

For reasons already covered elsewhere in this book, the management of a fishery and its environment continues to come under ever-increasing pressure. We must also be mindful that there are those who dearly wish to see the sport of angling banned; anyone who thinks that this is an idle threat just needs to look at what's happened to hunting in recent years.

The future success or failure of angling will not only depend on the attitudes of controlling clubs and associations today, but will also be highly dependent on the current youth coming through the ranks. My family has a long tradition with the sport of angling and many of my friends also have similar links, which is why they entered into fishing in the first place.

That's all well and good, but how do we attract more young people to the sport especially those that do not already have any connection with angling? In researching this book, I was both astonished and delighted with the work that some forward-thinking individuals and clubs have been undertaking in managing and implementing a number of youth development programmes.

I could have written many pages about my own thoughts on the subject; however, I opted instead to outline in detail some of the youth training programmes that have already been implemented by clubs and associations in Ireland which are proving extremely successful today. In this way I am using the book as a platform for other interested parties to adopt some or all of the training models described in the following pages. I would also like to promote the work being done by the club instructors, the unsung heroes of the sport, who receive very little recognition for their efforts, nor ask for it. I know from talking to these special people that the rewards come from the satisfaction gained through observing the young lads and lasses develop and learn about the sport and their environment. Passing on a lifetime's knowledge is both a wonderful gift to give and an even better one to receive. I just feel that these dedicated people really do deserve some form of thank you for the hard work and commitment they put in.

Too busy posing for the camera to notice there's a trout rising

A PASSION FOR TROUT

Mallow youths on a frosty morning at Ballyhass Fishery

LOUGHREA ANGLING CLUB

At the invitation of his club secretary, Robert Reilly put together a twelve-week programme to help train and develop the young members of the Loughrea Angling Club, which is based in County Galway. The programme was initially advertised in the local press and an introductory evening was held to inform parents and children about the course content. There was also the opportunity for the programme organisers to explain their aims and objectives. Parents were invited to attend any or all of the training evenings.

PROFILE OF A TUTOR

Robert Reilly comes from a family steeped in angling history. He first started fishing as a boy of just ten years old and has been a member of Louhgrea Angling Association all his fishing life. He has also been a captain of the Connaught team and has represented his province on no fewer than 17 occasions, winning four Inter-provincial gold medals along the way.

Robert fished in his first International in 1994 on the Lake of Mentieth in Scotland along with his brother Frank, and since then has gone on to represent his country on eight occasions. Robert won the coveted Brown Bowl in 2006 and received the ultimate accolade by being invited to Captain Ireland in 2007. He was also appointed national team coach in 2008 and will be providing the team with advice for the forthcoming spring and autumn Internationals.

The programme Robert devised is as ingenious as it is comprehensive. As I say, it could be adapted by any forward-thinking club secretary or, indeed, any other angler who feels, as Robert clearly does, that once you've taken so much pleasure from fly-fishing, it is worth putting a little back in. Each of the twelve modules explained overleaf is set to be just enough for the weekly meeting, so it's never too much for the pupils to grasp. There are numerous ways to measure the success of this programme. Thirteen children signed up for the first course, all of whom attended 100 per cent of the time on every module. What greater validation can there be!

Robert Reilly: winner of the coveted Brown Bowl

Louhgrea Angling Association's twelve-week training programme

Programme rules:
Parents must sign their children out after each training session
Be punctual for all training secessions
Children must register attendance on all evenings
A minimum of 75 per cent attendance is required for certification award

- **Module one**
Introduction to game angling
How fishing evolved from necessity to a sport and pleasure activity
A history of tackle up to modern equipment

- **Module two**
Understanding the various methods of fishing and associated equipment
Fly-fishing on lakes and rivers
Explaining and understanding various species of fish and the environment

- **Module three**
Entomology study involving river walk-and-kick sample
Insect collection, class examination and study
Understanding the lifecycle of an insect
Categorising insects

- **Module four**
Angling etiquette, good boating and river manners
Respecting the environment
Examining the concept of catch-and-release
How to handle a fish properly

- **Module five**
Personal safety management
Checking and the wearing of safety equipment
Maintaining safety equipment
Basic requirements and precautions before going out fishing
Entering and exiting a boat safely
Checking essential boat equipment
What to do in the event of an accident

- **Module six**
Preparing fishing tackle
Learning how to mount a rod, reel and line properly
How to attach line and leader
Leaders, different materials and when to use them
Learning how to tie knots, droppers and how to prepare a team of flies

- **Module seven**
Casting with a fly rod
Different styles of casting
Learning about rod actions
Learning how to assemble and dismantle a rod safely
How to maintain and look after equipment properly
Learning how to cast

- **Modules eight and nine**
Fly-tying
Introduction to fly-tying materials
Learning to differentiate hooks, and their uses
How to recognise different feathers and their parts
Preparing to tie a fly, good thread management
Tying three different patterns

- **Module ten**
How to read a water; what signs to look for
How to land a fish
Learning how to handle fish with care
How to release a fish properly

- **Module eleven**
Recap of the previous ten modules
Course exam

- **Module twelve**
Putting it all into practice
Coach trip to a fishery / cont..
Three hour fishing session, with additional coaching by organisers
Flies tied in the programme must be used on the fishing day
Meal for students and parents (with slide show of photos taken over the duration of the programme)
Presentation of certificates by programme organisers

Robert tells me he is exploring the concept of broadening the programme to include neighbouring clubs and perhaps even cross-fertilise the training between lake and river associations. Both Robert and his club, Loughrea Angling Association, are to be congratulated for their efforts in developing and training the youth of the area.

MALLOW TROUT ANGLERS
Based on the River Blackwater and founded in 1919, the Irish fly-fishing club in Mallow, County Cork, has a strong and a highly successful tradition of developing its local youth.

The initial training programme got under way in the early sixties under the Chairmanship of Tom Purcell and the tutelage of Dick Willis. Astonishingly, after 48 years of continuous attendance, Dick is still involved with the programme to this day.

The training delivered by the dedicated members of Mallow Trout Anglers does not differ greatly in content from the Loughrea model but does alter significantly in terms of length; the programme is delivered over several years until it is felt that the pupil is competent in all angling skills and safety.

The outcome of this programme is that many of the youths that initially undertook the training have returned years later to become tutors. Such loyalty and longevity by members ensures and continues the strong traditions and culture of the club to this day.

DICK WILLIS' PROFILE
Dick has represented his country on 23 occasions in both game and coarse angling and has also had the great honour of being captain of Ireland.

Dick was appointed team coach on no less than three occasions. He has collected nine Munster titles along the way on river, lough and coarse fishing championships. One of his greatest triumphs was winning the Fly-fishing World Cup on Lough Mask in 1966 but he has also won a staggering number of local competitions on his native River Blackwater and many other rivers during his illustrious fishing career.

By my reckoning, Dick has been 75 years of age for the last three years – all that whiskey consumed over the decades must finally be paying dividends. Despite the years and the whiskey, Dick has still not lost the competitive edge that made him so successful and such a renowned angler. On his return from England, Dick immediately set about organising a youth training programme within the club. This initiative, has resulted in Mallow Trout Anglers becoming one of, if not *the* most successful club in Ireland today. As I write, it has furnished 41 international fly-fishers: 26 seniors and 15 juniors – testimony to a hugely successful training programme that was instigated by Dick back in 1961.

PUTTING SOMETHING BACK
When Dick first started fishing the River Blackwater, there was were no youth facilities in the club and only senior anglers were allowed to compete in local competitions. This proved to be his main motivation in setting up the youth programme on his return from the UK.

Dick has never missed a winter with the kids since that first year and has devoted a huge amount of his time to the development of the local youth. His other motivation in setting up a youth programme was simply to put something back into a sport that has given him so much pleasure and so many rewards down through the years.

A young Dick Willis, with the World Cup trophy from Mask

THE FUTURE

Rutland Water provides fly-fishing tuition for everyone, not just adults

The technical end of the training workshops are carried out during winter evenings where the usual skills of fly tying, good personal safety management and basic competence in rod handling are taught. In spring, the youths are taken to the river to improve their casting and learn how to identify the various species of aquatic life.

In addition to learning river-craft, the pupils are also taken to Lough Lein in Killarney several times throughout the year. There, they are taught the basics of lough-style fishing and good boat management. The kids are also taken to the Ballyhass Fishery where they are taught entirely different methods, particularly those used to catch rainbow trout. These range from lure fishing to modern nymph fishing techniques.

The interest within the club for developing its youth is enormous. Members sacrifice many days fishing in a season and rotate their time in assisting the current Youth Officer for the club. Many parents who have no history of, or association with fly-fishing, regularly attend the training programmes and assist members on days out. Those that have assisted are far too numerous to mention, which in itself is a tribute to this highly successful angling club. Surprising as it might seem, the training programme has never been advertised, yet between 30 and 40 youngsters turn up every year. It truly is a great success story, and long may it continue.

Although I could never profess to show the same commitment as all of these club members, I once had the honour of being asked by the Irish youth management, to give the team a talk on reservoir tactics. The reason was that a Home International match was being held on Grafham Water. This was a role I had never previously undertaken, so decided from the outset that I would do my homework As luck would have it, I had been spending more fishing hours on Grafham than on any other water, so I was reasonably familiar with current methods

The Scottish youth team on parade at Grafham

and where the fish were concentrated. Having delivered the talk and answered various questions I joined the management team for a late pint before heading home. Before I knew it I was back the next day to take two team members out on the water and again, the following day, with two more. These young lads were an example to us all. Their attitude was excellent – nothing was too much trouble. They all worked into the wee hours of the morning and that was after a hard days' practice. There were no superstars or egos in the camp; they worked for each other and fully understood the team ethos. I was also amazed to see just how many parents had travelled with the team and who joined in to share the workload and add to the team spirit.

A STRIKING DIFFERENCE

Given the clubs and personalities mentioned here, the reader might assume that I am biased towards Irish organisations. This was in no way intentional and, from the outset, I did attempt to engage with clubs outside of Ireland to provide a more global view. Unfortunately I was unsuccessful and perhaps in hindsight I should have tried harder. That said, I do have an understanding of the internal workings of the Irish club-system. I am also fortunate that I know a great number of Irish anglers involved in the running of their clubs. And from this I've observed a striking difference between the way English and Irish fly-fishing clubs operate.

Much of it is due to the more commercial style of trout fishing in England where, aside from a few notable exceptions, tuition even for young beginners comes at a price. In Ireland, the clubs and associations have fewer constraints. The vast majority of the rivers and lakes are self-stocking and no rod license is required for trout fishing. As such, the clubs are able to offer either free membership or one that is heavily subsidised in order to attract young people to the sport of angling. This, of course, is taking away nothing from the sterling work that is being done by many clubs in Ireland. You still require people who are willing to give up their time for free, and pass on their experience.

A NEW BREED

The clubs and associations I have mentioned here – and those everywhere – who are actively engaged in youth development, are to be congratulated. These training programmes have been adapted not only to teach young people how to fish but also to enlighten them about how to respect and protect the environment. Young minds bring a fresh approach and new ideas that can only benefit their clubs and the sport as a whole. This new breed of angler will one day have a major influence in the future management of angling standards and environmental policies. Encouraging young people into the sport will avoid, in the longer term, a sterility of ideas at the very top of fishery management.

Wild fisheries, in particular, are a very fragile environment indeed. Teaching fishing can only serve to equip these young anglers to better appreciate these places, and perhaps to manage and protect them long after I have gone. I wish them luck, but I am minded of golfer Tony Jacklin's comment after he had driven a spectacular hole in one on a par three. Someone in the crowd remarked on how lucky he had been: "D'ya know?" he replied. "The more I play, the luckier I get."

A future star: Ireland's Mark Sloan, with a cracking Grafham rainbow trout

Youngsters enjoying winter fly-tying lessons

*numbers in bold denote photo plate

Index

FLY PATTERNS

Alder Fly	133, 134, **135**, 170, 174	
Amber Nymph	86	
Apps Bloodworm	85, 87	
Ant		
Black	186, **187**	
Brown	186, **187**	
Red	104, **105**	
Badger Grey	102, **103**	
Bibio	168, **169**	
Variant No 1 & 2	180, 181, 188, **189**	
Variant	64, 65, 172, 174, 176, **177**	
Bits		
Claret	12, **13**, 75	
Ginger	12, **13**	
Black & Copper	175-**177**, 195, 200, 201	
Mick's	176, **177**	
UV	176, **177**	
Black & Silver	122, **123**	
Black & Yellow	124, **125**	
Black CDC	184, **185**	
Black Jungle Cock No1- 3	168, **169**, 172, 174, 180, 181, 193	
Black Nymph, (Rod Tye)	26, **27**	
Black Spinner Nymph	122, **123**	
Blae & Black	175, 178, **179**	
Blae & Green	176, **177**	
Bloodworm	28, **29**	
Blue Damsel	86	
Blue Pennell	134, **135**	
Blue Winged Olive	97, 126	
No 1 & No 2	97, 98, 104, **105**	
Bumble		
Claret	68, **69**, 162, 163, 168,**169**, 174	
Golden Olive	68, **69**, 86, 144, 162-164	
Pretender	164, 168, **169**	
UV Claret	176, **177**	
Watson	180, **181**	
Butcher	134, **135**	
Variant	178, **179**	
Buzzer	20-22, 30-38, 73, 85, 142	
Black & Copper	34, **35**, 184, **185**	
Black & Grey	34, **35**	
Black & Grey No2	34, **35**	
Black & Pearl	34, **35**	
Black Bead	26, **27**	
Black Holo	26, **27**, 36, **37**	
Black Holographic	36, **37**	
Black No 1 & 2	184, **185**, 186, **187**	
Black Spider	28, **29**	
Blue Holo No 1& 2	34, **35**	

Buzzer *cont.*		
Bottle Green	26, **27**	
Boxmoor	33, 46	
Brown	28, **29**	
Claret	26, **27**	
Corrib	34, **35**	
Crisp Packet	22, 36, **37**, 63, 73, 74, 79, 85, 193	
Elinor	36, **37**	
Emerging Black	184, **185**	
Flash Attack	36, **37**	
Holo Quill	26, **27**	
Mick's Olive	28, **29**	
Olive No 1, 2 & 3	26–29, 36, **37**	
Olive	45, 144	
Parachute Black	14, 15, 186, **187**	
Parachute Olive	12, **13**	
Parachute Quill	12, **13**	
Pearl & Green	34, **35**	
Pheasant Tail No1	84, **185**	
Quill	26, **27**	
Red	36, **37**	
Red Holo No 1 & 2	34, **35**	
Red Spot	26, **27**	
Sean's	34, **35**	
Tiger	34, **35**	
Traffic Light	30, 36, **37**, 46, 73	
Zebra	28, **29**	
Caenis	97, 143	
Claret Clan Chief	164, 167, 178, **179**	
Claret Duster	95, 96	
Claret Rebel	74, 180, **181**	
Claret Rocket	176, **177**	
Coch-y-Bondhu	174, 180, **181**	
Cock Robin	144, 162, 163, 168, **169**	
Connemara Black	133, 142, 144, 147, 162, 163, 174	
Connemara Black Variant	178, **179**	
Connemara Nymph	186, **187**	
Copper Bug	122, **123**, 124, **125**	
Crayfish	121	
Cormorant	47, 79, 81, 87	
Black & Green	82, **83**	
Emerald	82, **83**	
Flash Attack	82, **83**	
Pearl	82, **83**	
Pseudo	75	
Red Holo	82, **83**	
Red Straggle	82, **83**	
Snow White	82, **83**	

Cormorant *cont.*			**Diawl Bach** *cont.*	
UV Black	82, **83**		Pearl & Green	38
Variant	82, **83**		Pearl Ribbed	42, **43**
Viva	82, **83**		Quilled	42, **43**
Zebra	82, **83**		Red Holo	41, 188, **189**
Cruncher	22, 24, **25**, 63, 73, 74, 79, 85, 114, 115, 184, **185**, 193		Red Spot	42, **43**
			Silver Ribbed	42, **43**
Cruncher No 1	24, **25**		Duck Fly	142
Black	188, **189**		**Dun**	
Fire	24, **25**		August	99, 100, **101**, 128, 129
Orange	64, **65**		Blue	116, **117**
Quill	24, **25**		Claret	104, **105**
Red	24, **25**		Iron Blue	99, 100, **101**, 108, 111, 116, **117**
Sooty Olive	186, **187**		Mick's	116, **117**
UV	24, **25**		Olive	100, **101**
Dabbler	48, 209		Pale Olive	99, 102, **103**
Black	63, 176, **177**		Pond Olive	10, 11
Golden Olive	176, **177**		September	97, 100, **101**
Green	62, 74, 86		Suir	102, **103**
Green & Orange	66, **67**		**Dunkeld**	63, 133, 152, **153**
Limeburst	59, 63, 68, **69**			172, 175, 178, **179**
Pearly	63		**Emerger**	50-57
Sunburst	63, 66, **67**, 74		AK 47	52, 73, 196, 197
UV Claret	62, 63, 66, **67**, 73, 74, 174, 195, 202, 203		Bibio	56, **57**
			Black Devil	54, **55**, 134, **135**, 178, **179**
Viva	66, **67**		Black Duck Fly	56, **57**
Warsaw	66, **67**		Dun	54, **55**
Daddy Longlegs	14, 15, 48, 49, 63, 86, 144, 209		Fiery Brown Wasp	54, **55**
Chocolate	70, **71**		Grafham Raider	30, 52
Fiery Brown	70, **71**		Olive Wasp	54, **55**
Flexi Legs	70, **71**		Mick's Wasp	52, 54, **55**
Foam Backed	70, **71**		Mick's	54, **55**
Octo	70, **71**		Olive Duck Fly	56, **57**
Pheasant Tail	70, **71**		Olive Emerging	56, **57**, 142
Red	70, **71**		Pale Green	188, **189**
Silver	70, **71**		Pale Olive	56, **57**
Diawl Bach	20, 21, 22, 38-43, 47, 74, 86, 120, 193, 195		Pheasant & Orange	54, **55**
			Pheasant Tail	56, **57**, 186, **187**
Black	188, **189**		Quill	54, **55**
Black & Blue	42, **43**		Red Holo	56, **57**
Black & Red	42, **43**		Sooty Olive	56, **57**
Blue	42, **43**		Stoker	54, **55**
Blue Holo	184, **185**		Stripey	56, **57**
Claret	42, **43**		Yellow Head	56, **57**, 160, **161**
Gold Ribbed	42, **43**, 188, **189**		**F Fly**	184, **185**
Green	41		**Fraser Nymph, No 1 & 2**	22, 24, **25**, 74, 86
Lein	42, **43**		**Fritz Damsel**	47, 74, 81
Mick's Olive Bach	42, **43**		**Ghost Nymph**	122, **123**
Olive	188, **189**		No 1 & 2	100, **101**, 102, 103
Olive Quill	42, **43**		**Gorgeous George**	144, 152, **153**

INDEX

Green Devil	188, **189**
Green Peter	143, 147, 160, **161**, 168, 169, 175
Red Arsed	63, 64, **65**, 162, 163
Rod Tye's	153, 154
Greenwell's Glory	96, 99-**101**, 107, 116, **117**
Dark	111, 114, 115, 124, **125**
Green	28, **29**, 93, 94
Grey Duster	14, 15, 143, 158, **159**
Grey Goose	122, **123**
Grey Wulff Variant	143, 148, 150, 160, **161**
Grouse	
Black	133, 134, **135**
Orange	112, 114, 115, 133-**135**
Orange & Green	**69**, 111, 112, 114, **115**
Red	112, 114, 115, 133-**135**
Hackled Whiskers	82, **83**
Hare's Ear & Badger	104, **105**
Hare's Ear & Claret	180, **181**
Hare's Ear & Orange	116, **117**
Hare's Ear No 1 & 2	28, **29**
Hare's Ear	21, 24, **25**, 58, 85, 119, 120, 122, **123**, 184, **185**
Hare's Ear Shuttlecock	75
Hawthorn Fly	14, **15**
Heather Fly	212
Hoglouse	78, **135**, 160, **161**
Hopper	16, **17**, 78, 79
Black & Orange	195
Claret	16, **17**, 75, 143, 160, **161**
Donegal	11, 12, 16, **17**
Emerald	16, **17**, 160, **161**
Fiery Brown	16, **17**
Grafham Special	9, 16, **17**
Green	212
Green Peter	16, **17**
Kilkenny	16, **17**
Mick's Black	16, **17**, 160, **161**
Orange	75, 160, 161
Orange & Black	16, **17**, 75, 160, **161**
Orange & Green	9, 10
UV Bibio	16, **17**, 75, 86, 211, 212
Warsaw	16, **17**
Hot Nymph	23, 24, **25**
Invicta	63, 66, **67**, 174, 180, **181**
Johnston	175, 178, **179**
Jonah Bug	122, **123**
Kate Maclaren	153, 154, 174
Variant	160, **161**, 178, 179
Kingsmill	168, **169**, 175
Variant	178, **179**
Mallard & Claret	68, **69**
Marlodge	133, 134, **135**
Red	134, **135**, 175
Reversed Red	176, **177**
Mattie's Mayfly	160, **161**
McGorman	174, 180, **181**
Mick's Sooty Olive	176, **177**
Mickey's Fry	64, **65**
Midge	
Black	99, 100, **101**
Brown	36, 37
Claret	36, 37
Olive	36, 37
Pheasant Tail	36, 37
Minkie	75, 78, 79, 81, 87
Montana Nymph	24, **25**, 58, 87
Muddler	7
Daddy	63
Gold	155, 156
Kate Maclaren	68, **69**
Murrough	
Mixed Claret	158, **159**, 143, 150, **151**
Muskins	24, 25
Muskins, Olive	24, 25
Octopus	68, **69**, 164, 168, **169**
Olive Bug	122, **123**
Olive Buzzer Ball	158, **159**
Olive CDC	136, **137**
Olive Shuttlecock	158, **159**
Orange & Black	124, **125**
Orange CDC	136, **137**
Parachute Claret	9, 10
Parachute Duster	14, **15**
Parachute Hare's Ear	14, 15
Parachute Olive	**158**, 159
Partridge	
Black	124, **125**
Gold	99, 102, **103**, 106, 107, 111, 114, **115**, 124, 125
Hot	112, 116, **117**
Orange	114, **115**
Pearly	116, **117**
Purple	112, 114, **115**
Silver & Gold	33, 134, **135**
Yellow	11, 66, **67**, 112, 116, **117**
Pearly Invicta	63
Pearly Wickham's	64, **65**
Peter Ross	133
Pheasant Tail Nymph (bead)	119, 120, 122, **123**, 124, **125**
Pheasant Tail Nymph	21, 23, 47, 52
Cove's	24, 15
Pheasant Tail (dry)	56, **57**, 102, **103**
Parachute	12, **13**

228

Pitsford Pea	72	**Sooty Olive (Carra)**	162, 163
Quill		**Sooty Olive**	28, **29**, 174, 193
Black	108, 112, 114, **115**	**Sparkler Booby**	81
Badger	97, 104, **105**, 110, 112,124,125	**Spider**	
Ginger	97, 99, 110, 112, 114, **115**	Black	73, 116, 117, 178, **179**
Hare's Ear	119	Black & Peacock	64, **65**, 174
March Brown	108, 111, 113	Black & Peacock Variant	178, **179**
Pale Olive	106, 112, 113	Blue Holo	186, **187**
Red	97, 102, 103, 104, **105**	Claret	102, **103**
Rough Hare's Ear	47, 74	Dark Olive	188, **189**
Sedge		Orange	99, 102, **103**
Black	133, 136, **137**, 158, **159**, 180, 181, 208	Pale Olive	188, **189**
Balloon Hare's Ear	133, 136, **137**	Sooty Olive	184, **185**
Caddis	100, **101**	Yellow	97, 99, 102, **103**
Chocolate Brown	143	**Spinner**	
Cinnamon	14, **15**, 63-65, 113, 136, **137**	Black	99, 111, 116, 117, 124, **125**
Claret	144,160, **161**	Blue Dun	100, **101**
Dark Brown	14, **15**	Jenny	104, **105**
Fiery Brown	48, 143, 150, 184, **185**, 195	Pale Evening	104, **105**
Gold	136, **137**	Pale Watery	128
Green	14, 15, 48	Red	99, 104, **105**, 107, 109, 110, 116, **117**
Hare's Ear	66, **67**, 136, **137**	Sherry	97, 99-**101**, 104, **105**, 127, 129, 217
Killarney Black	147, 174	**Stone Fly**	112
Orange	75	**Sunburst Blob**	74, 81
Red	68, **69**, 144, 158, **159**	**Tequila Blob**	74, 81
Red Caddis	136, **137**	**The Rebel**	160, **161**
Rusty Brown	14, **15**, 48, 143, 158, **159**	**Thunder & Lightning**	172, 174, 176, **177**
Silver	47, 49, 62, 64, 65, 74, 78, 86, 133, 136, **137**, 143, 195, 198,	**Thunder & Lightning UV**	68, 69
		Watson's Fancy	174, 178, **179**
Shipman's		**Welshman's Button No1&2**	158, **159**, 160, **161**
Black	12, **13**, 30, 45, 86, 143, 186, **187**, 195	**White Shrimp**	160, **161**
Olive	160, **161**	**Wickham's Fancy**	116, **117**
Orange	12, **13**	**Woodcock & Copper**	114, **115**
Yellow	12, **13**	**Woodcock & Greenwell**	112, 114, **115**
Silver Invicta	63, 64, **65**, 74, 79, 86, 148, 149	**Yellow Ordie**	164, 168, **169**
Silver Jungle Cock	142, 175, 180, **181**	**Zulu**	175
Silver Ross	124, **125**		
Snail		**CLUBS**	
Black	186, **187**	Cahir and District Anglers Association	90, 96, 128
Brown	12, **13**	Bangor Angling Club	167
Olive	12, **13**	Belcarra Fishing Club	145
Snatcher		Killarney Salmon & Trout Angling Club	171
Flash Attack	66, **67**	Lough Carra Angling Club	145
Red	66, **67**	Lough Lein Anglers	171
Olive	12, **13**	Loughrea Anglers Association	221, 222
Soldier Palmer	48, 49, 63, 66, **67**, 74, 86, 164, 165, 167, 168, **169**	Mallow Trout Anglers	223
		Mid Northants Trout Fishers Association	76, 77
Solwick	66, **67**	Partry Anglers Club	145

INDEX

PEOPLE

Boyd, Andrew	48	Farrell, Liam	91, 106, 131
Bram Kwak	175	Farrell, Tommy [brother]	91, 95, 128, 129, 132, 143, 153, 172, 204, 217
Burke, William	8, 142, 148, 167, 206, 213		
Callaghan, Michael	207	Farrell, Tommy [uncle]	91, 92, 131,
Causer, Keith	49	Foley, Pat	208
Causer, Margaret	49	Foster, Edward	22, 84, 210
Church, Bob	76	Foster, Harold	84
Church, Jeanette	76	Frisby, John	18, 19
Collins, Jim	76	Gathercole, Peter	9, 48
Cosgrove, John	165	Graham, Billy	208
Cosgrove, Kenneth	165	Hall, David	209
Cove, Arthur	58	Harte, Eddie	209, 213
Cresham, Philip	146	Henry, Seamus	167
Cullin, Steve	49	Hladic, Milan	209
Deane, Gerry	165	Horsey, John	209
Donavan, Dave	210	Hubbard, Ollie	138, 139
Draper, Bob	76	Huxley, Chris	145
Farrell, Davy	204	Huxley, Lynda	145

PLACES

Aherlow River	90, 108, 112, 133	Paradise Bay	165
Ballyhass Fishery	224	Munhin River	164
Blackwater River	108, 209, 223	The Black Lake	164
Cahir	90, 91, 97, 106, 108, 132, 214	Chew Valley Reservoir	209
Collinstown	207	Church Hill Farm	63
Carra (Lough)		Conn (Lough)	164, 173, 207
Annie's River	144	Corrib (Lough)	171, 172
Annie's Shore	147, 150	Draycote Water	23, 39, 44-49, 62, 210
Ballinrobe	145	Toft Bay	45, 48
Ballintubber River	144	Cornfield	45, 48
Claremorris	145	Dunn's Bay	45, 48
Castlebar	145, 146, 158	Flat Stones	45
Castle Carra	145	Leam River	44
Castle Island	147, 150, 158	Lin Croft Point	45, 48
Connor Point	147, 158	Rainbow Corner	45
Corrib Catchment	145	Elinor Trout Fishery	10, 33, 39, 41, 58, 84-87, 158, 210
Keel, River	144		
Moore Hall	142, 150, 158	Eyebrook Reservoir	10, 32
Otter Point	144	Farmoor I&II Reservoirs	32
Rineen	147	Grafham Water	1, 23, 30, 78, 81, 210
Carrowmore (Lough)	146, 148	Kingfisher Farm	18, 58
Bangor	164, 165, 167	**Lein (Lough)**	
Bellanboy River	164, 165	Killarney	20, 22, 23, 30, 39, 50, 52, 147, 170-181, 204, 207, 218, 224
Black Banks	165		
Bog Bay	165	Bog Bay	172, 173
Bangor	164, 165, 167	Brown Island	172
Glencullin River	164, 165	Cool River	171
Glenturk River	164, 165	Copper Mines	172
Owenmore River	164, 167	Cotteners River	171

Ingham, Roger	78	Pow, Ian	76, 78
Kinsella, Johnny	133	Purcell, Tom	223
Layton, Rob	77	Purtil, John	208
Linehan, Mick	208	Quirke, John	143, 209
McGovern, Anne	153	Reilly, Robert	207, 209, 221, 223
McGovern, Tommy	153	Rowe, Kevin	208
McPhillips, Frankie	11, 193	Rowe, Richard	153, 206
O'Brien, Malcolm	105	Ryan, Andrew	95,
O'Farrell, Danny	158, 159	Shields, Basil	213
O'Farrell, David	8, 10, 84, 147, 148, 150,153 158, 159, 165, 167, 172, 208	Sloan, Mark	225
		Sparks, Tim	77
O'Farrell, Michael [dad]	92-94, 98, 99, 106, 108, 112, 128, 131, 139, 165, 205, 206	Stevens, Mick	76
		Tye, Rod	142, 193, 208
O'Farrell, Michael [son]	158	Wallinger, Bob	45
O'Farrell, William	18, 95, 118, 119, 120	Wally, Paul	45
O`Reily, James	146, 208	Willis, Dick	99, 108, 207, 223, 224
O`Riordan, D J	171		
Poux, Pierre	92, 120		

Lein *cont.*		**Owel Lough**	207, 208
Crinagh River	171	**Pitsford Reservoir**	9, 22, 62, 72-77, 81, 209, 210
Deenagh River	171	Bog Bay	73
Flesk, River	171, 172	Creek	73
Finnow River	171	Little Half	73
Fossa Shore	172	North Farm Bay	73
Gaddagh, River	171	Sailing Club Bay	73
Gaureen	172	Stilton Point	73
Gweestin River	171	Stone Barn Bay	73
Hen & Chickens	172	The Gorse	73
Heron Stones	172	The Gravels	73
Innisfallon Island	172	The Pines	73
Laune River	171, 172	**Suir (River)**	39, 106, 126, 127, 129, 138, 193, 214
Loe River	171	Bakery Weir	91
Mahoney's Point	172	Ballyheron	93
Muckross Lake,	170	Ballyheron Weir	139
Muckross Shore	172	Camis and Golden	97
Purple Mountain	170	Carrigitatta,	96, 128, 129
Rough Island	172	Cottage Weir	138
Ross Castle	72	Darcy's Weir	106
Sand Bank	172	Devils Bit Mountains	90
Sweeney's Shore	172, 174	Liamy`s Lane	92, 109, 120, 126, 217
The Wash	172	Neil's Field	107
Victoria Bay	172	Ross's Slip	119
Loughrea, County Galway	221	Swiss Cottage	96, 97, 112
Mask (Lough)	129, 144, 146, 147, 171, 173, 206, 208, 209, 218	The Park	93, 96,
		The Point	131
Menteith, Lake of	209, 211	Walter Nolan's House	217

APPENDIX

CARRA (Lough)
Boat hire
Pat O`Reilly Tel: +353 94 9030879
Mob: +353 87 9348975 info@carraboathire.com
www.carraboathire.com

Joe Conroy, Brownstown, Hollymount,
Tel: +353 94 9541340
Peter Roberts, Kilkeeran, Partry. Tel: +353 94 9543046

Accommodation
Anne & Tommy MacGovern Tel: +353 949360359

CARRAMORE (Lough)
Seamus Henry (fisheries manager) Tel: +353 97 834487
Club website - www.bangorerrisanglingclub.ie

Accommodation
Bredge & John Cosgrove: boat & engine hire + gillie
Attavalla
Bangor-Erris
Ballina, County Mayo
Tel: +353 9783412, +353 877619198, +353 879884304
jandbcos@gmail.com

DRAYCOTE WATER
Permits-boat hire-fishing tackle-tuition
Fishing lodge Tel: 01788 812018 Fax: 01788 815711

ELINOR TROUT FISHERY
Permits-boat hire-fishing tackle-tuition
Edward Foster (fishing lodge Tel: 01832 720786
Email: ElinorTF@aol.com
Website- www.elinortf.co.uk

Accommodation
The Horseshoes, Titchmarsh Tel: 01832 733033
www.thehorseshoes.net
Pear Tree Farm, Aldwincle Tel: 01832 720614
www.peartreefarm.net

SUIR (River)
Permits
Cahir & District Anglers Association
Kevin Rowe
The Heritage,
1 The Square
Reiska Road, Cahir
Tel: +353 5274 42738 +00353 5274 42729

LEIN (Lough)
Boat hire
Eastern shore at Ross Castle, nearest to Killarney
Henry Cliften, Tel: + 353 60 66 32252
Western shore, near to the mouth of the River Laun
Sean Sweeney, Tel: +353 64 66 44207

PITSFORD RESERVOIR
Permits-boat hire-fishing tackle-tuition
Tel: 01604 781350
Email: fishing@anglianwater.co.uk

WEBSITES
Anglian Water
www.anglianwaterleisure.co.uk

Carra Boat Hire
www.carraboathire.com

Central Fisheries Board (Ireland)
www.cfb.ie
www.loughcarra.org

Killarney tourism website
www.killarney.ie

Peter Hartley's School of Fly Fishing
www.bsff.co.uk

ORGANISATIONS
CFB (Central Fisheries Board)
Confederation of English Fly Fishers
ITFFA (Irish Trout Fly Fishing Association)
TAFI (Trout Angling Federation of Ireland)
National Parks and Wildlife Services
NWRFB(North Western Regional Fisheries Board)
SRFB (Southern Regional Fisheries Board)
SWRFB (South Western Regional Fisheries Board)

BIBLIOGRAPHY
Anglian Water 2009 Guide
Arthur Cove's: My Way with Trout
Bob Church: This Fishing Life, first published in 2003.
Denis Kelleher: Another World on Mask
NWRFB: Towards a New Era for the Owenmore
John Veniard`s: Fly Dresser's Guide, first published 1952, fourth addition 1970. Reprinted 1972, 1973, 1976, 1977, 1979, 1981,
T C Ivens: Stillwater Fly-Fishing, first published in 1952. Reprinted in 1970, 1973